ELECTRONIC
SELLING

Electronic Selling

Twenty-Three Steps to E-Selling Profits

Brian Jamison

Josh Gold

Warren Jamison

McGraw-Hill

New York • San Francisco • Washington, D.C. • Auckland • Bogotá
Caracas • Lisbon • London • Madrid • Mexico City • Milan
Montreal • New Delhi • San Juan • Singapore
Sydney • Tokyo • Toronto

McGraw-Hill

A Division of The McGraw·Hill Companies

2 3 4 5 6 7 8 9 0   DOC/DOC   9 0 1 0 9 8 7

ISBN 0-07-032930-3

*The sponsoring editor for this book was John Wyzalek, and the production supervisor was
Suzanne Rapcavage. It was set in Vendome by North Market Street Graphics.*

Printed and bound by R. R. Donnelley & Sons Company.

McGraw-Hill books are available at special quantity discounts to use as
premiums and sales promotions, or for use in corporate training programs. For
more information, please write to the Director of Special Sales, McGraw-Hill,
11 West 19th Street, New York, NY 10011. Or contact your local bookstore.

This one is for Cyndy.

CONTENTS

Contents

Contents

Contents

PREFACE

Most executives realize the Internet is here to stay. They recognize it as a dynamic new medium of unprecedented range, power, and possibility; they also realize we're still in the opening stages of the Internet revolution. For many companies, how effectively they respond to the Internet's opportunities will determine whether they flourish or wither away in the coming years. Yet, few executives possess the basic knowledge necessary to make vital decisions in this arena.

This book provides what decision makers need—a nontechnical overview from the executive viewpoint, we minimized specific references to technology for two reasons.

One, the pace of technological advance on the Internet far outstrips the production time required for a paperbound book. It often seems as though today's cutting edge technology is obsolete tomorrow, and forgotten before Friday.

Two, and more importantly, decision makers never need know the time-devouring minutiae of electronic commerce or Web site production. Therefore, a detailed discussion of technology is beyond the scope of this book.

This book is built around a 23-step action plan that will guide the executive through the maze of decisions necessary to produce a successful Web site. Commerce on the Internet is a rapidly growing field, with new possibilities opening up on a daily basis. Rather than dwell on specific software packages that often become obsolete overnight, we concentrate on what to look for in a commerce package, discussing common shortcomings and pitfalls that apply to Internet commerce in general.

A brief listing of products and services available at the time of printing appears in the following pages. What about the flood of significant new products and services we can be sure will reach the marketplace after publication?

Your are invited to accesss information about them at the Internet site for this book. It's located at

http://www.jamisongold.com/eselling

Establishing cost-effective security measures should be one of the top priorities on any executive's mind when considering electronic selling. A thorough discussion of the several facets of security is presented here; it covers everything from customer perceptions to setting security standards capable of protecting both client and company.

Success in any field requires an understanding of what has worked in the past and what is likely to work in the future. Without introducing unnecessary complexity, we get down to the details of today's successful products and services on the Internet, cover proven methods of revenue generation, and suggest possible avenues for exploration.

Opportunities truly are limitless on the Internet. For those who question this fact, we have provided a number of success stories ranging from existing companies to new and unique Internet products and services.

We welcome suggestions and comments via e-mail. Send them to:

eselling@jamisongold.com

ACKNOWLEDGMENTS

Brent Phillips, chief technical officer at Jamison/Gold, LLC, made significant contributions, as did another J/G software engineer, Ken Vollmer.

This is very much Brian Jamison's and Josh Gold's book. My role as facilitator, scribe, and wordsmith depended entirely on their eminently practical know-how, vast technical expertise, and penetrating creative insights into the realities governing today's intensely competitive World Wide Web.

Thanks are also due our warmly effective editors at McGraw-Hill, Brad Schepp and John Wyzalek, and to many others at McGraw-Hill whose names I'll probably never know. Thanks also to our sagacious agent, Jim Trupin.

Thus this book has many fathers, but only one mother. Besides giving birth to Brian, my wife Kitty brought forth the basic idea of the book and then, whenever the fires of belief and creativity flickered, she fanned them into full flame again. She also selected, interviewed, and wrote most of the success stories in Chapter 8.

—Warren Jamison

While contributing to the conceptual framework and spirit of this book, the great majority of the work came from my partner, Brian Jamison, who spent countless hours refining and polishing it.

Thanks are also due Hauro Matsuoka for his guidance and teachings. As my martial arts instructor, Mr. Matsuoka has been largely responsible for the focus, determination, and strategic thinking that has driven my career.

—Josh Gold

I owe a debt of gratitude to my parents Warren and Kitty for their eternal love and support. This book truly would not have been possible without their hard work, expertise, and tolerance of my hectic schedule.

I also thank the entire team at Jamison/Gold, for their skill, creativity, and dedication to pushing the frontier.

—Brian Jamison

CHAPTER 1

Introductory Concepts

Before we plunge into the intricacies of electronic selling, let's do two things. First, a definition. We're using the term *Net Cash* (or *net cash*) to include all forms of digital money, whether DigiCash's Ecash, Cyber-Cash's CyberCash, or some other company's proprietary form of electronic cash. Second, let's take a few moments to explore the basic reasons why this churning new technology is taking the world by storm.

Why the Internet Is Today's Gold Rush

Imagine a low-cost medium through which even a one-person operation can sell goods or services worldwide. Imagine a medium through which giant corporations can offer the world's marketplace unlimited amounts of product information with minimal one-time set-up costs and also furnish technical support worldwide—all at low cost.

Such a medium exists. Internet technology already in place can meet the 24/365 sales and tech support needs of every-sized business. As such, it isn't a medium, it's an extra special humongous large market.

Jupiter Communications, the prestigious market research and marketing firm based in New York, says shoppers spent $1.3 billion online in 1996. Jupiter expects online consumer spending will exceed $7 billion by 2000. Although $1.3 billion can be dismissed as insignificant compared to the nation's $75 billion in traditional catalog sales, $7 billion can't. Neither can the projected growth rate, already running in excess of 50 percent a year. Add online selling's potential for even more explosive growth, and you have sound reasons why the Internet has set off today's gold rush.

Some estimates place the number of people capable of accessing the Internet at more than 100 million. Others place the number much lower. Although there's no consensus on the approximate number, four beliefs are so widely held they should be regarded as fact:

- Huge numbers of people can access the Internet.
- Users tend to be young, affluent, and obviously are among the world's most technically advanced.
- The number of users is increasing explosively.
- No end is in sight to Internet growth and its rapidly expanding impact on business and personal life.

No entrepreneur or corporate executive can safely ignore this immensely powerful change in the ground rules by which business will be conducted in the coming century.

The World Wide Web in Brief

Although the World Wide Web has already caused—and will continue to impel—enormous changes, it is simply a computer language. This language allows a constantly changing assortment of servers (computers) to provide attractively packaged information on request and to collect and process information.

The WWW is commonly confused with the Internet, a vast collection of networked computers. The WWW sits atop the Internet and is only one of many ways to communicate using this "network of networks."

Advantages, Opportunities, and Realities of Conducting Electronic Commerce

The advantages begin with the most clearly distinguishable difference between how turn-of-the-millennium business is conducted and the way mid-twentieth century business was done: ever-greater speed to meet the ever-increasing pressure of time.

Speed

At worst, e-selling is relatively instantaneous (minutes instead of days or even weeks compared to mail order). At best, it really is instantaneous, permitting sales of products or services and the collection of the resulting payments at computer speed.

As Secure As You Want It to Be

Security on the Internet is like securing your automobile against theft. In both cases, higher levels of security involve additional inconvenience and expense. Deliberately or by default, you choose the level of security you want after making as detailed a cost/benefit analysis as you feel the circumstances warrant.

Can Parallel Your Present Marketing Methods

Companies concerned about disrupting existing marketing arrangements can still avail themselves of some Internet advantages, thereby gaining invaluable online experience and exposure. Sales promotion and tech support can be pursued vigorously on their Web site, with sales leads automatically forwarded to the proper party in their present distribution network. Selling from the Web site can be deferred indefinitely.

CREDIT THE REPRESENTATIVE INVOLVED, OR MAKE INTERNET SALES COMMISSION-FREE.   Many companies see morale- and sales-boosting benefits in backing their field representative's selling efforts with Internet convenience. This entails making Web site sales commissionable.

Such companies won't make (or even see) distinctions between orders. They will be treated the same whether phoned in, snail-mailed in, e-mailed in, placed on the company's Web site, or written up by representatives on the company's order form and plunked down on the sales manager's desk.

This question will not arise in companies operating without exclusive territories or field representatives. However, most companies have complex distribution methods. They should carefully consider the effect of going worldwide (the reason it's called the *World Wide* Web) in search of online sales. Limiting their Internet activities to sales promotion—and excluding sales—may in many cases be the best alternative. In any case, the effect on existing wholesaler/retailer/salesforce arrangements should be taken into consideration before procedures to close sales on your Web site are activated.

SALES AND TECH SUPPORT OPERATION WITHOUT OVERTIME AND OTHER STAFFING PROBLEMS.   Web sites can operate on a 24/365 schedule at very little additional cost without overtime or staffing problems. Companies with customers in time zones several hours ahead or behind local time realize great advantages compared with trying to find mutually convenient times for telephone calls.

All inquiries, orders, and technical support requests will divide into two classes:

- *Orders and tech support requests falling within the company's sales parameters.* Internet sales should be fully automated so they can be processed—and payment, if any, collected for them—24 hours a day, 365 days a year. Similarly, tech support may be automated so customers can access written or graphic solutions to all foreseeable product problems whenever they choose to do so. This is especially helpful in the global marketplace, where local time in important markets may run half a day behind or ahead of the company's regular business hours.

- *Orders and tech support requests not fitting the company's established parameters.* Internet sales and tech support procedures may be set up to automatically capture as much information as possible about such no-go orders. This data can yield valuable sales leads if automatically forwarded to the proper field representative. It can also provide management with priceless clues to emerging developments and future customer needs.

Easy Entry into Export Sales

Companies with products suitable for export can ease their way into the profits, perils, and problems of international business on the Internet's World Wide Web. They can do this without incurring the large travel expenses usually associated with export business.

Nobody Owns It

Any individual or organization with suitable products or services and the minimal resources required to perform three functions can establish a profitable presence on the Internet.

- Furnish a server—or rent space on a provider's server
- Devise and develop a Web site, either in-house or with a firm of professional Web site builders
- Provide the staff to meet the response and fulfillment demands the site generates

No organization controls access to the Internet because nobody owns it. In this way the Internet is like the international waters of the world's oceans; restrictions and controls apply only to limited parts of it. Thus, the Internet, particularly with the advent of the World Wide Web, has emerged as the world's new frontier—in some ways it's the American Wild West reborn.

Once free of its academic and military origins, the Internet assumed a furiously developing, amorphous, everywhere/nowhere unreal reality. Indefinable and virtually ungovernable, the Internet will continue to expand and evolve simultaneously in many directions. As it does so, the Internet exerts a unifying force of ever-growing power on the world's peoples and economies.

Unequaled Cost-Effectiveness When Used Properly

Major corporations routinely spend tens and even hundreds of millions of dollars on sales promotion. By this standard, the costs of establishing and maintaining even the most sophisticated, cutting-edge Web site are negligible.

By any standard, sales costs on the Internet are insignificant when the products or services offered are well adapted to online sales. For many niche products and services, the Internet is the only cost-effective sales method available.

Frequent updates of the promotional pages are essential to maintain Web site performance. However, once the order processing system is correctly set up, tested, and proven in operation, it will require little or no maintenance.

2

The Getting Started Action Plan: Twenty-Three Steps to E-Selling Profits

Step 1: Determine the Scope of the Project: Decide Precisely What You Want to Sell on Your Web Site and on What Terms

Determining scope is really important whether you're taking a little baby step—just a toe touch—or going into the Internet with a major effort. In either case, the commitment, financial and otherwise, behind the project needs to be appropriate to the planned scope.

So, for a toe touch, you probably don't want to buy your own server hardware. You don't want to buy a computer. You'll probably want to go to someone who'll host the site for you at a relatively low cost.

Some people came into Jamison/Gold recently and said, "We're getting 20,000 hits per month and we're considering going up to a T-3 line."

As gently as I could, I helped them put this idea in perspective. A *hit* is one information request. Visitors typically record multiple hits during a single Web site visit. While 20,000 hits a month may sound impressive when viewed in isolation, it's more likely the number of people who visited is only a small fraction of your total hits. In fact, 20,000 hits might mean only 10 to 50 users per day accessing a site. A good number of visitors, but a T-3 line can accommodate thousands of simultaneous requests, far higher than necessary. A T-3 line—the largest Internet line you can get—carries a price tag to match: $50,000 a month. Lay the line cost against 20,000 hits a month and it comes to $2.50 per hit. It's just out of control.

If the scope of your Web site project indicates it will immediately start pulling millions of hits, you'll want to acquire your own hardware, your own Internet line, and have the staff to support it.

The cost-effective decision here has a lot of do with how you focus yourself. Once we go online with a Web site, we open the door to doing business with the entire Internet world. This brings up questions calling for careful analysis beforehand:

- Are we going to settle for merely putting up one of our print brochures?

- What's our market?

- If we are going to sell, we must know precisely what we will be selling down to every detail of packing, shipping, export licensing, and documentation where export will be involved. If it's information or product, we must think about what it will mean.

- Are we going to sell a lot of things?

- What terms? Are we going to be taking credit cards online or sending people our 800 number? Do they fill out a form for a salesperson to follow up? Or can they complete the purchase themselves before they leave our Web site?

- How many people can we expect will visit our Web site?

- What percentage of them can we reasonably expect will buy?

Accurate answers to some of these questions may be difficult to nail down, and the decision maker may have to fall back on educated guesswork. In any case, we need well thought-out answers to those questions so we can make appropriate decisions. Do this from the start.

If you aren't comfortable with answering these questions, you might want to consider scaling back your plan to establishing a foothold on the Internet to gather information. When Nissan Motors was considering its own Internet presence, we put up just one model, the Pathfinder. Using what we learned from the Pathfinder site, we were better able to craft a site based on the expectations of users when we did the full line of Nissan automobiles.

Develop the content of your Web site to fully exploit the advantages of this new medium. We rarely see this. We almost always see people making an online brochure. It's called *re*purposing, where you take existing promotional materials and simply translate them to the Web. This doesn't work. It's too wordy and it won't perform.

This book is about advantages of the Internet and one-to-one selling. You can make it possible for visitors to search huge databases of information quickly and find exactly what they're after. As long as it's indexed properly, it makes sense to provide more information than most people would want to wade through.

While you're providing all this detail, make sure you also provide advantages not as easily available elsewhere.

If you just put your brochure online, you give your visitors the feeling they've been cheated. Instead of building a relationship, you're tearing it down because you didn't attach any value to their going to the trouble to reach you online. If you give them no more online than they would have obtained just by picking up your brochure at a local store, you're moving away from the sale, not toward it.

However, if you offer special incentives, your latest product developments, or some neat way of looking at your product—some benefit or service appropriate to the medium—then your visitors won't feel shortchanged, and your Web site will be an effective sales promotion tool.

Be careful about using cutting-edge—and unproven—technology. Be careful about compatibility. Make sure your site is viewable by at least 80 percent of the market. Avoid requiring customers to download a massive file before they can use the site. Such delays are a huge turn-off to most people.

Step 2: Consider the Effect This New Sales Method Will Have on Your Existing Marketing Arrangements and Commitments

Make sure you won't enrage your end resellers by selling online. If you have lots of outside salespeople, you don't want to alienate them. Both groups will welcome the additional sales method if they are credited with the discount or commission on sales being shipped into their territories. It's not difficult to organize a sales crediting system based on zip codes.

Chances are you won't be setting up your industry's first Web site. If so, you can probably learn many of the things you shouldn't do by studying the mistakes your competitors have already made.

Step 3: Set Web Site Sales and Profit Goals and Budget the Funds Required to Achieve Them

Some people do this and have too high an expectation on what realistically they're going to get. Like they're going to make a million dollars in Internet sales. For a new site, it's not going to happen. If you've got something hot, you'll make money right away, but it's not like television sales. The money is not guaranteed.

In the beginning, be extremely conservative about profit expectations. You need to develop a following and establish a name. Expect to not make money for a while. At first, sales will merely trickle through. This is a building process; the flood comes later. It's not like a mall where you open the doors and people automatically stream in.

Budget the necessary funds to hang in there for a while. Few new ventures and programs in any area of business are instant successes; most have to build their audiences over time.

In addition to development funds, be sure to budget funds for media buys such as banner ads, online marketing, and PR—otherwise no one will know about your site.

Step 4: Determine the Level of Integration with Existing Company Systems

If you already have a system in place to handle automating some level of the process, you'll need to consider how you will integrate the existing system into your Internet presence. Whether it's an existing inventory database, computerized customer accounts, automated order processing or financial back end, sales tool or lead tracker, these systems have their own requirements and restrictions.

If, for example, you are using Oracle Financials in your current business, it might make a great deal of sense to link your Internet transactions into your master database as well.

In this case, make sure the database software you use for online transactions is compatible. This can be more complex than it sounds. Connecting to some of these legacy database systems sometimes isn't possible, or it's more expensive than the benefit received from a unified database will justify. Just going with the same vendor (such as Oracle) doesn't guarantee compatibility with your existing systems. Consult with your database administrator before going further in your process. A week of research on compatible database systems can really pay off. If you plan on this from the start you'll save plenty of trouble down the road.

Step 5: Decide Whether E-Selling Will Be Developed Internally or Externally

Making the wrong choice here knocks many company Web sites off the fast track to strong Internet sales. They may have something with the potential to sell extremely well on the Internet, but they never get rolling. Naturally, everybody who opposed the Web site project takes it as proving the Internet isn't a profitable sales avenue. But, just as it isn't the lake's fault when someone drowns there, it's not the Internet's fault if your Web site doesn't pay. The mistake is yours, not the Internet's.

External Development

External Web site development is probably the best choice for most medium to large companies. It's the best choice for the same reason most companies get television commercials made externally: it doesn't make sense to have a staff of incredibly specialized people sitting around.

Therefore, for the most profitable long-term results and lowest short-term cost, select the most creative and experienced external developer you can find, and have it create your Web site. Some managers are tempted to save money by going with the person who works out of the garage and says, "Sure, I can do it—no problem." These individuals appear to have a great deal of technical savvy and know-how; unless you're well versed in computer technology, they can wow you with the buzzwords.

However, an effective Web site can't be completed by one person—this is the reality. Think of Web site development as being on a par with creating a television commercial. Would you want one person doing every aspect of such an important project?

Because this is such new technology, many executives don't yet understand it can easily take 10 talented people to pull an effective Web site together. Each of those 10 people has a very specific core competency.

Smaller companies get burned by letting a self-trained hacker take it on. Sure, you'll get something, but it's not going to work well, it will look second rate, and it stands little chance of delivering the results you're looking for. Bear this in mind: from the first minute your site goes online, it's competing for business with the best on the Web.

Find a firm capable of meeting your needs. A firm with the human resources to take care of everything. It won't be cheap. There are a thousand or more medium-sized firms who can handle most things, and there's an unlimited number of hacker types.

It's most important to utilize people who have Internet experience. There are a lot of people jumping on the Internet bandwagon now coming from CD-ROMs, multimedia development, print advertising, and TV. They see this Internet gold mine and decide to hop aboard thinking it's easy. Well, it's not.

I wouldn't dare do a television commercial. I don't understand the ins and outs of it. This realization leads me to wonder what makes refugees from TV think they can jump into Web site development and pull it off easily.

Look for a track record. In your development contract, make sure milestones are inserted so you can evaluate along the way. Make sure you have a contract based on performance. If you have a six-month contract, don't wait until month five to evaluate how it's going. Make sure money is tied to the milestones and if the developers don't complete the project on time they lose money.

Software projects almost always go overtime and budget. Ours do not because we don't make promises we can't keep. Tie your Web site development to a schedule. Let's say the job costs $100,000 if we complete it within six months. For every week we're late, we're penalized $2000. Do this and the chances are you'll get a realistic development schedule and you'll likely get your site done on time.

You don't want a firm composed of a bunch of propeller heads (computer geeks who don't understand the market or product, much less your need to effectively communicate your brand's benefits and competitive advantages). These kinds of off-planet people can create great sites—according to their own nonselling ideas. But their sites melt like snow in a hot wind when they go online against the competition.

Other development companies come from advertising and they can talk all day long about brands and sticking with your existing campaign and making it look great—but once they go online their creation won't do anything. Technically, they won't be able to pull off the promises unless they have a talented staff of software engineers to back them up.

Except in the computer hardware and software industries, executives must develop a host of nontechnical skills to reach the top in their companies. When faced with decisions about developing a Web site, they're usually outside their areas of expertise. Understandably, the idea of turning the entire Web site and Internet commerce project over to their advertising agency presents an attractive option, particularly in large corporations.

This is often an eminently practical solution, particularly where the top people are already overworked and the firm's advertising agency has good experience with Internet commerce to their credit. However, the advertising agency will just hire a Web site development company to construct this site, and another layer of cost will have been added.

You need both computer expertise and advertising know-how to make your Web site perform well. It's tricky to find people who understand both—but it's worth the search. Expect to pay for it just like you'd expect to pay for a first-class television commercial. Anyone can make a TV commercial—just get yourself a video camera and shoot—but there's much more to making a commercial worth paying for airtime to run.

Make sure your Web site developer has the resources available to handle the job. Typically, many software developers take on more projects than they can handle. Make sure they have a solid track record. You don't want to be dealing with someone putting together their first site. The time when you had to pay someone to learn how to develop a Web site is long gone. The Internet is enormously more demanding today than it was just a year ago; so it's too late to make mistakes and put up a flaky Web site. Key questions for potential developers are as follows:

- Ask to see *all* of their Web sites, not just their pet projects.
- Find out what role the developer played in the creation of a site. Frequently, more than one company is used in large sites. One company will do the design, another the back-end programming, another will do online promotion, and still another will provide the server and Internet connection. Some companies have been known to take credit for more than they actually did on a given site.
- Ask who from their staff will be assigned to the project.
- Make sure you view sites using a standard connection, say a 28.8 modem. Don't let developers sneak in with a CD-ROM of gigantic images. You need to evaluate their work in the real environment, online with the computer/software/modem equipment most potential visitors will be using.
- Get references and check them. Ask if the developer was on time (and if not, was it the developer's fault?), if they went over budget, and did they fulfill their promises?

If internal development is chosen, make sure the assigned team has the expertise and resources to create an effective Web site. If external development is chosen, select an experienced firm who combines creativity with technical competence. Unless it's capable of attracting visitors and achieving sales on the fiercely competitive Internet, a Web site is a waste of money.

Internal Development

If you're going to develop internally and have your Web site server on your premises, at a minimum you'll need someone to take care of the computer itself and its inner workings. These people are called *system administrators.* If your budget is limited, compare the costs associated with programming your own site and providing your own server to using site-building software off the shelf and renting space on a provider's server.

You may think you'll use your existing system administrator. Chances are this person will be more than a little annoyed at having to take care of this particular setup. It opens up a whole new world and it's possible your employee may not be qualified.

Good system administrators are almost impossible to find. It's one of the most boring jobs you can imagine. Instead of providing a satisfying outlet for someone's creative urges, the job delivers high stress. You have to wear a pager to bed when you're on the Internet 24/365. If the system goes down at 4:00 A.M. on Christmas morning, your pager goes off. You have to race down to the office and fiddle with the server until it goes back online.

Being a system administrator requires an incredibly high level of knowledge. The only people capable of handling it are doing other things because they're really smart. To get a good system administrator you have to pay more than $100,000 a year at 1996 rates.

Beyond the system administrator, you'll need at least one software engineer at $60,000 a year to program the site. Make no mistake about this: at least one software engineer is the minimum for any serious Web site. For good reasons we call these talented people *software engineers,* not *programmers.* Web sites appear simple—this is part of the appeal and the fantastic success of the Web. It's true, any self-styled "programmer" can crank out Web pages using any of the hundred Web authoring tools on the market, just as anyone can write simple programs using off-the-shelf software. Software engineers are a cut above—they are classically trained in computer science and understand design methodology in addition to programming. They cost more but are well worth the extra investment. If you are planning on doing secure transactions or any level of order processing, you are making a big mistake if you don't hire engineers for the job.

Remember one key fact: Web sites are software engineering projects. Just because you can view Web sites on almost any computer in the world doesn't mean your Web site isn't a software program. It's not like printing a brochure where you can get a freelance artist to lay it out and then take your pick among thousands of printers and get beautiful copies in any quantity you want.

Creating a Web site is a software project; if you don't treat it as such you'll get burned. You'll run into delays; your site won't be up to the technical expectations of the very sophisticated people who frequent the Net;

your site will pale in comparison to other sites and it probably won't pay its way or even work.

If you're talking about commerce, you're talking about engineers, probably more than one. You may have a database engineer, an engineer who writes the host software, and an engineer to write the client software. Even if you're using a commercially available package, you don't just push the button and fill in the blanks. It's a very complex project.

A lot of companies have these people on staff, but you just don't take the person who's backing up the computers at night and say, "Here's what you're going to do in your spare time." If you're lucky, that person will quit when you delegate the extra assignment. If you're unlucky, he or she will stick around and pretend to do it until you catch on: nothing's happening except your firm is falling further and further behind in the race to adapt to the new conditions.

Now for the creative aspect of your site: You need everyone else required to produce a brochure but they *must* have Internet experience. Copywriters, artists, and layout people are also needed. They have to specifically understand the Web—its capabilities as well as its limitations. If you get regular print ad people, they inevitably end up trying to do online print ads. I've seen this happen dozens of times. They make gigantic graphics. They look beautiful on the projection screen when the printcentric people demonstrate their site plans for you. You'll love it—but it's not the real world of the Internet.

Once you go online, you slam into the real world, where most potential visitors to your Web site have standard Internet connections. This means your beautiful home page will take 3 minutes to load and 99 percent of your visitors are gone within 15 seconds.

Your copywriters have to understand hypertext so they can take advantage of its power. Your layout people have to understand the language of the Web, from which techniques work across all computers to which design no-no's make your site scream, "We don't understand this Internet business!"

And, on top of all the people already mentioned, you need a director to make sure it all happens.

Many companies hire a *Webmaster,* whose job encompasses all of those previously mentioned. Far from solving every problem, the decision to do this often results in important areas not being adequately handled. There's a simple reason for this: one individual can't possess every core competency required to meet all these responsibilities.

It's a different story after your site has been created; then one Webmaster can possibly maintain it. However, it's unrealistic to expect just one person to create a commercial-quality Web site in a reasonable time.

Step 6: Establish a Relationship with a Bank Possessing Ample Capability in E-Cash Transactions

Eventually banks lacking thorough Net cash experience and capability will be a rarity, but this is not true today. Make sure you select a bank with the expertise to handle your needs. If you plan to sell on the Web and automatically collect credit card or other payments online, you need a bank set up to receive those collections online, credit your account promptly, and keep you posted online. A list of banks advertising Internet commerce capability is given in App. B.

If a Web development firm is hired to produce your commerce site, it should be able to assist in the establishment of a relationship with a bank. However, if your firm already accepts credit cards, your present bank may be your best connection. Working with it may avoid having two bankcard relationships, one for over-the-counter or catalog sales and one for Internet sales.

Step 7: Determine the Appropriate Security Level for Your Planned Net Cash Transactions

This is important. Security involves the eternal struggle between convenience and safety. Imagine a horizontal line. On the left, there's the height of convenience, on the right the ultimate in security. If you have the ultimate in security, you take blood samples, fingerprints, and run multiple authorization checks. You have to pass 15 levels of checks when you walk into each room.

The other way is to have access without identification. Somewhere in between those two extremes is where you want to be. It depends on what you're selling and the concerns of the customers.

Certainly you'll want to lock the server in some secure place and use some form of encrypted transactions—such as PGP, SSL, or BBN Planet's Merchant Advantage system.

This is discussed in more detail in Chap. 7. You don't want to go too far into super security or people won't bother to use it.

Here's the most important thing to remember: Internet commerce is still more secure than any other kind of transaction. As long as you have basic security in place, making a purchase on your Web site is far more secure than paying for dinner with a credit card in a restaurant.

We just had lunch at California Pizza Kitchen in Marina del Rey. Probably at least three people saw, or could have seen, my credit card number while the payment was being authorized over an unsecured telephone line without counting the people on the other end of the line. There are more breaches of security involved in credit card purchases of the ordinary kind than most people realize. We're all used to them; we accept them because there's no other way we can use credit cards.

Then the Internet comes along. It's new, it's different; it's easy to imagine bogeymen—vicious hackers lurking out there in cyberspace who are eager to rip you off. Many of us decide it's far riskier than the credit card usage we're familiar with, when in fact the opposite is true, or at worst the two risks are about equal.

With Internet transactions, you send your number yourself, nobody else need see it at the point of origination. Systems are readily available to allow you to encrypt the number, send it to a trusted third party, who then completes your purchase from the vendor without giving your credit card number to the merchant.

As a result of the knee-jerk reaction of many consumers to the idea of sending their credit card number to merchants, Internet commerce is developing along far more secure lines than are used in other kinds of credit card transactions.

Step 8: Choose and Test Your Payment Collection System

Not only choose it, at the earliest possible opportunity, set up several transactions as near real life as you can organize. Use those transactions to test how well your first choice for a payment collection system works. Avoid skipping lightly over this requirement. If you do, you're likely to run into serious problems after you're online, costly, time-consuming, customer-annoying ones. If you are going to run into problems in this area, it's far better to thrash them out before going online.

And by testing, we mean test on every platform you can and with every method of making payment you plan to accept. Do you want to exclude buyers with Macintosh computers? If not, test the order form to make sure it can handle Mac orders.

What about buyers offering DigiCash tokens or transmitting Cyber-Cash encryptions? Do you want to process orders placed through Netscape browsers without foul-ups?

The methods of collecting or paying money over the Internet fall into five classes, arranged in order of practicality and need for most Web sites right now: credit card sales; e-cash sales, cost-effective small payment collection capability, checkless transfers, and EDI (electronic data interchange). Discussion of each method follows.

Credit Card Sales

You can't overlook the vast purchasing power of credit cards over the Internet, not with more than 300 million credit cards in the wallets of Americans. For start-up businesses and others having difficulty qualifying for credit card account status at their bank, there's a quick solution: merchant credit card services.

For more details, see the section entitled Spotlighting Credit Card Processing Companies in Chap. 6 and App. A.

You should be aware that accepting credit cards over the Internet poses the same risks as accepting them over the telephone. With telephone or Internet sales, the merchant generally bears the cost of fraudulent transactions. For this reason, verification systems such as VeriSign are strongly recommended. See Chap. 7.

UNENCRYPTED CREDIT CARD NUMBERS. All Web sites should be prepared to accept unencrypted credit cards in payment of purchases when supplied via the Internet just as so many companies do over the phone, frequently through well-advertised 800 numbers.

Many have been doing this for years with only minor problems. However, the many horror stories about theft of numbers should serve as a wake-up call to such businesses. The prudent course is to make sure your firm isn't accumulating databases of credit card numbers because they are likely to draw criminal activity the same way spilled food draws ants. The numbers should be encrypted or stored in a secure computer until the sale is completed, then promptly erased. This vital duty should be performed by reliable people supervised by a responsible executive.

However, with the rapid growth of encryption such as SSL built into the popular browsers, merchants will receive fewer credit card numbers in plain text.

ENCRYPTED CREDIT CARD NUMBERS. The original limitation to encrypting credit card numbers to defeat theft and misuse on the Internet has been overcome. No longer is it essential for the buyer to download special software. Some of the popular browsers such as Netscape include this feature.

Here's how it works: let's say Archibald cruises the Web looking for a good deal on tennis balls. Archie finds what he's looking for at the Balls-R-Us Web site, decides to buy two cans of his favorite tennis balls, and clicks on the purchase icon to jump to an order form. His computer and the seller's computer swiftly negotiate and agree on encryption keys and protocols. When Archie types his purchase information, all of it—including his credit card number—gets encrypted before it's sent. At the seller's end, the message arrives in the form of encrypted gibberish to be automatically deciphered into plain text so the order can be processed.

A hacker tapping into the line to steal credit card numbers would find it virtually impossible to do so. However, the seller has Archie's credit card number, which means the number could be stolen from the seller's office. However, the seller can set up procedures to tightly control who has access to credit card numbers. Certainly they can be eliminated from shipping and billing documents.

This level of security is far greater than any restaurant or store can offer to its customers who routinely hand their credit cards to a waiter or clerk to pay for a purchase. Whether this high level of security at virtually no inconvenience to the Internet buyer will satisfy large numbers of them remains to be seen.

Again, encryption does not reduce the risk of fraud to merchants. What reduces this risk is verification—electronically establishing the purchaser's identity.

Security is taken to an even higher level by systems requiring both buyer and seller to use the same software. The software of at least one firm, CyberCash, is free to consumers. Probably all future systems requiring identical software at both ends will also have to provide it free to consumers, whether included on free browsers or downloaded from the Internet without cost. As the concept of strict protection of credit card numbers becomes more widely understood, few consumers will buy from any Web site not offering a free and almost effortless way to guard against credit card crime.

Your Web site order form, therefore, should be designed to work smoothly with every popular browser or software encryption system, or you will lose a growing percentage of buyers as people become more knowledgeable in this regard.

For more information, see the section entitled A Quick Overview of Encryption Methods, Most of Which Are Available Now in Chap. 7.

E-Cash Sales

DigiCash, a Dutch company headquartered in Amsterdam, has made great strides in developing a system for the anonymous payment of money over the Internet. Receiving Net cash from a DigiCash customer is nice work if you can get it because it's immediately spendable and can't get charged back to you. The rub here is on the other end—the buyers must withdraw R-cash (real bucks) from their bank account and store them in their computer. When they buy from your company, they send an encrypted message to you. As a DigiCash merchant, your computer is able to decipher the message, extract the Net cash, and send it to your bank for immediate deposit.

Net cash systems claim they offer anonymity to the buyer. Consider an online order paid by anonymous cash tokens. The order includes instructions to ship to Seldom Seen Smith, 123 Old Soak Road, Butte, Montana. Chances are the purchaser is none other than the elusive Mr. S.S. Smith himself.

Some Web site owners say DigiCash gives the issue of anonymity far more importance than it deserves in the practical world of selling and delivering noncontroversial merchandise. No matter how much the Net cash companies belabor the anonymity issue, from a practical standpoint the chances of preserving the purchaser's anonymity go out the window when a Ship To address is given. Nevertheless, Seldom Seen's credit card number wasn't compromised or even at risk in the Net cash transaction because no human saw it, only computers did. From this important standpoint, his interests were amply protected by impenetrable cryptography.

For more details see DigiCash in the Spotlighting section of Chap. 4 and in App. A.

Cost-Effective Small Payment Collection Capability

Both CyberCash and DigiCash have workable systems for making extremely small sales. DigiCash mentions charging two cents to participate in a game; CyberCash talks about making sales practical from a low of a quarter to five dollars. Obviously, volume is the key to profits here—after all, a million sales at $0.25 produces $250,000.00 in gross revenue.

Checkless Transfers

Pioneered by the Checkfree Corporation, this system makes it convenient for consumers to pay bills electronically, without writing and mailing checks, and it does this for pennies less than the cost of a stamp to mail the check. However, the number of consumers who have established an account with Checkfree enabling them to make checkless payments is a tiny fraction of the people who have credit cards. Add the capability to accept checkless payments to your Web site after the need for it develops; until at least 1998, you can probably safely ignore this complication.

For more details see Checkfree in the spotlighting section of Chap. 6 and in App. A.

EDI (Electronic Data Interchange)

Considering the pace of change in computer technology, EDI is ancient, having been developed in the 1960s as a means of speeding the exchange of specifications and shipping documents. It was quickly seized upon as a means for exchanging all sorts of data. By the mid-1980s, the use of EDI technology was growing at the rate of 45 percent a year. Now more than 90 percent of Fortune 1000 companies use it extensively. In fact, so great is the power of EDI networking it's likely to become *the* way interorganizational business is conducted, if it's not already there. Major retailers such as WalMart require their vendors to be EDI-capable. The DOD has long relied on EDI to communicate with defense contractors.

All companies who sell to other companies should be prepared to handle EDI transactions, though not necessarily through their Web site. However, EDI is not a practical avenue for sales to consumers or small businesses.

Step 9: Select a Server/Software/ Connectivity Combination Powerful Enough to Service the Expected Load

How do you determine the expected load? If you're going to be doing massive transactions you'll need a powerful server, fast software, and lots of bandwidth. A powerful software and server combination can easily cost you $300,000 to $500,000, with $50,000 per month additional for bandwidth. Smaller sites can get away with a fast Pentium and software for $10,000 to $30,000, plus $500 per month in bandwidth. You can even start out without buying anything at all by renting everything for just a few hundred dollars per month. There are a number of service providers who offer various server/software/bandwidth solutions.

Make sure each of the three options—server, software, and bandwidth—are balanced. An Internet connection is only as strong as its weakest link. It won't do you any good to have a fast server trying to stuff information down bandwidth the size of a straw. Likewise, massive bandwidth and a slow server is pointless. Though a fast server will speed up even the slowest software, the reverse is not true. Many software packages can overwhelm low-end systems.

You might want to get a second opinion since it's so important. This experience can be likened to buying a car—it's easy to spend a lot of money on frills. On the other hand, you don't want to get something too slow. If the system is not fast enough, you're not going to make any money. Imagine if you spent $50,000 on a commercial, and it ran in slow motion; people wouldn't watch it. If you had to wait a year to get your product catalog, no one would want it.

Like on-hold service—if you have people waiting five hours to get technical support—it's not only ridiculous, it's a sure way to drive customers away. In this day and age you need to supply technical support immediately.

Step 10: Develop the Content of Your Web Site to Fully Exploit the Advantages of This New Medium

This doesn't necessarily mean you have to rely on all the latest—and often unproven—programs. Software known to have performed well for a year or two clearly is a safer bet than stuff on the bleeding edge. I have two rules to recommend to your consideration here:

> *Bleeding Edge Technology Rule 1: Don't blindly trust promises to deliver from software companies.* Use proven leading-edge technology such as animation and sound to increase the persuasive power of your

selling messages. Beware of using sexy-appearing (*sexy* meaning exciting) bleeding-edge technology. Most of the latest innovations don't work in the real world. For example, when we put together the proposal for the Sony PlayStation Web site in early 1995, Java was the buzz. Everyone was talking about it. We thought it was a great idea. Unfortunately, it didn't work. Many companies were promising it was going to work "soon," but it was mid-1996 before it started working reasonably well, and then only for limited uses. Had we gone with Java, we would have been in big trouble.

Bleeding Edge Technology Rule 2:   You can usually do it better with existing stuff.   As it turned out, we came up with a new use for existing technology and were able to deliver terrific results. It cost the client less, and we delivered the site right on time.

Step 11: Index Your Web Site's Content for Quick, Easy Visitor Access

I can't tell you how many times I've been on sites with poor navigational paradigms. It almost seems as if the site designers are trying to make it impossible for users to find anything. Most of the large sites are like this. Try and find something on Microsoft. If the designers at Microsoft are using the same interface today as they have from the beginning, you'll soon get lost. But on the other hand, there are some sites where it's a breeze to find things and the designers have intelligently indexed the information. They have search tools to enable you to find what you're looking for quickly and easily.

Let's define the difference between a search engine and an index:

An *index* in a Web site is like the traditional book index: it's a listing of items in the Web site with an indication where each one can be found.

A *search engine* allows you to enter a word or series of words, and then presents you a list of places where your words are located on the site.

Indexes and search engines complement each other, as they appeal to different styles of browsing. An index is a useful starting place for first-time visitors, while the power of a search engine allows more advanced visitors to escape the limitations of an index and locate the precise information they're seeking.

If your search engine merely mirrors your index, it's nothing more than a useless confusion to the visitor. As with everything on your Web site, each element must add usefulness or it shouldn't be there. If you index your site and break it up into widgets, gadgets, gommies, and how to contact us, it's great.

The search engine should help visitors go further. It should be able to assist in locating a purple gommie with an XQ option; if not, it should explain why or point them in the right direction. Make no assumptions. It's important to analyze how people will move through your site, and then make it very easy for them to do so.

Step 12: Optimize Your Web Site's Graphics

Optimizing is the process of fine tuning your graphics for the Internet. Many Web sites look beautiful but take forever to download. The folks at Macromedia have a Vanguard Gallery which has the coolest stuff with

Good design of a Web home page.

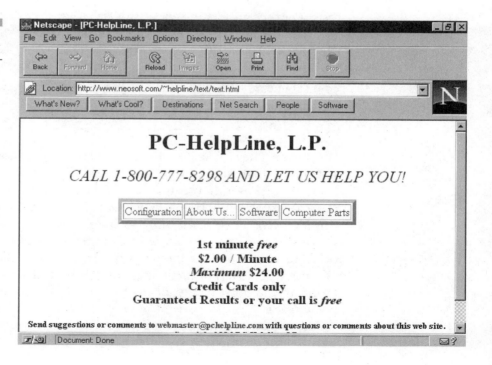

My browser is set on the standard view most people cruising the Net will be using. That is, a small monitor with all the default options which further eat up screen "real estate." It doesn't provide a lot of viewing space, which means good Web site design aimed at consumers takes this reality seriously. In other words, site designers don't have a lot of space to work with.

Concern for this problem is evident here. What I like about this page is

- Everything important fits within the first bit of information you get.

- So, we have right at the top, Who We Are: PC Help Wanted

- Right below is an 800 number. "Call and let us help immediately."

- Next appear some links configuration about computer software and other things this company offers.

- Below—but still in the first view the visitor sees—is the important stuff—first minute free, then it's $2 a minute and so on. The company only accepts credit cards and guarantees results.

- Another great thing about this site: it gives an e-mail address to a live human being so you can make contact by e-mail if you prefer not to call. Right away you have two ways of contacting the company and a link about it taking you to more information.

- There are no graphics and it doesn't matter. It just gets its information across perfectly.

Shockwave. They categorize the recommended speed for accessing the site, 14.4, is the highest award for the fastest experience—meaning you can enjoy the site even if you have an old 14.4 modem. On the other end of the scale are absurdly large files which take forever to download. They call this level *Ethernet Plus,* meaning to enjoy the site it basically needs to be sitting on your desktop computer. (*Ethernet* is a local area network capable of delivering millions of bits a second.) So, you can look at some sites such as the Virgin Entertainment site, which is beautiful but has an Ethernet rating. If you don't have your own personal T-1 connection to the Internet, forget it.

The Nissan site we created received a 14.4, meaning we tested it on the most common modem speed in use today: 14,400 bits per second. We

Terrible design of a
Web home page.

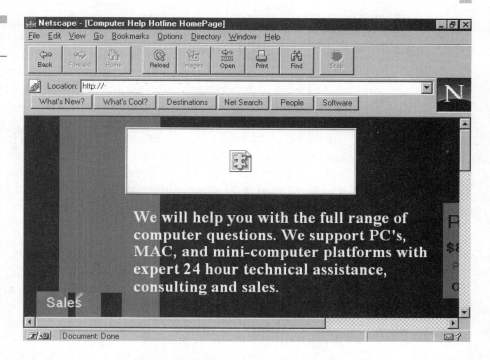

Let's look at this page at the same resolution as Good Design used, in other words the standard size most Web visitors have. At the top of the page appears this big white box enclosing a strange little puzzle device. How many people know that this puzzle icon means you don't have the piece of technology required to see this page?

The people who put this site together assume you, being an early adopter, will have this high-technology link—yet they're doing technical support. Early adopters don't really need this kind of technical support. It's the perfect example of technology for technology's sake.

They do say they'll help you with a full range of computer questions, but there's no way to reach them. Most people don't even realize you can scroll the view in a browser. As a result, the visitors who are most likely to need this firm's services will just give this dysfunctional page a glassy-eyed stare and go, "Ummm, forget it. I'm outa here." Nothing on the page makes me want to stay, nothing tells me how to use the scanty information offered.

Put your upfront information in a window most people normally see. Cut to the chase—or you're out of the running.

spent a lot of time and effort maximizing the experience for the average user. The effort was worth it. You've got to optimize your graphics. You've got to make sure it looks pretty but also make it so people can access it fast.

If I were to do a beautiful four-color picture for a one page print ad in a magazine, you're looking at a 50-megabyte file. You can't do it on the Internet. The math is easy. The average connection to the Internet runs about 1K (1000 bits) per second on a 14.4 modem. There are 1000K in a megabyte. So a 50-megabyte file would take about 25,000 seconds, or about 6.9 hours, to download! Fortunately the information stored in the photograph is more than you need. For example, magazine articles print out at 1200 to 2400 dots per inch (dpi) and have a very small granularity. Hold up a print ad and you're lucky if you can see the individual pixels, or dots.

Most monitors are at 72 dpi, which means anything over 72 dpi is wasted—the computer just throws it away. Those extra dpis not only are wasted, they still have to be downloaded, which takes much longer without accomplishing anything. Many inexperienced graphic artists who don't understand the Internet make this blunder. They create graphics at 150 dpi or more and wipe out the Web site with a beautiful picture no one will ever see because you can't resolve the higher dpis on screen.

Print is typically *24-bit true color*—16.7 million colors can be viewed simultaneously—it's photographic quality and beautiful. Most browsers can display no more than 256 colors which is 8 bits. Each bit takes up space so an 8-bit instead of 24-bit image is nominally 3 times faster to download. So, you're looking at a third decrease if you go from 24 bit to 8. And you're looking at more of a decrease if you drop from 300 dpi—it's more than a third.

Step 13: Develop a Comprehensive and Aggressive Web Site Promotion Plan

If you build a beautiful Web site and don't promote it, no one will come! It won't matter how gorgeous, technically advanced, informative, convenient, and value-packed it is. Nobody will see it!

Lycos, a well-known search engine, claims to have cataloged 30 million Web pages as of late 1996; HotBot claims almost 60 million; a more modest Magellan claims to have indexed 2 million. Whether the actual count is under 100,000 or over 60 million, obviously a huge number of Web pages are out there—far more than anyone could possibly visit. And all of them compete for your potential buyers' limited time, interest, and money. It's not like television or radio where you run your commercial and a certain number of people are certain to see or hear it. Put your ad in a magazine and someone will see it. But except for a minuscule few who might hit your site by accident and be gone with another quick mouse click, no one ever sees your Web site unless that person deliberately seeks it out.

So you've got to let your target audience know where you are. Promote, promote, promote. Especially, miss no opportunity to promote your Web site on the things you control. Here are three equally vital Web site promotion rules:

Web Site Promotion Rule 1

Put your URL everywhere you can.   Your address, called a *URL* (Universal Resource Locator), will often be something like http://www.yourcompanyname.com.

Adding it to the things you pay to produce will add only insignificantly to their cost, but can return large dividends in the form of greater traffic to your Web site, giving you additional opportunities to sell the visitors.

- Display your URL prominently on all your packaging.
- Display your URL prominently on all your non-Internet advertising. It's an easy thing to do, although you may have to lean on your advertising agency to get it done. Don't settle for the brief flash of the URL often seen on TV commercials; make sure it stays on-screen for at least 5 seconds. Give interested people a chance to memorize it or copy it down.
- Display your URL on business cards and stationery, on brochures, catalogs, presentations, and on every piece of paper you can.
- Put your URL on your voice mail system and technical support system.
- Add your URL to your company's e-mail signature and to your fax transmission sheet.

Web Site Promotion Rule 2

Get yourself listed on every search engine. A number of sites provide for free or for a fee an automatic listing with the major search engines. (See App. D.) It's a good idea to use several of them. Make sure to follow the rules, as you may not be notified if you mess something up. These automatic listing services ask somewhat technical questions—if you aren't positive about the answer, don't submit. If they ask for a brief description, say, in 20 words or less, make sure you stick within the limits. At best, a noninterested person will edit them. Extra words might simply be chopped off by a processing computer. Or your request might be denied.

When you describe your offerings, make sure to list yourself as the *official* site (if you are the official site). Remember, there are most likely unofficial sites out there maintained by individuals. Keep your description extremely brief and be sure to mention what unique service or information you are offering. You're writing a tease here, trying to lure the picky Web surfer to your site, so get creative. Don't put overt sales pitches in your description, because many search engines prohibit this.

TIPS FOR SEARCH ENGINE PLACEMENT. When people use search engines, the results of their queries are displayed in a listing. Ideally, your company would be listed at or near the top of any relevant keyword search on all the major search engines on the Web. To achieve this requires attention to each engine and a certain amount of luck and timing.

If you search for the same thing on different search engines you'll turn up different results. Not only is the order in which the results are displayed different, but frequently one engine will turn up references another does not. This is simply because the wealth of information on the Internet is so large and changing it cannot all be contained in a single database. Each engine uses its own unique methods to catalog this vast amount of data.

Although a number of technical tricks can be played to increase the visibility of your site on some engines, this too is changing all the time. A constant battle goes on as the operators of engines seek to prevent wily developers from circumventing their methods of prioritizing search results.

You can help to assure your site gets as close to the top of the list by visiting each search engine site and examining their guidelines for submission. Don't wait until you go live to submit to the search engine; some take weeks to process your request.

Some search engines don't accept submissions. For them, make sure all of your Web pages contain some relevant information in text so when the automated robots from search engines come across your site, they can properly scan and index your information. Any words represented as graphics will not be seen by these robots, so be sure you have text as well.

Web Site Promotion Rule 3

Find all the places your typical customer accesses and get linked there.

■ Get listed with all the related companies in your field.

■ Do something a bit flashier than your competition so you'll definitely be among those accessed.

The Internet almost certainly has existing groups involved in some way with your market. Interest groups, dedicated individuals, knowledge resources, and discussion groups are ways your market might be present. Where do you find these groups? Use the large search engines—type in your market or key words and phrases and see what comes up. Try several combinations

There is another extremely important reason to become involved. If you can, dedicate someone for a couple of hours a week to spend time being part of these groups. Sports groups, gardening groups, wine tasting groups—whatever fits your product. Assign this person to monitor and interact. Suppose a competitor, a disgruntled customer, or a sociopath posts a message on the Internet saying Jumping Joe's Wines are terrible, and you're Jumping Joe's grandson who runs the business now. The complainer might claim the people who jump in the vat to stomp the juice out of the grapes have athlete's foot, gangrene, or worse. You want to respond quickly and show that this archaic practice went out when your grandfather retired. Today, at your winery, the grapes are machine-pressed under highly sanitary conditions.

Slander and other issues you'll want to deal with can come up at any time in your areas of interest on the Internet. It's vital to respond quickly and effectively because people—including both potential or existing customers—often take things like this very seriously.

Remember the Intel-Pentium bug disaster? It was started on the Internet by one person. Here's what happened:

Someone called Intel and requested a replacement of the defective chip. Intel refused. So, the guy got on the Internet and posted a particularly scathing message and started getting people stirred up. Pretty soon the media picked it up and blew this disgruntled customer's complaint way out of proportion. It became a major disaster for Intel because Intel didn't have the proper Internet controls in place. It didn't have anyone monitoring the right Usenet newsgroups who could put the Intel spin on whatever popped up. If it had, it could have caught it before the media did and averted a PR disaster of major proportions.

Step 14: Test Your Web Site

Make sure it looks sharp and works well when accessed with the arrangements most visitors will use to reach your site. Make any indicated adjustments.

In 1996 two big browsers were fighting for control of the market—Microsoft's Internet Explorer and Netscape. There's also AOL and a host of other smaller browsers. They are mostly compatible but not completely, so it's difficult to get 100 percent unless you're doing text only.

Most sites should try for 80 or 90 percent of the total Internet audience. Some sites catering to early adopters can occasionally get away with targeting less. If you have a site today compatible with Internet Explorer and Netscape you're getting 90 percent of the audience. Check it under those two browsers even if you're not going to be able to do some of the whiz-bang stuff because some people are using the old versions. Just be sure it works.

Make sure to test your site out on older versions of browsers as well. For example, there are still going to be a lot of people out there using Netscape version 1, even though Netscape has issued several later versions.

Any good software developer will test those browsers, and, if there's a problem, they'll notify you about it and allow you to make a choice or just do it automatically for you.

Step 15: Test Your Tracking and Reporting Software

Test it thoroughly before you go online—debug your site before the world hits it; problems in your Web site would reflect poorly on your firm's technical competence. Make sure you're properly tracking it and getting the information you want. Be certain you have set out in advance how many people are hitting the areas, what's working, and the reports are readable and in understandable formats because a lot of untested reports won't make sense.

Make sure you can understand the reports before they go online. If you don't understand them, go back to the programmers or site builders and tell them you don't understand it. What's a hit? What does this mean? If you're not happy with it, fix it before it goes live.

If tracking and reporting aren't being done consistently on your site, time and money are being wasted. You're losing one of the main advantages of the Internet—being able to get feedback in the form of highly useful and up-to-date reports. You don't get such feedback from magazine ads. At best, you only know approximately how well it's doing; at worst, you don't have a clue. It's the same with radio or TV commercials; mostly you take results on faith.

By contrast, feedback methods on the Internet are already powerful, and they're improving every day.

Step 16: Test Your Form-Processing and Order-Taking Systems and Software

Make sure they're convenient and readily accessible by every kind of computer. You might want to do a focus test and make sure people can quickly see how to use your forms and complete purchases. You're in business to collect money from other people; make it easy for people to purchase from your company and to give you their money.

Some of the online sites make it difficult to buy. It should merely be a click and you're there, with an easily completed order on your screen. Simplify, simplify, simplify. Avoid programming your site to ask unnecessary questions before it can close a sale. Run your surveys later with online promotions or by e-mail; this too can be programmed to occur automatically. Work out the bugs before going online.

If you are interfacing to existing systems, check to be sure orders can be placed, edited, and deleted without duplication or loss.

Step 17: Test the Cash Throughput of Your Banking Arrangements

Make sure you're getting your money on time. If your electronic deposits are supposed to be there in 24 hours, test this system before putting your products up for sale online. If you have to change banks, it will be far easier to do it before your Web site goes active, than after. See App. B.

Step 18: Protect Your Server Against Unauthorized Access

Make certain your server is physically and electronically protected against unauthorized access to sensitive databases such as customer credit card numbers.

If you're hosting the site yourself and if the computer is on your company's premises, consider your exposure. If you're collecting credit card information you have an obligation to take prudent steps to prevent the data from being stolen for fraudulent purposes. Failure to do so could be costly in terms of legal expenses, awards for damages, bad publicity, loss of customers, and other unpleasantness.

Put your server in a vault. Lock it away and don't let anyone get to it. If someone with criminal intent copies the numbers and other data, you can find yourself spending more time stomping on snakes than growing your business.

If you're locating a site with a provider, make sure they lock it down and it's in a secure area. Be certain your firewalls are in place. *Firewalls* act as a barrier between your company's computers and the Internet. They help keep hackers from gaining access to your sensitive data. Although a detailed firewall discussion is beyond the scope of this book, some information about them is given in Chap. 7. No commerce site should be without firewall protection.

Step 19: Activate Your Web Site Promotion Plan

Before you go live, activate your promotion plan. It takes weeks to get set up on search engines. It also takes time to establish relationships with other Web sites.

You should be talking to people who are into your product area as soon as you have a clear idea when you'll be able to go live with your site. It makes these people feel special to be in on the start-up.

From people who possess specialized knowledge in your field, you can get valuable input on the process of activating an effective Web site. Maybe they'll identify key points you might otherwise miss. Another long-term dividend accrues from involving key figures in your field in the start-up: they'll be allies for life.

Step 20: Go Live on the Internet

Do all the fanfare you can: issue a press release; put it on the business and PR wire—make a big deal about it. Mainstream media probably won't pick it up because it's no longer newsworthy to simply put up a Web site, unless there's a special hook for the story. Give your fanfare the strongest possible push anyway. Many people subscribe to electronic clipping services to monitor the wires looking for information they are interested in. And the trade magazines in your field are likely to use a piece based on your announcement.

Be sure as many people as possible know about your exciting new Web site. If you have a newsletter, make your Web site the lead article before you go online, after you go online, feature it in every issue.

Announce it on your voice mail. Most people think at this stage their Web site job has just about finished. However, the job really begins at the next step.

Step 21: Update—Beginning As Soon As You Go Live—with New Contests, Special Offers, New Products, Intriguing Promotions, and an Intensified Web Site Publicity Campaign

Keep your Web site growing. Keep adding new features, new reasons for people to visit it. You might think if you do a good job developing and testing your Web site before you go online, you won't have anything new to add to it for a long time. The contrary seems to be true more often: once you're online you start getting a flow of reports and ideas for improving. Act on them. Your Web site should be better tomorrow than it is today.

Tell people when you're going to be changing the site, as in: "The next update will be Wednesday, (date)."

Even if your changes are minor, keep making them. Freshness is the key to Web site success.

Step 22: Set up and Maintain a Regular Schedule of Frequent Updates

Don't let this vital marketing duty get lost in the turmoil of daily demands. Make it someone's job to frequently update your Web site. Take it on yourself to make sure this gets done. If you let it slide onto the back burner, your Internet customer base will slip away to the competition instead of growing steadily—or even explosively.

Step 23: Modify Your Marketing Staff Assignments and Structure to Be Sure Frequent, Repeat-Visitor-Causing, E-Selling Updates Will Continue As Long As the Grass Grows and the Internet Flows

Make certain you're continuing to attract repeat visitors. If people aren't returning, try to find out why. How can you find out? It's really very simple: you have all the tools necessary to do the job at almost no cost and with very little effort. Here's how to send a "We've missed you" message to everybody who qualifies:

■ Pull up a list of every customer who hasn't logged in again or bought anything for whatever time period is appropriate to your business.

■ Draft a one-size-fits-all e-mail "We've missed you" message. With a bit of software legerdemain you can have your computer pull up what each customer bought and when it was shipped. Crank this information into your e-mail messages to personalize them.

This is important: analyze your lost customer file by product bought. Studying this information can alert you to serious quality or price problems with specific items you might not otherwise notice.

■ Tell them you appreciate their business, and you want to deserve their business. If they don't feel you do, you would deeply appreciate being told exactly why. Of course this opens your firm up to taking a lot of heat and possibly getting demands for refunds or replacements. But what's better? Letting angry customers stew in their own acid, or encouraging them to tell you what angered them so you can do something about their complaints and take steps to prevent the same thing from happening to other customers?

■ Look on your regular "We've missed you" message procedure as a powerful instrument for uncovering weak links in your operation. Just make sure you reply promptly to any customer who reports a problem. If you take too much time responding to customer complaints, you risk letting a mild complaint fester into an angry one. This means you have to staff this activity adequately. It's shortsighted to look on such an activity as "soft," in other words, as useless overhead. Properly conceived and run, this small subsection of your marketing department can produce priceless "hard" results.

■ The "We've missed you" message should be an ongoing procedure, perhaps carried out monthly, quarterly, or semiannually. In order to keep each round of messages fresh, tie the wording to the season or some event.

　■ "We haven't heard from you since last spring."

　■ "We haven't heard from you since the Olympics."

　■ Or even, "We haven't heard from you this year."

■ Offer something to former customers who take the time to answer your "We've missed you" message: free product, entry into a special contest, a one-time discount, in any case, something of value appropriate to what you sell.

For most businesses, discovering exactly why former customers stopped buying is vital. So is finding out exactly why first-time buyers did not become repeat customers.

Equally important is keeping regular customers buying. To this end, offer a service for people who come back, whether it's an ongoing newsletter e-mailed to them with inside tips, new offers, special prices, or discounts. Chances are your best prospects are the people who've already bought. Cultivate them, prize them, reward them for coming back again and again. The Internet's World Wide Web is today's most powerful method of building repeat customers. Work it diligently for all it's worth!

Consider this fact: a good Web development company can take care of most of the above issues, tasks, and opportunities listed in these 23 steps. The World Wide Web has already become a teeming jungle, where vast riches are concealed under baffling layers of foliage. If you want to move quickly through the undergrowth and find your company's rewards, enlist the services of the best guide you can find: an experienced, multi-talented Web site development firm.

Organizing Your Web Site for Net Cash and Credit Card Sales

Let's get right to work on organizing your Web site to take maximum advantage of the Internet's great potential power to boost your company's sales and profitability. The key things to remember as you set out to do this are three simple and painfully obvious but all too often overlooked facts:

- The Internet is not TV, it's not a magazine ad, it's not direct mail, it's not radio, and it's definitely not a billboard on the highway or a logo banner in a sports field.
- The Internet is an entirely different medium from all the others. It has its own unique and unforgiving realities, limitations, and requirements.
- You play by the Internet's rules or you automatically lose.

Automate Replies to Standard Buyer Questions

You can program your Web site to be an alert sales agent that never sleeps. So, just as you supply your living salespeople with all the information they need to counter client objections and meet people's needs—work what you know people will ask about your product or service into your Web site. You want to distill this down to key points and put it up on the site in a logical way. It may be as simple as the five most common questions people ask. In this case, just have a link called *Frequently Asked Questions*. (They're called *FAQs* for short.)

Typically, this section is laid out in a question and answer format—it's a standard Internet document and it says, Question: How many Bugaboos does it take to make a Gadget?

Do it in a logical way so people can search for it and find the information easily. If you handle standard customer questions well right from the start, you're already much closer to closing a sale.

A lot of Web sites put up an online brochure no more interactive than a Sears catalog or a flyer somebody sticks on your windshield. The designers don't say to themselves, "Now we have this great new medium enabling us to involve prospects in dialogs about what we want to sell them. Let's make the most of it."

Take time and meet with the various groups in your organization. Find out what it's really like in the trenches where your sales battles are fought.

Ask questions such as these:

- What are our current customers asking for most often?
- What are the key questions prospects are likely to ask?
- Can any of these questions be answered on the Web site?
- What are our customers' frustrations and wishes?
- Can these be addressed on our site?
- Is there a unique pool of information or service we can provide for our customers in the online environment?
- What sort of people will be looking at our site?

Ask these questions first of your own staff, then go further. Ask potential clients, existing clients, the media, vendors, prospective employees, and related industries. Those are some possibilities; in your unique situation there are probably others. Imagine yourself as a member of each one of these groups, one at a time. What would you be looking for from this site?

Categorize for Easy Access

Now take all of this information and categorize it. You'll want no more than six top-level areas to your Web site, or you run the risk of overwhelming your customer. These areas might be

- Order form
- Company information
- Product information
- Product comparisons
- Customer service

Already you're establishing dialog. Someone can look at these top-level points on your home page and say, "I've done business with these people for 20 years. I know about them so I just want to place my order."

Another customer could say, "I've been getting my gadgets from Widgets, Inc. and want to know how you stand up against them." And so on. Think through who the people are who'll be coming to your site and how can you immediately point them in the right direction—toward buying your product.

Use the Power of the Web

Make it simple. The Web is at least two-dimensional—use this power. A lot of companies have a huge document of hundreds of words and they assume people will page through it until they find the right information. The client won't do it. You have to organize your information in increasing levels of detail.

How you organize your Web site is critical. This Web site may be your only contact with this person. Maximize it and respect their time. Don't assume someone will spend an hour reading through text. Imagine you're a salesperson and you're in front of a really impatient person. Be aware of a vital fact: you only have a few seconds to interest this person, so you'd better distill your message down to the most powerful essentials. Then, give the person the opportunity to ask for more. If they want it, provide it. If they don't want more, ask them to buy. Set your Web site up to operate on those lines.

Avoid the urge to add too many levels of organization to your site. Make sure useful information is right up front and that each level deeper in your site adds detail and information. Don't save up your key points until the third click into your site. People rarely get below the second or third level of a site unless they're deeply interested.

So, up front present top-line statements about quality control or whatever points make it work for your product or service. Put it out there in easy, short, understandable bits. Keep it short—short sentences, with a minimum of choices. You might use a question-answer format or a bulleted list of statements.

For example, your home page might start with an introductory paragraph and these five bullet points:

- What is a *Gadget?*
- Why our Gadgets are the best
- Order your Gadgets now
- Contact customer service
- About Gadgets, Inc.

Each of these points would link to another area with another level of information. The first area might consist of a few brief paragraphs with another bulleted list such as

- Aerospace Gadgets
- Computer Gadgets
- Pet Gadgets

- Why our Gadgets are the best
- Order your Gadgets now

Each of these points might have a sentence or two below them and also be linked to their own pages. The point here is not to overwhelm but to guide and inform. There is a place for extensive information on your site, but it is not at the second level. Here, information should, at a minimum, consist of the key points you want to make along with links allowing visitors to investigate further if they wish.

Notice also we've included the top-line points from the first page in our second level. Make it easy for visitors to navigate your site! When you finish describing why you're the best, provide a way for them to order. Don't make them go back to the home page or go into a major search. Give them every opportunity to order easily.

Navigation Bars

A great way to add this functionality is with navigation bars (*navbars*). Navigation bars are one of the most commonly understood methods of moving through a site.

Think of navbars as miniature versions of your top-line areas you've made available on every page of your site for the visitor's convenience. Keep them small, easy to understand, and unchanging.

On the Nissan site, the navigation bar and the Nissan logo sit on top of every page. The bar has six areas—the Nissan logo which takes you back to the home page, the four main areas of the site, and a link to a keyword search capability. You can quickly find the information you want because we laid out the site clearly and summarized it in the navigation bar. You gain the advantage of branding each page with your corporate or product logo as well as utilizing a well-understood way for people to navigate your site.

A navbar is an enhancement to standard text-based navigation; it's not a replacement. If you decide to use a navbar, make sure you keep text links

At the Nissan site, the navbar summarizes the site's information and provides a clear path for users to navigate.

as well. Many people view sites with graphics turned off. Your navbar won't be visible to these visitors, so you need to provide them with a text-based method of navigating.

Navbar Rules

If you must use icons, use easy-to-understand icons. Don't make visitors waste time trying to decipher the meaning of a strange picture. Always append text to every icon you use, no matter how universal you may think the meaning of an icon.

Put the navbar on every page (an exception could be your home page). Keep the number of items on the bar to a minimum.

Navbar No-Nos

On many sites, you see changed navbars every time you visit a new area on the site. This supposedly helps users know what area of a site they're visiting. However, your visitor has to wait for the new navbar in each area to download. Pointless delays can drive your customers away. Get rid of them.

One-to-One Automated Marketing

For example, let's say we're selling CDs on the Net. You may be interested in classical music and particularly in Beethoven. The first time you visit our site you might look under the Beethoven section—we record this information. The next time you come back, our computer accesses the customer database and throws up a page saying, "Welcome back. Just so you know, we have a new Beethoven CD just released by London Phil-harmonic." This has been called *one-to-one marketing*. You can't do this with a TV commercial, a print ad, or a radio spot. If you try one-to-one marketing with direct mail, it's intrusive and a large percentage of it hits the trash unopened. But on the Web you're not intruding because they came to you. And when they did, you welcomed them with a word of friendly involvement in their interests. People like to be remembered and welcomed; but they don't like to be intruded upon.

No other medium allows you to do this. We're talking about making a television commercial on the fly for each specific viewer. Imagine if you could monitor people's television habits by computer. While they're enjoying a program, your robot could see them drinking Coke and eating potato chips. So, all they'd get would be commercials for snack foods.

For another example of one-to-one marketing, go to Yahoo or any other large search engine on the Web. Search for a common word such as *computer*. It's no coincidence when you see a computer-related banner pop up on the top of the screen. The advertiser paid for the word *computer* there. Type in *car* and you'll get an ad from an automaker such as Nissan.

You can take advantage of this power on your site through some form of registration.

All Web sites track where people go in a log file. The log file records every request made. There are some great programs and services out there to process your log files and give you back reports remarkable for their detail. However, if you take the extra step and incorporate registration, you can track how your Web site is being used much better. You can begin to accumulate information of great value in establishing stronger relationships with your customers or clients.

Tactics

Give something away and you'll get people to sign up for your mailing list. We've gotten tremendous responses for all the promotions we've run. It's still the golden rule: if you offer a tangible product, people will sign up. Tangible product giveaways are best; the second best tactic is to offer a special service.

There are two methods of collecting registration information: authenticated registration and invisible registration. Choosing between them is your first decision. Both methods have their advantages and disadvantages, as discussed in the next section.

Registration, Surveys, and Tracking: Tactics and Benefits

Registration, surveys, and tracking are closely related on the Web. Though you can obtain much useful information by analyzing the raw data recorded by any Web site, registration opens up a new and higher level of possibilities.

Authenticated Registration

Authenticated registration means your visitors have to enter a name and password combination each time they visit your site.

Two points of view regarding authenticated registration are often put forth. One camp states everything on your Web site should be accessible to everyone. Supporters of this view maintain it's not a good idea to require registration to gain access to certain areas of your site. The other side sees it this way: unless you perform some sort of registration, you lose several of the chief benefits of the Web. Specifically, you lose the precise tracking of visitors necessary for one-to-one marketing and automated relationship building.

The truth is, authenticated registration makes sense for only a few sites. Provided it's handled properly, you can overcome most of the obstacles. As we will see, for most sites, invisible registration can provide many of the advantages of authentication.

Certainly you'll want to use authenticated registration if you are providing a fee-based service. Authentication might work for non fee-based services so long as the service cannot otherwise be obtained without authentication elsewhere on the Web. You might also want to use authenticated registration for promotions with giveaways attached. Be warned—you'll lose quite a lot of people up front by requiring them to register or fill anything out before they can access your site. Another fact to keep in mind: a very high percentage of registrants who are given a password will immediately lose it.

Invisible Registration

Invisible registration tracks who visits your site without requiring the visitor to enter any information. It's another way to gather information on a Web site and set yourself up to carry on one-on-one marketing. It's possible to track who's coming in and remember what they've done and what they're interested in much the same way as authenticated registration, but without requiring users to fill out any forms or remember any passwords. Because there are many ways to do this, and new ways to do this are always being invented, we call this *invisible registration*. This means of registration generally involves passing a small token stored on the visitor's computer. You can then check for these tokens whenever a person returns to your site (providing the visitor is using the same browser and computer).

Invisible registration is not suitable for fee-based services, as it is not a secure method and is not *transportable*. This means each individual computer is tracked, not each individual.

Online Surveys

One of the primary objectives of an online promotion is to gather information. People will fill out entire surveys if there is a possibility of winning something, but how do you get them to remember their passwords?

The solution is simple—tie participation in the promotion to the one piece of unique information every user of the Internet possesses: his or her e-mail address.

This has two advantages. First, you are collecting e-mail addresses for possible follow-up by e-mail to turn them into customers. Second, everyone will be able to either remember or easily get their e-mail address.

Whether or not online survey information is statistically correct is another story. Online surveys can be valuable in determining general interests. However, data gathered in this manner should not be compared to true surveys conducted by professionals. Online surveys are generally less expensive than focus tests, test marketing, or other means of collecting data, but they do not compare to full-scale studies with carefully controlled sample sizes.

Another thing you can do is to have a mailing list—some call it a guest book. Because these generally do not offer any benefit to the person filling them out, responses should be treated as a very hot lead and immediately followed up.

Tracking

Once you have tracking information, put it to use. Evaluate your site at least once a month after it goes online. Look for trends:

- What areas are most popular? Least popular?
- From which pages do people most often leave our site?

Ideally the answer to the second question will be the page where orders are confirmed. If people are leaving frequently from a different area than this, you've just located a page, and perhaps an entire area, in serious need of rethinking and improvement.

■ What percentage of visitors place an order?

Keep polishing and refining your site after you launch it. Repeat visitors expect to find new information and new ideas from your company. Your updates don't have to be daily, but you do need to update your site frequently if you're serious about attracting repeat visits.

Process Consumer Credit Card and Debit Card Purchases Automatically

Obviously, you can automate your entire sales process on your Web site. But do you want to? Here are several things to think about when considering this question.

Cost

Putting up a Web site can be extremely cost-effective. However, adding the necessary software and technical expertise to automate credit/debit card purchases increases the investment significantly—one can easily spend $50,000 to $500,000 on the required elements. This brings up a key question: *Will your clients use it?*

Possible Disruption

Does accepting and processing credit card orders streamline the ordering process for clients?

Would this new and territory-intrusive selling method interfere with your existing distribution methods and relationships?

In other words, would you be burning bridges with retailers, distributors, or your sales force?

Automate Your Post-Sale Follow-Up

The technology of the Internet opens up tremendous possibilities for post-sale follow-up. You probably captured the client's e-mail address when you closed the sale, meaning you can send the client product updates, electronic newsletters, notices of sales, and other promotional material at little or no cost.

However, with those possibilities comes a tremendous potential for backlash. Internet slang for junk e-mail is *spam*. If you spam your customers, you might as well call them up and ask them to use a competitor.

The key here is to make sure your follow-up e-mails are perceived as useful or as expressing care on your part. Here are some spam-free guidelines for effective e-mail:

- Ask before sending!

- Always give every customer the opportunity not to hear from you. As your clients submit their e-mail addresses, tell them you'll keep the information confidential and give them a box to check if they do not wish to receive e-mail from you.

- Offer useful information or a legitimate follow-up.

- Don't just send an e-mail detailing your product offerings or yelling loudly about a sale.

- Send useful information only—tips on maximizing your product, for example. It's okay to send a follow-up after a sale along the lines of "Thanks for purchasing one of our XL-500G gadgets. If you have any questions, I'm here to help."

- Make sure a human being signs all such e-mail. Make it personal.

- Calculate the normal replacement cycle of your product or service. If it's three months, early in June, e-mail everybody who bought in March. If your product's cycle is three years, e-mail them in two years and nine months.

- Never send an e-mail out asking the person to come back with no reason.

- Put something interesting up there. Woe to the company who does not update its site—people will never return.

- Keep it short.

- If you have a lot of great information to share, keep it on your Web site and just let the client know it's there. Don't send more than a single short paragraph of information.

- Include an explicit address in your e-mail. This allows the recipient to click on the address and go immediately to the site in question.

- You need experts on this because the wrong syntax—a period in the wrong place for example, can cancel out this whole process. You need experts monitoring the pulse beat of your Web site—people who understand the process in technical detail.
- Don't send anything more than once.
- Always use a proper return e-mail address.
- A fake return address is the sure sign of spam. You wouldn't print a fake phone number on your product, don't do it in e-mail.
- Always give clients the ability to remove themselves from your list.

Include a statement such as this at the end of every e-mail you send out: "If you wish to be removed from our e-mail list, reply to this message with a subject including the word REMOVE."

Your technical folks can automate this process.

Automate Your Tech Support

This is so awesome. It's one of the best uses of a Web site for any company. It's automated tech support or customer support. People call up Gadgets, Inc. with busted gadgets. Gadgets probably break most frequently on Friday at 5:01 P.M.! Or a first-time buyer gets a brand new gadget out of the box and only has a chance to look at it after work on Friday. Opening up the box, the client finds the scroungemong is missing, or the parts aren't going together properly. The customer is sitting there seething for 72 hours muttering, "Dammit, those airheads can't get a simple part in the box. How irresponsible can you get?"

This is not the way to build a loyal clientele.

They can call up your voice mail hell: "Thank you for calling Gadgets, Incorporated. If you have a Gadget, Model 9, press 1, etc., etc." Everyone hates how the recording goes on and on.

Customers can call up a company's fax machine; first they have to request the list of available documents. The company then faxes the customers the long harangue, wasting all their fax paper with a 30-page summary of what's available. Then clients read through this tome of crap which was formulated by propeller-head engineers who really don't grasp what the customer is feeling or needing. Probably these engineers are intellectually and emotionally incapable of understanding what a less technically minded person goes through trying to use their product or understand their turgid writings. The company's marketing group fights its battles with engineers, trying to create under-standable, customer-oriented tech support. If the firm is headed by an ex-engineer or someone with an accounting background, the best marketing can hope for is a compromise. What develops is a bad system from the standpoint of building a larger base of satisfied, loyal customers.

Once the first-time buyer gets the approximate fax document he or she hopes might help, it's never explained correctly. Does the buyer want "Installing and configuring the Gadget 24X" or "Tips and Secrets of the Gadget 24X"?

So, the client orders via fax what he or she hopes will be the helpful document and, theoretically, it gets faxed back promptly, thus allowing the client to pore over a maze of paper. Clearly, this is a poor form of customer relations.

Enter the World Wide Web to solve this customer-killing problem. You probably have people who are answering pedestrian questions about your product or services because most customers are too lazy or busy to look up the answers in the manual. Typically, engineers are fond of saying *RTFM* ("read the fragging manual." (We know, we know, usually an older participle is used to modify "manual.")

We just did a focus test and 90 percent of people who called technical support didn't read the manual. 90 percent!

Automate this and put it on the Web—steps for installing your product. It's your manual online. Make it simple, but don't just take existing pages and throw them up there on the screen. Put thought into it and make it easy for people. What do they need to configure the Gadget 24X? Sometimes, in the back of good manuals, there is a section describing little problems and their solutions—troubleshooting scenarios, such as the green light comes on but the screen doesn't light up, and then, three possible solutions. This is ideal for the Web. Make your site as interesting and interactive as possible. Walk the problem-afflicted customer through the steps; make the solution clear and easily understood.

You can go a little further. For example, in the case of software, if you know you have a problem you want to show people how to handle, a bug fix, for example, walk them through the step and if it turns out they need the software fix, show them how they can download it right away, and boom, it's done! Your customer thinks you're great.

If it turns out there is sometimes the same problem with the Gadget 24X—the flippy knob breaks—ask customers to enter their name and address and—only if absolutely necessary—the serial number for the 24X they bought, and then tell them a new flippy knob will be sent right out to them free of charge.

That's it. You don't have to call. You don't have to run through all the frustration. And, come Monday morning, that little report gets spit out on Pete's desk saying, "Joan in Kansas City needs a flippy knob. Send it to her. No charge."

It's automatic. It's automating your tech support. You don't need some technical support person sitting around at 8:00 P.M. on Friday answering calls. The only point when a live person has to step in is to send out the defective part. So, you've prequalified them for true technical support.

Make sure to say on the site, "If none of this works for you, then you can reach one of our technical support people. Send us an e-mail and we'll respond by e-mail from technical support." Many companies do this. Your tech support people correspond by e-mail. Your support engineers will love this because they can do it at their pace and their time and summarize exactly what needs to be done. They can also gradually accumulate a database of carefully written responses to common problems, and continually become more efficient. You can be sure they'll like this approach better than answering the phone. Most engineers hate handholding nontechnicals.

Customers appreciate this because they get back a list. Managers love this because they can monitor what's going on, thus allowing them to gauge trends and react promptly to them. "Wow, that 24X has a lot of busted flippy bits. We should do something about that."

Sun MicroSystems is an example. It's a gigantic computer company but it saves a million dollars a year by moving a lot of technical support onto the Web.

Tech support really should be done on your Web site if you have a product. You're making a mistake if you don't. It infuriates me when, after buying a product and visiting the company's site, I discover they don't have a clear system for retrieving information about the product I just bought. That makes me wonder why I bothered to buy from them, and to solemnly swear I'll never make that mistake again. Obviously, they don't care about me. They're not organized or they'd realize this and make their presence on the Web count.

Eliminate Voice Mail Hell with Automated Customer Service

If we had a time machine, I'd like to find the guy who invented voice mail and change his life a little bit. At the point in his life when he was deciding whether to become a dentist or an engineer, I would give him a firm but friendly nudge toward dentistry! Voice mail has got to be one of the worst inventions ever. I understand why it's being used—companies need to make money. Frequently a company's management blinds itself to midterm sales realities by fixing its gaze solely on what affects the bottom line on the short term. If you're a relatively large company, you have to have a number of people just answering the phone, and it's costly. It's cheaper to put a computer in place. Then you know exactly what's going to be said every time and how your company will be represented. You can immediately and efficiently route calls.

We've all come to expect voice mail hell. The only thing I think voice mail is good for is when you want to deliver bad news. You call up at 6:00 A.M. and leave the message that Widgets, Inc. lost the job, and you get the hell out of Dodge! You've delivered the bomb. It's the best solution possible for political office situations. You can be the messenger of ill tidings without being ripped. That's the only benefit I can see.

The downsides are (1) it makes your company cold and featureless, (2) it makes your clients think, "Oh, no, here we go. I have to suffer through listening to the nine options, decipher which one is right for me, or try to find someone's extension."

Even worse are the systems that tell you to punch in someone's last name—and you don't have a clue how to spell Dwanga, Tschepsich, or Schyler!

If you're going to have a voice mail system, first have it say something such as, dial zero and you'll reach a living breathing person.

Second, tell callers you have a Web site that can answer most of their questions. Give its location. Be sure it's said slowly and distinctly.

Third, go on with the other options that are available by voice mail. If I hear the long list right away I hang up.

Save your money on the 800 number and encourage customers to hit your Web site. If you have a properly designed Web site, it's awesome to deal with because you can immediately get what you need.

Basic customer service representatives are not the highest paid people in the industry. Typically, there's not a lot of pep and enthusiasm that comes along with a customer support rep. It's not the best face your company ever puts on.

You can design the Web site any way you want; you can brand it with your logo countless times; you can put your best foot forward. All you need to do is take the time to do your Web site right or spend the money to have a qualified firm do it for you. Organize your site to handle buyer questions and customer service intelligently. Make a big thing about customer service on your home page. Try and serve the client on that Web site. Discover what they're looking for when they call your customer service lines. Then incorporate that information on your Web site. Your customer support people are just reading off a digital text file anyway. So, take all that and put it on the Web properly. Put links in so they can buy more products, too.

Don't make your valuable customers go through steps they don't need. Whatever they have to do should bring them immediate results and benefits.

Think about how you react on someone else's site. Distance yourself from the good feelings you have toward your own company. A lot of sites are built along company-centric lines: this is our company; aren't we great? Where's the meat? Get to what your customer wants to know, fast.

Items You Must Include to Have a Powerful Web Site

Keep things consistent.

If the color scheme changes, make sure it changes consistently. A lot of people have different ideas about graphic design but there's some pretty well accepted things about graphic design that are universal. Use the same colors.

You must include a way for people to reach you. I see it all the time where it's difficult to find a phone number, it's difficult to find an address, and impossible to locate an e-mail address. Some sites have a Contact Us section to their navigation bar; no matter where you are on the site, you click on that to contact the company. List live people who can be reached by phone, fax, e-mail, or snail mail; give their names, titles, and addresses or numbers. Make sure you have all the different mediums easily available so your customers can contact you.

Please make sure you include your e-mail address and make sure someone checks the e-mail on a daily basis. It's impressive for a customer to get a reply the same day, even if it's just automated. You can program a reply that says, "Here's your automated reply; if you need to contact a human being send mail here. In the meantime, here's some more information for you that might help." Almost no one does this.

If you're going to be processing the credit card automatically, make them wait until the authorization comes through.

If you click onto 777film.com for tickets to a movie, you are asked to stay on the page or your tickets won't be confirmed if you leave. After a brief wait, you are told the authorization has gone through and you're set. Even if the customer is the best in the world with a platinum American Express and buys from you all the time, maybe this is the time AMX randomly shows call Center on the authorization. It is understandable why it does this, but make sure you keep the customer online until the sale is confirmed.

Nothing is worse than placing an order, then two weeks go by and you wonder what happened to the order you placed. Maybe you go back to the Web site to check, and it shows your card was declined. You're now mad as hell for not being advised of this immediately when the order was placed. Or maybe you forgot where you ordered from and can't find the site again. Companies should send customers an e-mail confirming the order!

I placed an order with a record company over the phone and gave my credit card number. They told me I'd see my CD in seven to ten days. After two weeks went by, I called to ask about the order and they said they had some bad information—the wrong card number, it turned out. I've never done that again because it was a bad experience and totally unreliable. Like most people, when I buy something I expect the seller to use some intelligence and commitment to seeing that I get what I ordered. If it won't do that, who needs it? There are plenty of other companies who will jump through rings of fire for their customers.

Make sure people can come back and check the status of their order. Either, the order's being processed and is en route. Or, "Oops, there's a problem and we're delayed two weeks."

You can set it up where an e-mail is automatically sent advising the status. It's the little details that make the difference.

Make sure you have an adequate description of your product. You can have a simplified order setup but make sure customers can click on that and get more information. You don't have to have the detail on each page, it's probably elsewhere on your site, but make it convenient to click it up at a moment's notice. It's the cross-linking that a lot of people have trouble getting their brain around because they're used to thinking in a linear sense. Hypertext requires a new level of thought. You have to consider all the possible connections and do your best at linking those connections. You want to test it and make sure people like it.

Software Companies Offering Low-Cost Ways to Create Do-It-Yourself Electronic Commerce Web Sites

CashGraf Software

2901 58th Avenue N.
St. Petersburg, FL 33714
Phones:
    Corporate Headquarters: 813-570-5555
    Corporate Fax: 813-578-0238
    Toll Free Sales: 800-872-3902
    Solution Center: 813-528-2579
    Solution Center Fax: 813-526-5053
URL: http://www.cashgraf.com
Contact: Larry Deaton, president and CEO

A leader in providing complete, easy-to-use software for small businesses including small offices and home offices, CashGraf offers functionally rich solutions that are endorsed by the commercial banking community.

"After years of intense research, product design and programming, the company was formally founded in 1992. Ca$hGraf Software, Inc. is committed to providing the public with highly functional and cost effective software applications.

"These applications will work with Microsoft Windows and Windows 95 and require an absolute minimum amount of effort to become immediately productive. At Ca$hGraf Software, Inc. we believe the only true value any software product has to offer is the amount of real world productivity it allows the user to enjoy. With that concept in mind, we offer a true alternative for the software consumer that provides maximum productivity at reasonable prices."

Corel Corporation

URL: http://www.corel.com
Phones:
    800-772-6735
    613-728-3733
Ottawa, Ontario, Canada

Corel offers several reasonably priced products to help you design your own Web pages. CorelWEBDesigner, $99.00, is an authoring kit that let's you avoid learning HTML. Another Corel product, CorelWEB.Gallery, contains a library of over 8000 backgrounds, buttons, clip art, and separators.

First Virtual Holdings

See Chap. 6 for complete details.

iCat Corporation

See Chap. 6 for complete details.

Netscape Communications Corporation

See Chap. 6 for complete details.

The Distinction Between Debugging and Testing and Why They're Both Important

When you're programming, you're always debugging. For example, let's say I'm writing a program to allow painting on the Web, which we did for DreamWorks. I write a few lines of code to this effect: "Whenever you draw, draw in black." Then I run the program and the line it draws is blue, not black.

The process of debugging is figuring out how to make the blue line black. *Debugging,* in other words, is getting the program to do precisely what you want it to do after you think you've done it. Any part of the code standing between the programmer and the desired result is a *bug.* Debugging is simply the process of getting the bugs out.

Once the application is done and it seems to work okay, the process of testing can begin. *Testing* is where you smash on the program in all sorts of different strange ways you hadn't thought of before, and you discover all sorts of interesting bugs.

For example, my paint program might crash if you double-click on it. Maybe double-clicking is something I never tried during the programming process. This is why testing is so important. You uncover all sorts of problems, big and small, lurking in the shadows. You'll also discover things like, "We need an eraser here." So, testing can reveal desirable additions, as well as problems after the original programming process has been completed. Testing allows you to uncover bugs never even conceived of by the person or team writing the program.

After you've written the program—let's say it takes you three weeks—you could profitably spend three weeks testing after the program is "done." As used in the preceding sentence, *profitably* refers to the advantages of uncovering and curing bugs before they raise all sorts of ruckus with your customers. It's well to face a well-known fact: *Customers universally have a very low tolerance for problems caused by bugs in new programs they just bought or Web sites they're trying to buy from.* The low tolerance for bug pain extends to users of shareware and freeware programs. Computerization is frustrating enough, users tend to believe, without having insufficiently tested programs driving them nuts.

How much testing is necessary? It depends on the complexity of the program. A very simple Web site may only take you an hour to test because there are just a few pages. You just want to check to make sure the pages work on different browsers.

If you have actual programs running on the Web site such as commerce, you're going to want to test all sorts of things. Like, what happens if I click on Submit, and then press the Stop button? What happens if I enter something and then back up and hit Okay again? Does it duplicate my order? Does just one shipment arrive, but I get double-billed? Or do two shipments arrive, but I don't get billed at all?

What happens if I add the same item to my order more than once or even run up an order for 30 of the same thing? Does the program ask me to confirm my choices? Or does it not say anything when the possibility of error appears? In all these cases, experienced merchants will tell you the customers tend to believe the merchant is trying to rip them off. The most profitable way to cope with these possibilities is to head them off in the testing stage, before you have to contend with a flood of confused shipments, customer complaints, demands for refunds, and refusals to pay.

Lots of things can go wrong here and you want to check all the way down the line. Is the database that was designed to track orders actually tracking? Are you collecting sales tax and shipping charges correctly? Are the orders and charges being processed correctly in every detail? Is the money being collected getting credited against the right purchaser's account?

Let's say I want to write an application to sell every variety of flamigommies known to humans, and you're on my list of big flamigommy users. Besides putting my program up on my Web site, I plan to mail everybody on my list a disk containing my catalog of flamigommies and the program for buying them.

Before I can do this, I'd have to make a basic decision. Am I going to write this program for every computer out there or for only Windows or Macintosh? Those two, of course, use different operating systems. You can't just write a program for Windows and expect it to immediately work on Macintosh. Each operating system has its own set of requirements a program must meet if it's to run smoothly.

This is where the Web comes in. Because the browser acts as an interpreter and reads this universal language, it usually presents you with the same information regardless of the platform you're using. I say *usually* because if it did it perfectly you wouldn't have to test. But the reality is, different browsers make slightly different interpretations of the information.

For instance, some of the older browsers won't center pictures. So, if you have a site where you were heavily centering pictures, it would look awful when you scanned it with some old browsers.

Others have problems with more advanced things—tables, for example. Java adds multiple levels of complexity. Every time you add a level of complexity, you better make darn sure you're checking your entire site under different browsers and also under all the operating systems popular with consumers: Windows 95, Windows 3.1, and Macintosh. For consumer sales, you may or may not want to check it under the various flavors of UNIX.

A plain Web page is incredibly simple—you've got text and maybe a hyperlink. So all you have to check is whether the text comes up and the hyperlink actually links. When you start designing the page using formatting, tables, and graphics you add a level of complexity. Now you have to make sure your site looks the same under all possible viewing conditions.

A part of our testing procedure involves viewing the entire site on all the popular browsers. We go further than this because we view under different environments as well. Let's say we're going to use Netscape, Microsoft Internet Explorer, and AOL. There are more, but let's just say we're going to do these three. Each one of them can run under several different operating systems. (The operating system is generally more important these days than the manufacturer of the hardware. Today, you can run Windows NT on a Motorola-based PowerPC from Apple, an Intel-based IBM-compatible Pentium computer, or a DEC Alpha, among others.)

For example, Netscape Navigator will run on Windows 3.1, Windows 95, Windows NT, numerous flavors of UNIX as well as on the Macintosh. Every one of these combinations of platforms and browsers are potential bug breeders.

In a perfect world, it wouldn't matter if you're browsing from a PC or a Macintosh. In the real world, the information can't be guaranteed to come across exactly the way you want it to, even if you're sticking with the very basics.

It gets even more complicated if you get into enhancements such as tables, which allow you to do very nice formatting, or if you want to do animations. If you're talking about using Java, ActiveX, or any of these added-on technologies, you further complicate issues.

A Java application is truly a program, whereas HTML is a mark-up language—it's not really programming. There's a big difference between the two.

Java promises to run any given program the same across all operating systems. In other words, you don't have to write separate versions of a program for each operating system. Sounds simple. In reality, things work a little bit differently. If you can get Java to work, you have to tweak it and test it and find out if it works on every browser supporting Java and under every operating system you want people to use. You may find out it doesn't work on a Macintosh after spending months programming it to work under Windows 95.

If you don't test it out, you'll have Macintosh owners throwing rocks at your storefront. Or even worse, lots of users will hit the site, find out it doesn't work, and they're gone forever. While Web surfing, I've done this a bunch of times, particularly with Java.

The point here is to not skimp on testing and to test thoroughly before you launch your Web site and start finding bugs the hard, hassle-heavy, and most expensive way.

CHAPTER 4

Internet Selling Pitfalls and Alternatives

Although Internet commerce is in its infancy today—it's a lusty infant, and it's growing far faster than any normal child could. Some predict worldwide sales on the Internet in the range of $400 billion a year before this millennium ends—and already the next one is almost upon us.

While the potential of this new method of doing business is explosive, it's still far too early for most established companies to seriously consider abandoning present methods of promoting and selling. However, it's already well into the time when all companies with an eye on the future should be seriously involved in exploiting this amazing new medium.

If properly handled, Internet commerce can coexist with traditional selling methods. This should be the goal in the overwhelming majority of companies. Only in a few limited areas will Internet commerce entirely replace traditional selling methods during the careers of people now working. However, the next two decades will see a huge change in how Internet selling is regarded. All but a few sales organizations will come to regard it as a necessary and highly useful tool for cutting costs and expanding the effectiveness of their existing people and methods. It's coming in the future. In the present, the final years of the twentieth century, whether Internet selling can be immediately profitable depends on two basic things:

- How well the product or service is suited to the requirements and opportunities of the Internet world.

- How wisely and vigorously the company adapts to the requirements for Web-selling success. Companies who recognize how a new medium requires new thinking and new methods will probably succeed. Companies who ignore the new medium's unique characteristics will certainly fail to achieve satisfactory results from their efforts to sell on the Internet.

Pitfalls of Internet Selling

Here are the most likely pitfalls to trap the unwary no matter what kind of Web site they seek to create.

The Unrealistic Schedule Pitfall

Most Web sites are developed under extremely short deadlines—typically four to eight weeks. Short deadlines can work for nonselling sites. Don't let a deadline push you to release early. Get time estimates from several developers—even if you're developing in house—to reality-check your schedule. Allow weeks to work the bugs out of your system after it is "done" but before you go live. For whatever reason, clients often say, "You've got two months maximum to get this site up."

If you're just doing a regular Web site, you're all right. But if the site will be used to transact electronic commerce, two months is not enough time. It can easily take four weeks just to determine the right way to proceed—who'll do the hardware and software and program it efficiently.

A lot of executives get caught up in transient things such as an upcoming convention, trade show, or some other important event they choose to use to impose a short deadline. They get freaked out, rush to the wrong decision, and make a costly mistake. It's important not to let an event-imposed deadline dictate your schedule for going online to do business. At least 9 out of 10 event-imposed deadlines aren't nearly as important in retrospect as they appeared to be in anticipation.

With a regular Web site you can put up a few pages and it's done. With commerce, the potential exists to run yourself out of business. Commerce Web sites going online half-baked can lose orders; they can double- or triple-bill customers (thus ensuring they'll never buy from you again). Untested commerce Web sites have been known to bill customers erratically or not at all, to lose data, and to mess up the database so thoroughly the errors can't be corrected by audit. A huge number of things can go wrong when you develop software. The ratio of debugging/testing time to programming time should be budgeted at least at a 1:1 ratio.

Whoever you're interviewing about creating your electronic commerce Web site, make sure that designer not only allows time to write the program, but also sufficient time to debug and test it as well. Debugging can easily run above 50/50 to 60/40 or even 70/30. It's far safer to insist on ample debugging time in advance rather than have an uncontrollable amount of troubleshooting time jammed down your throat later.

Especially, beware of the developers who say, "We don't have to test because we do it right the first time." Easy for them to say. Keep in mind whose reputation with your own customers and whose company resources are at risk. Soon after you start doing online business, you'll find out how far off the mark you've let the bugless wonders put you. The day of reckoning dawns like thunder when time-sensitive problems pile up faster than you can deal with them.

This is a classic case of the wisdom of learning from the experience of others rather than insisting on taking the fall yourself. Testing is a critical stage; shortchange it at your peril. You should have a whole team of people, from experts to novices, running through the Web site giving you feedback.

The Bleeding Edge Pitfall

A commerce site is no place to experiment with bleeding edge technol-
o ̧ : Stick with the tried and true to drive your business—databases, server
software, hardware, and vendors. Bleeding edge is cool in some situations.
For some sites it makes a lot of sense, particularly if you want to attract a
segment of computer users known as *early adopters*. These folks are
attracted to the latest technological goodies for the technology alone.
However, a commerce site is not the place for this. Stick with software
known to work smoothly.

It may sound great to work with the latest and greatest release in software, but often the latest software doesn't work very well. We can go so far
as to say, "On electronic commerce sites, stay away from any version 1.0
software, which is notorious for bugs with the potential to cost you a fortune."

Also be advised of a software trap. Some software developers are
painfully aware how labeling their product *version 1.0* saddles the release
with a stigma. So they call the first release version 2.0 or whatever and still
claim bleeding edge newness for it.

Let's not be naïve. Many software developers feel tremendous pressure
to get to the marketplace early, so they give debugging their best quick
shot, and then throw their latest creation into the marketplace. They gain
three important advantages by rushing a new software product to market:

- They reach the market first or at least early enough to share in skim-
  ming the cream of better-margined early adopter sales.
- Customers will put the new release through its paces in hundreds of
  different combinations of hardware, operating platforms, and applications—far more combinations than any company could afford to use
  in product debugging.
- Customers bear the cost of this testing, not the software developer.

Thus, it's unrealistic to expect any version 1.0 to be bug-free. Although
they are typically ridden with bugs, you can probably get by with version
1.0 on a regular nonselling Web site. But do you want to trust your commerce to version 1.0 of anything? Screwups on order taking and billing
aren't the only risks. Version 1.0 could have big security holes hackers will
gleefully charge through to rip you off.

It's been the same since the first Stone Age cave dweller tied a stone to
a short stick and made a weapon. The version 1.0 ax didn't work at all

smoothly the first time it was used to bonk a leopard—the stone flew off and left the hunter with nothing but the short stick. That designer didn't get away with it.

The second cave dweller, watching from some distance away and scratching a bulging forehead, decided doing business with leopards called for a better ax. So, after devising a method of firmly securing the stone to the stick, this designer gave version 2 of the new ax a thorough debugging by pounding any convenient skull with it until it proved to be a dependable design. When the second hunter encountered the leopard, the ax brained it with one blow.

The Automated Office Pitfall

Don't be deceived by unrealistic promises made by technology. Despite what some people are claiming, it's simply not possible to have a Web business run itself. Though it's possible to automate many aspects of business, some key interactions with your clients must be handled by direct communication with an employee. Until we see major breakthroughs in artificial intelligence, you'll need to provide people to handle many standard business functions—customer service, many areas of technical support, returns, complaints, suggestions, and the like. It's a very good idea to use the Web to partially automate all these functions, but it cannot entirely replace people. Someday, certainly; today, no.

Always provide a means for customers to contact your firm directly, be it via phone, fax, e-mail, or snail mail. This may sound obvious, but it's startlingly common on the Web not to provide any other means of communication.

Show respect for your customers and proclaim your reliability by giving your customers five ways to reach you: e-mail, fax, telephone, mailing address for overnight express or snail mail, and, of course, your Web site.

If you doubt the importance of this, make a quick study of a few Internet businesses. You'll probably discover about the same situation I did: at least two out of five of them make it extremely difficult or impossible for a customer to reach a fellow human being in the form of a live employee.

Many legitimate firms make themselves look like scam artists to a significant number of potential buyers by failing to give their location (mailing address) on their Web site. Gigantic corporations whose names are familiar to everyone can get away with this; smaller firms can't. Tell people where you are as well as who you are. It's a subtle but effective confidence builder. Never forget a basic fact: people have to trust you before they'll buy from you—no less on the Internet than over the counter.

By my own far from comprehensive count, only about 1 company in 20 provides a phone number where contact can be made with a live human being. And, in many of the 5 percent of cases where human contact can be made, it only happens after fighting through the interminable waits and confusion of voice mail hell. Most automatic answering systems appear to be designed to frustrate and infuriate customers enough to turn them into excustomers. It's hard to understand the management philosophy behind such a policy.

We've discussed only a few common Web site mistakes; there are others. As a result of these mistakes, large numbers of Internet sellers disappear without a trace after only a few weeks or months online. Web sites born too weak to live are many; realistically conceived and operated electronic commerce Web sites are few.

Don't be deceived by unrealistic promises made by technology promising your Web site will run itself with no one watching over it. If you're selling something online, the reality is, at some point a significant percentage of your customers will need to talk with a human being. If you're going to succeed, those customers better be able to reach a breathing person without going through the mental torture of a fiendishly conceived voice mail barrier.

The Lame Product Pitfall

A lot of companies go online with a product or service and don't make it better, easier, or faster than offerings already on the Internet or available elsewhere. Let's say you have a database of movie reviews. Several free databases of movie reviews are already on the Net. For your database to have any chance of success, it must have something unique to attract people or make advertisers want to be on your site. Maybe you're featuring a major critic, special promotions; maybe you do it better, faster, or with more glitter and glamour. In any case, you must have an edge or your Web site won't fly. The best edges give the customer more convenience for less money.

The Freebie Elsewhere Pitfall

A staggering amount of data and services are available on the Web for free. If you're planning on charging for access to your online information, entertainment, or services, make sure the same things aren't already available free of charge on the Internet. If it's already free, there must be compelling reasons why someone would come to your site and pay for access to what you have to offer.

Selling on a Secure Server

Electronic selling falls into only two categories: products and information/services/entertainment.

Selling Products

As of late 1996, the Internet offered no widely used way to sell to consumers other than with proprietary electronic tokens or by credit card. Accepting credit cards for purchases is by far the most popular method. However, the next few years will see a rapid increase in the variety of payment methods. Alert Web site sellers will adopt many of them. The goal always should be to make purchasing as convenient as possible for every significant group of potential buyers.

Product selling (and often service selling, as well) breaks down into two capability categories: single item sales and multiple item sales.

Single Item Sales

Single-item-sale Web sites are easily set up and straightforward for consumers to understand and order from. A simple click on the Buy button sends them to the order form, where they type in their purchase information; click the Submit button; and it's done. The chief advantages to the merchant: it's quicker and less expensive to set up. All you need is a secure server and a few Web pages. The disadvantage: you can only sell one item at a time.

Multiple Item Sales

This is the most accepted and generally the better method. It's more expensive because you have to have software for a database, a shopping cart, and more sophisticated programming to calculate shipping charges and sales tax. It all adds to the cost. However, for most companies, it's the only viable option.

A key merchant advantage: companies can offer an unlimited number of items—for example, Amazon Books lists over one million titles (see Amazon's story in Chap. 8).

Customer advantages include being able to select more than one item and being able to change their minds—add or subtract from their orders—until they click the Execute button. This is the shopping cart concept.

THE ESSENTIAL SHOPPING CART. On catalog Web sites and on any site where a choice of items is offered, shoppers should be provided with a *shopping cart.* This software feature permits addition or deletion of products customers might wish to buy until they finalize their purchase by clicking on the order form. Without being assured of the shopping cart's escape and revision features, many Internet shoppers are unwilling to select items.

The shopping cart, essentially an easily created list of items a consumer considers buying, permits the consumer to easily add or remove items or modify quantities. If you were in a supermarket and the shopping cart you were pushing down the aisles had a trapdoor preventing you from changing your mind and putting a selected item back on the shelves, you'd be turned off. Chances are you'd walk out of the store, never to return. It's the same situation online; your customers must be able to add and revise their orders until they reach a final decision about buying. Here again, it's the same as in a supermarket; you can easily add and subtract items from the supermarket's shopping cart until you reach the checkout counter.

THE ESSENTIAL ORDER FORM. Unless it's easily filled in, it becomes a business killer instead of a business builder. For maximum results, make buying as easy as possible for the customer. To this end, successful Internet sellers generally avoid cluttering their order forms with survey questions or unnecessary graphics. If you want to conduct a survey, do it by e-mail after the sale.

Multiple item or catalog Web sites are particularly effective for small-ticket items such as books, CDs, software, theater tickets, travel reservations, and specialized gear and parts of all kinds.

The method of choice for payment on the Internet is by credit card and will probably remain so until standardization occurs on digital money. Chapter 7 covers this in depth.

Selling Information/Services/Entertainment

The methods of selling information, services, and entertainment on the Internet are more varied than is the case with products. Here are the most common methods:

- Subscription
- Advertiser supported
- Pay as you play (pay per view)
- Time based

SUBSCRIPTION. The consumer selects a service level and is charged a fixed amount for services within the chosen level, generally a flat monthly fee, with no break for under usage but additional charges for running over the limit. Outstanding examples are two Internet service providers—America Online and CompuServe.

Services of this kind make an important assumption: not all their subscribers will use their services at the same time. This is not unique to the Internet. On big holidays or when there's a Richter 7 earthquake in California or a hurricane in Florida, the long-distance telephone lines are jammed. Similarly, if every car in town hits the road at the same time, nobody goes anywhere.

I can't think of any system capable of serving all possible consumers at the same time; it's neither necessary nor economic to have such grossly overbuilt facilities. Nevertheless, Internet service sellers can charge each subscriber for full use of whatever they're offering in the certain knowledge they only need to prepare to service a small percentage of them at any given moment. It's a way of making a great deal of money. The control is competition; if your service gets overloaded too often, your customers will go elsewhere.

ADVERTISER SUPPORTED. Another way to have a profitable information/services/entertainment Web site is to be advertiser-supported or sponsored. You provide your information free to site visitors and sell banners or graphics on the page to advertisers who want to reach your particular audience.

Visitors to your Web site see an interesting advertiser's banner. If they click on it, they're transferred to the advertiser's Web site, where the banner-buying company has a good prospect of selling them.

Banner charges can be set up in three basic ways or in some combination of them:

1. *Flat monthly fee.*   Easiest to set up and administer, but doesn't automatically provide feedback to advertisers showing how much traffic their banners are generating.

2. *View count.*   Advertisers can be billed based on the total number of visits to the banner-selling Web site, whether or not the visitors react to the advertiser's banner. This is similar to many kinds of print advertising pricing based on circulation.

3. *Link count.*   Advertisers can be billed based on the number of times visitors to the banner-selling Web site link up to the advertiser's Web site. This is usually the most useful information the advertiser can get. However, from the banner seller's viewpoint, this has its disadvantages. It reflects on the pulling power of the advertiser's message rather than on the advertising-supported Web site's ability to attract traffic.

This method of harvesting revenue on the Internet has a downside: many Web sites are chasing the limited number of advertisers willing to spend money on Web banners. In this way, it's like magazine advertising, the market is limited. However, unlike the great uncertainties of print or broadcast advertising—where effectiveness is often impossible to measure with any degree of accuracy—Web site exposure can provide computer-counted reports of activity and computer-generated lead lists.

Competition is keen for the limited number of advertising dollars. The best opportunity to catch some of them belongs to the search engines. Then there's ESPN, CNN, and NBC news services. As a result, the average company faces a daunting challenge to swim upstream against this swift current.

Let's say I want to start an entertainment company and on the basis of this I'm going to try to get advertisers. It's possible and a lot of exciting things can be done. But I'm not entirely convinced it could be profitable; success depends on doing something unique and compelling. Done right, it could be fantastically revenue-explosive.

To move ahead along these lines, get a good group of people together, and do your own programming. An example of this is located at http://www.thespot.com. The originators combined a serial like *Beverly Hills 90210* and a Web page into a totally new form of entertainment. It's about a mythical beach house in Playa del Rey, California, where four beautiful girls and four handsome guys hang out. Visitors get to read their private diaries with pictures and they're updated frequently. This site gets a lot of hits. As a result, a number of copycat serial Web sites have developed, including many with ample advertiser support.

It's even easier to attract sponsors than in the television industry. Let me tell you why. If you have a good idea, you can pitch it in your spare time, put the site together at a relatively low cost, and put it up on the Net. If it's promoted effectively enough to catch on, you'll be able to prove heavy traffic and have advertisers coming to you. Your next move could be to a beachfront home on Maui because the Internet is one of the few places where people actually do beat a path to your door with sacks of money if you have a better mousetrap.

It's incredibly difficult for people who aren't TV insiders to put together a television pilot and get it onto a network. In realistic terms, it's beyond the realm of possibility. Not so with Web sites. If you've got some good people and a great idea, you can make it work with a very low investment. It's very exciting because success doesn't depend on getting a nod from a network VIP.

However, we're not pushing serial Web sites; they're just an example of what can be and has been done. A vast number of possible uses of technology haven't been invented yet, and a very good shot at riches awaits anyone who can invent and go online with a new form of entertainment. Many respected experts say we haven't designed the right model yet. So, we should be creative and take these examples as a starting point.

Advertiser-supported sites are good information resources. It may make sense to tie yours into a brand. If your company has a valuable set of information, for example, specialized maps, you can sponsor this information yourself on the Web and either give it away and sell advertising or charge users for it.

PAY AS YOU PLAY (PAY PER VIEW).   Another method of selling information, entertainment, or services is *pay as you play.* Customers pay either for each page, for each downloaded picture, for each game they play, or for each nugget of information they access. This works very well if you have a lot of similar features people may want to choose from. With a large database of information, say a thousand or more documents, another wrinkle becomes practical. Provide abstracts they can read for free, but if they want the real meat, they have to pay for it. New methods of collecting payments may make charges for as little as a few pennies per buy cost-effective. See Chap. 6.

TIME BASED.   In theory, time-based charges work much like a phone call—you pay per unit of time. The Web site would track the exact amount of time someone spends there and a time-based charge is made to the credit card whose data and validity your computer has already captured and verified.

Here's a key fact standing in the way of this: the Web is stateless. This means you don't have a constant connection to the computer you're receiving information from. Let's say you're hitting a server from your computer and receiving news information from the *L.A. Times*. Your request for front page headlines opens one connection to the *Times* server, and the server then transmits the information, after which the connection is closed. The computer is no longer communicating with you. So it's not really possible without maintaining an open connection to the server to track how much time is spent.

Since the Web makes it difficult to maintain an open connection, it's not a good idea to try to base charges on open connections. Every connection to a server bogs it down because the server has to have a process running with every open connection. Each server can only support x number of simultaneous connections, depending on the hardware/software combination used. The Web works well because it is stateless; people open up a single connection, get their documents, and the connection closes automatically, thus freeing up the server to accept another connection.

I would recommend against any sort of time-based billing arrangement unless you can be sure a constant connection is kept with your server. A variation on time-based billing might work if you say, "For $5, you can read any 30 pages. Once you're through those 30 pages you need to spend another $5." The complication is in setting up a method to make sure the customers get every one of the 30 pages they pay for, but no more.

Harnessing Web Site Power If You're Not Ready for Internet Sales

After studying the pros and cons of Internet selling as they exist at this time, many companies adopt a wait-and-see policy. This doesn't limit them to the three most popular image-destructive alternatives: (1) putting up a few information-starved pages on the Web, (2) having a site with the infamous "under construction" tag, or (3) being conspicuously absent from the Internet. ("Hey, we're high tech. We got a computer around here someplace, and we're gonna put our mailing list on it soon as we find somebody who can run the durn thing.")

No question about it; a bright, customer-oriented Web page stamps a company as being on the move, up-to-date, future-minded, and headed for greater things. But many companies find the prospect of completing sales on the Internet very complex for good reasons peculiar to themselves. Such companies can choose among several alternatives.

Product-Listing Web Sites

Some companies can build business simply by listing all their products or services even though they must refer buyers to local distributors or ask them to call their orders to an 800 number. This allows you to put your catalog, no matter how large, in the hands of every prospect without printing a page or spending a dollar on mailing costs. You can also update an online catalog as often as you wish at almost no cost.

Compare the low cost and rapid update possible on a Web site with the cost and inflexibility of collections of bound catalogs such as Sweet's or your own catalog mailed to distributors and customers. You're probably years away from being able to dispense with either of these traditional means of product promotion, but as soon as possible, display your URL prominently on print catalogs and other literature, along with a statement to this effect: "For latest updates, visit our Web site at http://www_____com."

You can merely list products by name, description, stock number, and price. But for maximum promotional power, give as much additional information as possible for each item. Unlike printed catalogs, adding details to help them specify the right product involves very little additional cost—often merely a typist's time to enter the information into the product database.

If you don't have enough catalog items to justify a database on your site, templates can be used to allow cutting and pasting information into pages much like you cut and paste information in your word processor.

When appropriate, provide each product listing with an illustration, ideally of the product in use, or a schematic to provide more buyer-useful details than a photograph could. Keep the size as small as possible, and give the visitor an opportunity to view a larger, more-detailed picture.

Promotional Web Sites

Unfortunately, the vast majority of Web sites merely relate company history and a little product information, much of it lifted verbatim from press kits and print catalogs.

Typically these information-only (often *boring*-information-only) Web sites offer visitors no reason to return. Generally they don't even offer any reason for a visitor to remain connected longer than the few seconds it takes them to realize they've reached a Web site unworthy of their attention. Such Web sites often feature extremely slow loading illustrations and generally lack easy-to-use indexing to direct visitors quickly to areas of special interest.

Many companies put up a doomed-to-failure information-only Web site, discern no results, and decide the Internet is vastly overrated as a sales or promotional tool on the basis of their Web site's poor performance. They have difficulty accepting why: their message fell short, not the medium. Discouraged by their initial, ill-advised Internet adventure, these companies often cut themselves off from the enormous opportunities available in electronic commerce.

A promotional site can be a powerful sales-building tool in fields where closing a sale requires the services of a live representative, often in a face-to-face meeting. Automobiles, airplanes, yachts, land and real estate of all kinds, and large appliances are some of the candidates for promotional Web sites.

In order to reach their full potential, such sites must offer visitors reasons to visit repeatedly. Along with product specifications, the site should offer information about how products are used, maintenance tips, and far more details than are ordinarily included in print brochures. However, this information must be well organized so visitors can quickly find what interests them at the moment and skip over details of no interest to them.

THE ESSENTIAL DEALER LOCATOR.   In many cases, the primary object of the Web site is to induce prospects to visit a dealership. Unless it's made easy for the visitors to locate nearby dealers, the Web site will probably fail to improve sales.

Dealer locating systems are easily set up by zip code. We pioneered the dealer locator concept on the Nissan Pathfinder site—visiting prospects type in their zip code and receive the three nearest dealers in their area. This is a prime example of providing a unique service to your customers, in this case, saving their time while boosting your sales results.

THE ESSENTIAL TRAFFIC BUILDER/SUSTAINER.   If your Web site merely offers nothing but vast quantities of product information, you're probably going to be disappointed with its performance.

Give visitors reasons to be glad they clicked on your Web site; give them reasons to return. Contests or games are often effective if well done and particularly where they further involve visitors in the company's products.

If appropriate, offer to send e-mail to visitors announcing new products, special prices, contests, and drawings.

Informational Web Sites

The Web is about information. The medium is ideal for providing real-time or archived data. Likewise, it appears ideal for selling valuable information. However, since most information available on the Internet is free or advertiser-supported, Internet consumers resist directly paying for information up front.

If you have access to potentially valuable data, consider offering a part of it as a free resource. ESPNet is an excellent example of this strategy. This site provides a wealth of sports-related information to visitors for free. Consumers may subscribe to the service and receive even more information.

Online Demands: Seller and Buyer Requirements

The ultimate goal is to make online demands rest fully upon the seller. This is not possible today. CC (credit card) requires the least amount of buyer effort. The chief obstacle is the perceived threat of credit card theft on the Internet. Overcoming this obstacle to the continued growth of Internet commerce requires education, coupled with alternative means of ordering (800 number, email request, salesperson will follow up on phone, and so on.)

Some consumers, and perhaps many of them, are reluctant to send their credit card number over the Internet today. This attitude will gradually dissipate as more people come to realize the Internet is inherently more secure than handing their card to clerks and servers in stores and restaurants.

Going well beyond the more secure environment built into the Internet, many companies have made fraudulent use of credit card numbers extremely difficult. As a result, credit card thieves will gravitate toward easier areas of operation.

Secure Server Solutions

With electronic commerce still in a state of rapid change and development, predictions of what standards will become dominant in the next few years are chancy at best; at worst, they'll be dead wrong. We can show who the early leaders are. It's a safe bet some, if not all, of these companies will be at the forefront well into the next century.

Secure merchant-to-consumer Internet commerce methods can be divided into two areas:

- Credit card acceptance systems as provided by Atomic Software, Microsoft Internet Security, Open Market's Secure WebServer, Netscape's Secure Server, and others
- Electronic cash solutions as provided by America's CyberCash or Holland's DigiCash

Here is a company who can help make your credit card transactions simple:

Atomic Software
2837 Peterson Place
Norcross, GA 30071
Phone: 770-417-1228
URL: http://www.atomic-software.com
Contact: Thomas McCole, president

Atomic, whose target market is small- to medium-size businesses, provides credit card authorization software for Windows 95 and NT servers.

Others are listed in Chap. 6.

Companies who can provide systems that will permit you to sell over the Internet for Net cash (various forms of electronic cash) are as follows:

CyberCash
2100 Reston Parkway, Third Floor
Reston, VA 22091
Phone: 703-620-4200
Internet: info@cybercash.com
URL: http://www.cybercash.com

CyberCash Sales and Marketing:
303 Twin Dolphin Drive, Suite 200
Redwood City, CA 94065
Phone: 415-594-0800

Fax: 415-594-0899
Contact: Cheryl Sullivan Lester, director of merchant marketing
Phone: 415-413-0155
E-mail: clester@cybercash.com

CyberCash has solved the problem of providing security for Internet commerce. In its system, consumers encrypt their card numbers automatically and send them only once to the trusted third party, Cyber-Cash.

They can then place orders with any merchant subscriber to the CyberCash system. CyberCash receives the order, strips off the credit card number, and sends the order on to the merchant, along with payment verification. These automatic operations are usually completed within 20 seconds. In other words, all this security can be provided for Internet commerce as quickly as a store can process a purchase made by credit card.

In the Internet transaction, the merchant never sees the customer's credit card number. Any such purchase is vastly more secure from the buyer's standpoint than handing the card over in a store, gas station, or restaurant.

For more information about the products and services available from CyberCash, see Chap. 6.

DigiCash
Netherlands World Headquarters
Phone: 31.20.655.2611
Fax: 31.20.668.5486
E-mail: info@digicash.nl
URL: http://www.digicash.com

United States
Phone: 212-909-4092
800-410-ECASH (800-410-3227)
Fax: 212-318-1222
E-mail: office.ny@digicash.com

Australia
Phone: 61.2.375.2316
Fax: 61.2.375.2121
E-mail: andreas@digicash.com

For more information about the products and services available from DigiCash, see Chap. 6.

Microsoft Internet Security Framework
At press time Microsoft had just announced its electronic commerce offering. For later information, call Michael Kim at 206-703-0403.

Netscape Communications Corporation
Mountain View, Calif.
Phone: 800-638-7483
Fax: 415-528-4125
E-mail: http://www.netscape.com

Netscape offers a "complete online merchandising solution" called Netscape Merchant System. For more information about Netscape products and services, see Chap. 6.

Open Market
245 First Street
Cambridge, MA 02142
Phone: 617-621-9500
E-mail: winkowsk@openmarket.com
URL: http://www.openmarket.com

Open Market's Secure WebServer can support up to 5000 simultaneous client connections, providing fast access using HTTP, Secure HTTP, or SSL to communicate with all standard browsers. Open Market offers several other products to facilitate Internet sales. The firm has an impressive list of partners and customers.

CHAPTER 5

How to Succeed at E-Selling

Get a Solid Grip on What This New Medium Provides—and Demands

The Internet is unforgiving in its insistence on favoring only those products and services that fit its requirements. Things that don't fit the Internet fail utterly; things that do fit can score big. Scoring big on the Internet means ringing up sales growth percentages in excess of 30 percent a month, rates that most companies would love to experience annually.

Ninety-nine percent of the sites out there are pathetic and boring. The people responsible didn't consider what the medium is all about. If you properly consider the medium, you'll be able to capture business and keep it. A well-done and well-promoted Web site, just like an engaging TV commercial for a needed and competitively valued product, produces solid business. The difference is that the TV commercial's pulling power will steadily decline, while a good Web site, if imaginatively updated frequently, will continue to build customer relationships and create sales.

Some TV commercials you watch, more you don't. You notice the clever ones, but most of them have DDD (they're dismal, disgusting, and degrading). If you don't eat fast food, don't have heartburn or headaches, don't need to lose weight or gain hair, don't have athlete's foot or certain other itches, and don't drink beer, most advertisers are firing blanks at you anyway. Increasingly, people use VCRs to filter out commercials or simply leave the room when they come on—only two of the ominous trends afflicting TV as we know it today. With the network audience continuing to shrink and Internet buying continuing to grow, major changes are inevitable.

Ken Wax, writing in *VARbusiness*, July 15, 1996, about Web sites, makes a good point by saying, "I don't know what gold is buried underneath. What I do know is that I'm bored—so goodbye."

That's exactly what we want to communicate here. Even more than couch potatoes with their twitching thumb on the remote, Web surfers literally have their mouse in their hand with a finger constantly poised to send them soaring off your site, never to return. You can't bore them, you can't bury them in pages of text that do nothing for them; they are not a captive audience.

Visitors to your site have two basic choices: they can click to find out more, or they can click out. Which they're going to do is largely your decision, made far in advance when you decide whether your site is going to be excitingly interactive and useful to the visitor, or whether you'll settle for a useless, company-centric site no one stays on for long.

Wax says people are fickle. "They're just as likely to zap themselves away from you to faraway places, rather than proceed along the sales cycle."

This is true, if your site presents itself as a sales cycle. The typical mindset is, "We're going to have an online brochure here. We're going to give them our standard sales pitch, only we're going to be clever about it, we're going to reword it in a digital format."

Wrong. That's not what you want to do.

You want to envision what users are coming for. If you're selling watches, you don't want to make them wade through the long harangue about your craftspeople. Sure, some people will be fascinated to read that your highly skilled artisans work in modern plants tucked away in the mountain valleys of Switzerland and are descended from generations of Swiss watchmakers. Give visitors a link they can click on to read all about your precious craftspeople.

But for most visitors, just get to the point and serve the customer. Certain issues are uppermost in many people's minds when they consider buying a watch. Make it easy for visitors to read how you address those issues. Organize your responses in several levels so the visitor can get the gist of your response to each issue off the top line, and can then dig deeper to quickly come up with more detail.

Wax writes, "Guess who else has a Web site? Your competitors have them too." What he's saying is, since you've got me clicking, it's easy to visit them, too.

Actually, it's not that easy. It's not as if every Web site is indexed to its competitor—who would want to do that? Here, Wax misses the point entirely. If your competitors have a Web site, it's even more important for you to not only have a Web site yourself, but to have an even better one. Wax says, "If you have a solid customer, it's madness to encourage them to go to a vehicle that invites them to discover details about competitors."

This makes no sense. No company can prevent its customers from learning about its competitors. What it can do is make its own products and services competitive in every way, and then present them in a more exciting, more interactive, more useful fashion on the Web.

Wax says, "Sending customers for pre-sale issues [to a Web site] is a knee-jerk action to avoid."

We disagree. The Web is ideally suited to presales because most visitors can be regarded as prequalified. They do this themselves, simply by showing enough interest in your company to visit its site.

It's a really good idea to get your Web site address out there because it's the easiest way for someone to reach your firm. It's easier than making a phone call to an 800 number because the information offered is usually offset by an annoying wait unless your customer service number dials right through to a human.

If you put your presales on the Web, you can design exactly what you want stated on different issues. You are assured it will reach people in precisely the form you desire. The alternative is to have customer service personnel respond. Their response may or may not stay close to the company line.

It's my understanding that in most companies, presale and brochure requests get thrown to the junior salespeople. Call a company for something and you'll probably wind up in presales information, where—if you're persistent enough to hang in until you reach a person—it's always just somebody sitting on the phone all day long who knows a little bit about the product but doesn't know it in depth.

Offer E-Selling-Compatible Products and Services

Everything that fits e-selling falls into one of these three categories:

1. *Direct appeal to Internet users.* This includes all the products and services that appeal directly to the Internet kind of people—computer hardware and software, peripherals of all kinds such as personal digital assistants like the U.S. Robotics Pilot, keyboards, mouse pads, and any product or service computer enthusiasts typically want or need.

Salable information products delivered over telephone lines—downloaded by purchasers—comprise a subgroup of this category. Already highly concentrated, the enormous profit potential will result in steady and perhaps explosive growth in this area.

2. *Price-driven purchase decisions.* When you know precisely what you want, the Internet often is the perfect place to get it—a fact that has rapidly growing implications for sellers of anything remotely suitable for Internet sales.

Let's say you own a computer store. Your good customer Jill, an architect whose office is just down the street, comes in to look at laser printers. You show her several models and she seems to like a Hewlett-Packard Laser Jet XIX. You discuss price and delivery, do all the usual things to close the sale, but Jill goes away without buying.

Back at her office, Jill tells an assistant to check the Internet for prices on an HP Laser Jet XIX. In a few minutes, her assistant locates a supplier who will deliver the identical item by express the next day at a substantially lower price.

Many people would feel that Jill's action is unethical, even dishonest, in pretending an interest in buying, thus taking up the dealer's time, without any intention of making it worthwhile. Others might feel the dealer had the chance to sell Jill on the idea that having a local dealer to service the printer would be worth the extra cost but failed to do that, so it's the dealer's tough luck. In any case, ethics have been known to lose in head-to-head confrontations with price savings.

Regardless of how you view such situations, a new reality is already making itself felt: Internet selling by low-overhead firms is having, and will continue to have, an increasingly powerful effect on many kinds of retailing.

Once your customers zero in on the make and model they want, their purchase options no longer are limited to a nearby store. The whole nation, and increasingly, the entire world, enters the picture. More and more, customers will turn to the Internet as *the* place to find the best price for many of the things they want to buy. Already it's a far more attractive option than fighting through the time-wasting phone call hell far too many companies shortsightedly inflict on their customers today. Competition-conscious executives will occasionally phone their own companies to see how well average callers fare, and they take corrective action if the wait is more than a few seconds. It makes little sense to spend enormous amounts on product development and promotion and then enrage potential buyers by refusing to recognize how much they value their own time.

3. *Microniche products and services.*   *Microniches* are markets whose appeal is limited to a very small audience, generally one that's too small to be reached profitably by any other means offline. Distributors aren't interested, and conventional advertising is too expensive compared to the achievable volume.

To purveyors of niche products or services, the Internet offers a low-cost alternative to direct mail or attendance at obscure trade shows and meetings. It provides a low-cost way to make niche offerings available to a huge audience. Among that huge audience will be found some members of every specialized group of buyers imaginable.

For example, if you have a line of calligraphy brushes designed for haiku poets, you can be assured of reaching the haiku market effectively on the Internet. Why? Because the vast reach of the Internet certainly includes several groups for haiku fans. I found the following haiku sites in under two minutes of searching on the Internet. Many have links to dozens of other sites. Do your own search on any niche group or try these sites if you disagree:

http://glwarner.samford.edu/haiku.htm

http://www.obs-us.com/people/sunny/haiku/

http://mikan.cc.matsuyama-u.ac.jp/~shiki/

http://www.ori.u-tokyo.ac.jp/~dhugal/haikuhome.html

http://www.lsi.usp.br/usp/rod/poet/haiku.html

http://home.sn.no/home/keitoy/haiku.html

Hundreds—perhaps thousands—of niches boast larger groups of enthusiasts than haiku poetry. In spite of this, these larger groups are still too small for profitable promotion via yesteryear's media. Hang gliders are another example of a niche market with great Internet potential. The entire market composes perhaps 10 to 20 thousand pilots, demographically placed dead-on for access to the Internet.

However, just because everybody uses a particular kind of merchandise doesn't mean it will sell strongly on the Internet. Clothing has a limited sales opportunity on the Net because buyers want to see how it looks on them and check the fit. Anything you need to touch, taste, or feel faces an uphill battle on the Internet.

Many kinds of commercial equipment and machinery, along with specialized sport and hobby gear, lack the sales potential to justify a fraction of the advertising budget spent on mascara, beer, or potato chips. Yet, on the Internet, detailed specifications, action photos, and virtually unlimited amounts of testimonials and selling copy can be made available at low cost.

Link Impulse Buying with Sites of Interest

Linking is one area where only big corporations have been doing it right. Even they need to be more focused. I'll give you a perfect example of focused linking.

Take gamespot.com, a Web site for video games that's completely advertiser supported. It covers the hottest, most cutting edge information about games. It has reviews and insider tips and interviews for people who are specifically interested in video games. So, it's a niche market—a big one—a several billion dollar niche market. It carries ad banners on the top of the Web page which are basically billboards for video games.

It has no magazine, no newsletter or TV show—just this Web site. It just came online a couple of months ago. It got together some big names in video game magazines, so it had top promoters, great graphics, and a good concept and came out with the largest number of advertisers anywhere for its market. It really did a good job. If you're reading a review of a game on gamespot, you can either download a demo of the game right there or a little ad comes along with the review, describing a similar game you can purchase from a video game manufacturer. If you click on that picture, it will link you to the video game manufacturer's Web site where you can get information.

Now, the natural extension of this would be the ability to actually order that game once you've moved over to the video manufacturer's site. I'm not aware of any manufacturer's site that does this right now, but it's certain to be happening soon. However, a number of independent resellers do offer games directly over the Internet.

All subjects and interests are represented on the Internet. This example could be about gardening or anything where there's a Web site specifically targeted to an interest. A company should put up an ad banner—visitors to the site can click on that banner and be taken to the Web site of the manufacturer to buy the product outright. This is only being done in a few instances and should be done much more. There's tremendous potential.

So, anyone interested in selling products on the Internet should say, "Where are the people interested in my product hanging out on the Web?" Suppose we're selling gardening tools and accessories. We search for gardening sites, gardening clubs, and associations who promote gardening, whatever. Let's say we find the International Order of Elite Gardeners, the IOEG. It sounds like our kind of people. So we negotiate a deal with the IOEG to pay it x dollars for a *link banner*, that is, a graphic on its Web site. When gardeners click on our IOEG banner, they jump to our site where we have well-organized information about our gardening tools. These banners are really cheap to make: they're just small digital pictures. Usually, you get them free or pay a fee, which can be a flat charge, a percentage of the sales that result, or x amount for each time someone links to your site.

Playboy has a Web site with advertisers. I understand it's a bonus for advertising in its well-known national magazine. Take out an ad in the magazine, and it throws in a banner on the Internet. You can also purchase Web advertising, but very frequently the ads are add-ons or discounted because it's a new medium. There are many ways to structure these advertising deals.

Fight Unidirectional Communication

Nearly half of all Internet users make a mistake when typing their e-mail address on a merchant's Web site, thus providing an address that doesn't work, according to First Virtual Holding Corporation. This *unidirectional communication,* therefore, constitutes a huge loss of potential business.

Consider making a statement to that effect on your registration page. Consider asking for visitors' phone numbers "to be used only to advise them if their e-mail address doesn't work." Consider offering a special benefit to those who give you a correct e-mail address. Consider asking for mail addresses so visitors can be notified by snail mail if their e-mail address doesn't work.

Promote Your Web Page Aggressively and Relentlessly

Promotion is broken up into two areas: online and offline promotion. If you have a Web site and you manufacture a product, by all means, give the Web site address on all your products. Get it out there. If it's not out there offline, then people won't see it. Get the Web site address in TV promotions, literature, everything, and do it quickly on your brochures, flyers, business cards, and letterheads. This does two things.

1. It positions your company as a winner. You're hip to the technological age. You'll be considered an early adopter—a fast-moving company.

2. It's a fantastic way for a company to quickly get a lot of information about itself and its products or services to consumers.

Online promotion has many different aspects. The most important way to do it is to make sure you're listed in search engines so buyers can find you. To get listed on many search engines can take up to six weeks because there are thousands of pages added constantly, and it takes time for the search engines to index them; even the search engines are struggling to keep up. But there's more than just search engines. You want to get to related sites.

Humans like to classify things. So, thousands of people on the Web have a particular interest and they've done research and found a lot of areas featuring whatever interest they have. Then they put their list up on the Web where people who share their special interest can get to it. Search engines are typically linked to lists of this kind. A way to get around the long waiting period to get listed on search engines is to go to these smaller sites. You can get listed there almost immediately. These sites are already listed on search engines. These pages frequently have an area devoted to links. So, find these sites and send people e-mail to tell them about your great site and ask if they'll list you.

Most people maintain these lists for free. Go to a search engine such as HotBot and search for gardening. You'll see something like Archie's Gardening list of links or Cosmer's Mega-Link List of Gardening Web sites. Get listed on those sites, and you've listed yourself in a search engine.

Seek out all of those lists and get yourself listed on every one you can. When we say *promote your site relentlessly,* we mean keep doing it. Don't stop because a month later you may have been removed from the list. Maybe three other companies have replaced you. Perhaps there are new, better link lists. Keep in contact with the people that maintain those lists—they can be your greatest friends. Any one of them could be president of a gardening group and be very helpful to your business.

Having people on your side on the Internet is highly intelligent. There's an issue of damage control. You want to make sure you're in touch with people who are interested in the products on the Web and that they are on your side. Rumors fly rapidly on the Net and they can destroy a company.

The medium is about reaching individuals. It's about fostering one-on-one relationships. With a television ad, you can't have an individual relationship.

If you run a promotion or some sort of giveaway, there are several lists on the Web that will list you simply because you are running a promotion. It's a good way of promoting your site if you want to attract general interest people.

The important thing is, *even if you build a great Web site, if it's not promoted effectively, no one will come.*

There are millions of Web pages and there's no real way for anyone to get a grip on what you're doing unless you take steps to promote the site.

It's like a party. You can rent Dodger Stadium, spend a zillion dollars on champagne, music, and hiring the Cirque du Soleil to perform. But if you don't get the word out, no guests are going to show up unless they happen to be driving by the stadium at the time.

If you do a TV commercial you're guaranteed some people will see it. But the Web has an ocean of information, far more than anyone can wade through. If you don't take the time to wave the flag and shoot fireworks into the sky, no one will find you. I can show you thousands of pages that have only been accessed 30 or 500 times, even though the firms have clearly put a lot of effort into their sites. But they failed to promote them; so, they're flops, drains on the company's resources when they could have been a profit center with shrewd promotion.

In the movie "The Jerk," Steve Martin's character put his name in the phone book and gets excited when he sees it in print, thinking it would lead to great things. That's no more naïve than a company putting a page up on the Internet with no intention of promoting it, and expecting great things.

Get on the Right Search Engines So Buyers Can Find You

It's free to get listed on search engines. However, it takes time and money and experience to get ad space with search engines or related Web sites. You have to know how to approach these people. If you come in green, they'll stomp all over you and want lots of money. If you come in like a veteran and say, "Let's work something out," they'll be cooperative.

Make sure you understand the big search engines. Things change and the fortunes of the search engines rise and fall like the tide. They're all struggling to get a grip on this exploding Web. It's almost like the word processing wars. Some of them seek to do different things. Yahoo seeks to classify the Web; it doesn't pretend to index the entire Web. Yahoo indexes in selected sites like a Dewey decimal system. It has a professional librarian with a degree categorizing the Web, which makes Yahoo a pleasure to use.

On the downside, it doesn't remotely have all the information on the Web. It's a poor choice when you're doing broad research or you want to see what's available. It's better when you know what you want to explore or nail down. HotBot, Excite, Lycos, Alta Vista, among others, all have their pluses and minuses, and they're changing constantly. The point is that you need to get listed on all of them, and you should be aware which ones are the hottest.

The Web is very dynamic. Some of it is growing and improving, some of it is shriveling and dropping out. This adds another level of complexity to the problem of staying listed in all the right places.

There are a few different approaches search engines use to grapple with this problem. Most search engines use programs called *bots*—short for *robots*. They're not robotic programs but search programs that go running around hitting different sites and bringing information back and assembling it.

For example, Excite attempts to categorize by subject and uses an interesting grammatical database to make correlations between different words. It's very complex and occasionally yields puzzling results. You may be searching for automobiles and you'll turn up references to peanut butter!

Then there are the storage engines that attempt to store an abstract of every page on the Net, such as Alta Vista. They maintain a massive database—searches can frequently yield upward of 100,000 matches.

The important thing to remember about these tools is this: they are without a doubt the first step for anyone's attempt to search for information on the Internet. The foundation of Web promotion is listing your site on the major engines.

The major browsers are also good places to get listed, if possible. When you fire up Netscape, it brings up the Netscape home page. This is extremely important. Its home page has pointers to many interesting

Different search engines return different results. Compare the results from a HotBot search to those from ohter engines.

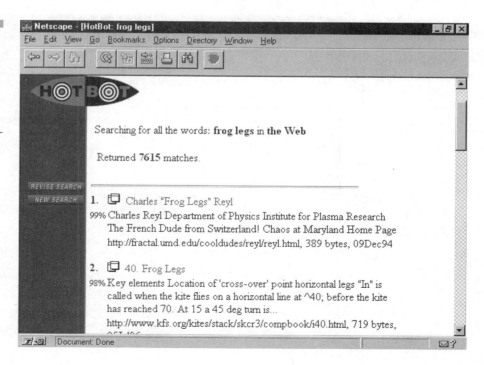

Excite categorizes by subject and shows a very different search result.

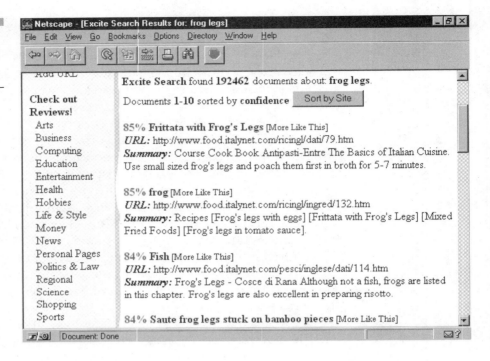

Alta Vista maintains a huge database and sometimes returns thousands of matching entries for a search.

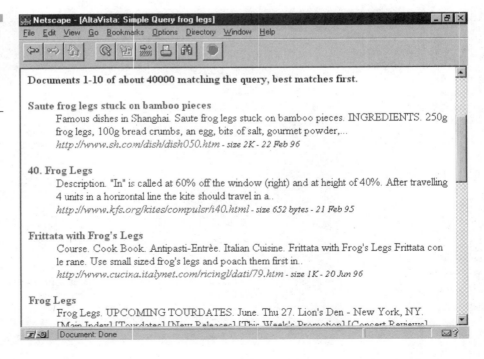

The Netscape home page is one of the most visited sites on the Web. A listing here is a guaranteed traffic generator.

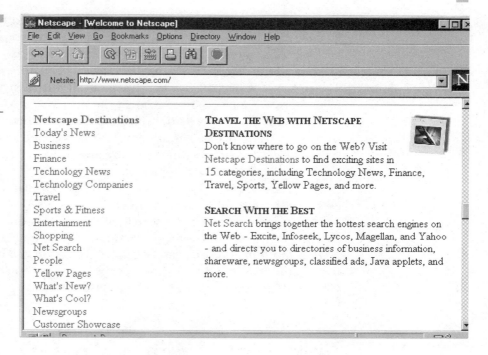

things on the Internet—but not all. Netscape decides what goes on this page, naturally.

Unless you modify Netscape (it's trivial, but most people don't know or bother), the Netscape home page is in your face each time you start up Netscape. Since (at this time) 70 percent of everyone using the Web is using Netscape, it has a lot of power in this arena.

Survey the most popular browsers in use. They could be Netscape, Microsoft, or another one. The search engines linked directly to the browser start pages should be your first choices. Those are the first places people go to. Try to strike up a deal with Netscape or Microsoft. Find a way—whether you have cool stuff on your site or useful information or are willing to pay a listing fee.

Shotgun-Position Your Page on the Web

Shotgun positioning is a broader approach. It comes about when you say, "Here we have some people interested in role-playing games; it's not too far a stretch to think some of them will be interested in playing our collectable card games." It's not a direct market, of course, but a related market that in many situations will be profitable to work.

You roll the dice in this area. However, it's been done with great success. Try to buy a volleyball at a beach volleyball tournament. Instead of volleyballs, what's for sale? Beer. And in the next booth, people are handing out free samples of soft drinks. This came about when somebody in beer marketing recognized a simple fact: members of the beach volleyball subculture are into partying in a big way, and lots of them like beer. This is more toward the shotgun approach.

The true shotgun approach is to get a large popular Web site that about everyone goes to. The most frequently accessed Web sites, in terms of broad demographics, are the search engines. You would place a headline banner on one of these sites, on its main page—the first place visitors go.

This shotgun approach can be quite effective, especially if you are establishing a brand. It's another way to expose many people to your brand—whether they actually take the extra step and visit your site or not.

Frequent Updates Pay Off

It's important to know that the Web is dynamic; people expect it to change at a very rapid pace.

People expect magazines to change every month and the newspaper to change every day. The Web is more like a newspaper than a magazine. While your page doesn't have to change every day, you want to make sure that your site is updated as frequently as necessary to keep it fresh. If you're doing news, you need to change it more than once a day, otherwise people will buy a newspaper or they'll go to a bigger news service.

If your product doesn't change often, you still want to change the site once in a while. When I take a look at a site and decide I like it, I'll *bookmark* it, which saves that location in the software and makes it easier to revisit. It may take me two or three weeks to return. If it seems the same as when I last visited, then I never go back. No new information, so who cares? It's pointless.

Changing the site doesn't have to be a big undertaking. It can be as simple as changing the color. I would change the graphics fairly frequently and I don't say this because we do development. (It could be argued that because we do some of this, we want to make more money by increasing the frequency of updating sites.) In reality, these sorts of updates are extremely inexpensive. A properly designed site can be given a facelift quickly and easily.

The value of the data is in direct proportion to how new it is. If your data is an hour old, it's very valuable. If it's a week old, it's not as valuable. Data older than this is only useful as reference material. For technology, I go to the Web because when I get *Byte Magazine*, or any other magazine, material isn't just a month old—it's three months old. *Wired* magazine should be called "Unwired" because it does articles six months in advance. The games are ancient history by the time the magazine is on the streets, compared to what's on the Internet; a game is old in my mind after a week. I hit the Web site at wired.com for the latest info.

Netscape and Microsoft issue press releases every three days to keep their products fresh. Even if the enhancement means little overall, it's the freshness of the information that grabs attention.

If you're running a small business, you can't dedicate the resources to constant updating, but here are two simple ways of keeping your site fresh:

1. When you design a site, try to design with alternate color schemes. You can do a page for each color of your logo and every couple of weeks change the color. It's simple to do and makes your site look fresh and new every week.

2. Consider developing several alternate images for your home page. Keep the layout the same, but change an image or two every time the page is loaded. This, too, can be done inexpensively.

Companies often put a lot of effort into a new site and then hang it out to dry by never changing it for four or five months. Users will never visit again if they see that it doesn't get updated. You wouldn't do this on any other media, so why would you do this on the Internet?

The Internet is not a print ad. When someone takes the time to come to your site, this is a fantastic thing. A customer has walked into your store. Some stores don't care, you can walk in and right back out. Others—usually the most successful stores—want to keep you there. They also want to entice you to come back.

When people visit your Web site, it's as if they got into their car and drove to your company's office or flagship store. It's not like they're casually leafing through a magazine and happen to see your ad. A Web site is very interactive, so you have to take advantage of that or you turn that unique advantage against yourself. Web surfers won't put up with it.

If you spend enough money, you can register almost every visitor who comes to your site. Software is available that will greet you by name and say, "We noticed you were interested in our XL-250 Whatsis the last time you visited. Now we have our new improved XL-360 Whatsis that won't wrinkle, ravel, or rip under the roughest usage. If you're interested, click here for more information."

If you say the site will be updated next week, make sure it is or you'll lose the contact. If you make a promise, keep it.

Special Offers

Decipher makes collectible card games. When it restructured its site, it ran a promotion where visitors could get free cards. Freebies are magnets for people, especially when they aren't normally available. Whether it's a discount, a special product, a hat or T-shirt, or free admission to an event, giveaways build traffic enormously when they're promoted well. All the typical marketing approaches work here. People are special when they come to you on the Internet as opposed to responding to a TV ad. You have a possibility for a long-term relationship, so do everything you can to develop it.

Provide Advantages to Internet Buyers

Providing buyer advantages is especially important. There are a lot of things that the Web can do as an advantage that other ways of selling cannot do. One of the great advantages is you get instantaneous information. On the FedEx site, you can enter your tracking number and it tells you where your delivery is—fantastic. Another advantage consumers value, even though it's very low cost to the company providing it, is the Net's ability to let people know immediately when a new product they've expressed interest in is available.

Use the Internet's Great Usefulness As a Test Market

Be careful about making product announcements by e-mail; that is, be sure they only go to people who have requested them. It's unwise to spam people (send them unwanted e-mail). There's a lot of opposition to the possibility of the Net becoming like snail mail, where a stack of junk mail hits your mailbox twice a week—and it's all stuff you just throw away. If visitors ask for e-mail newsletters or product announcements from you, it's a cost-effective customer relationship builder. It's powerful, and many of the people on your list will tell their friends. It's inexpensive to try out things on the Internet. You don't have to worry about ad costs, you get rapid feedback, plus information you wouldn't normally get.

Buyer Advantages

Use the technology of the Web. Because you have hypertext, which allows for people to make interactive choices about the information they want, and Java, which allows you to write programs, you can do things such as interactive comparisons. So, if your product is better than another product, you can use this medium to dynamically and interactively explain why. You can't really do that in a brochure in an entertaining fashion. Instead of bullet charts, you can allow people to investigate your product deeper than it's physically possible to do in a small brochure or even a large catalog.

Other advantages are having resources on your site people can use and keep coming back for. Offer something besides your product to draw people. It can be anything, but preferably something regularly updated that would keep people coming back, such as a column written by a knowledgeable person or information linked to the product or service. This can be a guide updating ins and outs or how to do this to make the most of the product. Success stories, testimonials, all these things are great draws that can get you additional exposure elsewhere.

If you want to get listed on a gardening site, offer to write a column regarding gardening or related services. Offer to have the Joe Montana of gardening answer your customers' questions online. Or, offer a forum so people can write questions on gardening. Web site success lies in making your site have value. Provide an interactive bulletin board where customers post questions and answers. If you have a staff of people and a company newsletter, a lot of such information could be used on your Web site. It will only take a small 15 or 20 percent additional time for the employee to keep this up. Dedicate the resources and do it or there'll be a lot of disgruntled people who, instead of coming back, will head straight for your competition.

Put Your Catalog Online at Low Cost

Nearly all companies should carefully consider the idea of having their entire line available on the Internet. Because of the insignificant cost of doing so, every item in even large product lines can be described. In most cases, this can be done in sufficient detail to enable visitors to make a purchase decision; in which case clicking on an icon should bring up an order form.

A key element in making this a success is intelligent organization of the products, which most companies will already have done in their paper catalogs. On the Net, go further. Set up a simple search engine to locate products under every name you've ever heard people apply to each product. Say you're listing tools. Wrenches should be found by a search of at least the following names: monkey, crescent, movable jaw, Gripco, plus every other brand name in the field.

Particularly if style is an important element in your product line, you may want to add photographs of your products. However, if you do this, bear in mind that many people will visit your site with graphics turned off. Therefore, they will only see text. So, make sure the text can stand alone.

An example of software to facilitate putting your catalog online is provided by iCat Corporation.

iCat Corporation
1420 Fifth Avenue, Suite 1800
Seattle, WA 98101-2333
Phone: 206-623-0977
Fax: 206-623-0477
Product information: 800-558-4228
Internet: jodis@icat.com
URL: http //www.icat.com
Contact: Jodi Sorensen, Marketing Programs Manager

iCat Electronic Commerce Suite

The iCat Electronic Commerce Suite is a package of iCat products that allows a business to build a commercial Web site. The Electronic Commerce Suite allows the company to set up a catalog online by creating the HTML needed to display its products.

Key Features

Has the ability to import data from any database

Supports extensive product information such as tables or complex specifications

Predefined templates

Supports all media formats including text, graphics, sound, movies, and Adobe Acrobat PDF files

Optional dynamic page creation (on-the-fly)

Secure online ordering: payment security via SSL, HTTPS, CheckFree Wallet, First Virtual, and other leading systems

Optional real-time credit card authorization

Customer preferences such as personal, editable shopping lists; in-product searches; and real-time order placement

Customizable electronic billing forms

Capability to receive, process, and track orders 24 hours a day

iCat Suite's cost (which follows) is low enough to level the playing field for small companies seeking to place their catalogs on the Net without budgeting six figures or more to do it. However, large companies also use this software. For example, Office Depot relied on the iCat Electronic Commerce Suite to put its 10,000-product catalog online.

iCAT COMMERCE PUBLISHER SYSTEM REQUIREMENTS

486, Pentium, or higher PC running Windows 95 or Windows NT

Any Macintosh, Power Macintosh, or Macintosh-compatible running System 7.0 or later

16 MB RAM and 15 MB free hard drive space

iCAT COMMERCE EXCHANGE SYSTEM REQUIREMENTS

Any Internet server software and any of the following systems:

Windows NT 3.5.1 or later

Macintosh OS 7.0 or later

Sun Solaris

SUN OS

SGI Irix 5.3 or later

Digital Alpha NT

Price: $1,495.00 (as of September 1996).

Windows or Macintosh.

Includes the iCat Commerce Publisher and iCat Commerce Exchange.
CD-ROM catalogs require the iCat Commerce Player (to be available
in spring 1997), which is sold separately, and allows you to build
your catalog on CD-ROM.

Web Sites with Help for Small-
to Medium-Sized Enterprises

These three Web sites offer a variety of help to businesspeople.

1. *http://www.toolkit.cch.com.* Provides useful information in the areas
   of business planning, finance, and much more.

2. *http://www.americasbrightest.com.* America's Brightest is a trademark
   of

   America's Brightest LLC
   1223 Wilshire Blvd, Suite #352
   Santa Monica, CA 90403
   Phone: 310-656-8714
   Fax: 310-656-8716
   E-mail: info@americasbrightest.com

   This Web site offers several newsletters, personalized counseling, travel
   tips, background checks of employees, a database of "perfect employees for your current job openings," help with PR, and legal assistance
   through a newsletter.

3. *http://www.entrepreneurmag.com.* Among other things, this Web site
   by *Entrepreneur Magazine* allows visitors to chat with several business
   consultants. Could be a business saver for small companies in need
   of specific advice.

Net Cash Payments Service Providers

The first half of the 1990s saw a rash of new companies emerge with innovative ways to exploit the vast potential of Internet commerce. Today, the problem for nontechnical executives seeking to bring the benefits of e-selling to their own companies isn't finding help, it's choosing among the many options available.

The first requirement of e-selling for cyber payment, as opposed to selling for r-cash (the folding money in your pocket) or cc-cash, (credit card cash) is to get what you need.

Get What You Need

As a company who accepts credit cards over the phone to complete sales, you routinely get an approval number before completing the sale. At the very least, you need to build a similar routine into your Web site sales.

You also want to make it as difficult as possible for a hacker to penetrate your Web site and change it, capture credit card numbers for fraudulent use, steal your sales data, or, for no apparent reason except malicious mischief, mess it up. This important subject is discussed in detail in the next chapter.

One simple, low-cost way of minimizing some of these risks is to transfer each day's harvest of credit card numbers and sales data to an offline computer, zip file, or other storage system. Obviously, this only accomplishes the objective if the offline computer or storage unit is not connected by LAN to any online computer. To preserve security, the transfer must be made by having a trusted person hand-carry the data on a disk from the online computer to the offline computer, and then immediately erase the transfer disk. The offline computer or storage unit should be kept in a physically secure environment such as a vault. All information on the offline computer can easily be further protected by encrypting it, with the decryption key restricted to as few people as possible.

The vPOS solution from VeriFone handles this problem automatically (http://www.icd.verifone.com).

Avoid What You Don't Need

You don't need hassles from banks or lawsuits from customers claiming an employee of yours stole their credit card number and ran up charges, destroyed their credit, and caused them grievous mental agony and life-threatening stress. If they can prove your employee did it, you could be hit with a major judgment. Even if you win the case, the legal fees could be formidable. Check to make sure your insurance covers this risk.

Minimizing inconvenience to your customers should be a primary goal in organizing your security measures. To this end, have your Web site order form ask as few questions as possible. This is no time to attempt to gather demographic information on your buyers. Remember, every question you ask beyond what you must have to complete the sale will kill some sales.

What the Next Decade Will Probably Bring

The turn of the millennium almost certainly will usher in tremendous changes in retailing. Thousands of small firms all over the world will be selling direct and building loyal clienteles for their specialties. Net cash payments will flow over the Internet in ever-increasing volume. Retailers who ignore or fight these trends will lose market share; retailers who embrace these new paradigms of selling will prosper.

The line between manufacturers and retailers, already slightly fuzzy due to the advent of factory store complexes, will blur even more as selling direct to consumers becomes more attractive to both consumers and manufacturers. Competition will force many reluctant manufacturers to move in this direction to protect their market share.

Not only will manufacturers increasingly sell direct to the ultimate consumer, they will increasingly sell direct to the retailer. Thus the heaviest impact of Internet-driven change will fall on wholesalers, who will see more and more volume flowing around them rather than through them. The only wholesalers to survive this streamlining of distribution will be firms who provide genuine cost-effective service both to retailers and manufacturers.

Universally Accepted Standards: The Missing Key to Explosive Net Cash Payments Growth

Over 315 million Visas and MasterCards were in circulation in the mid-1990s, with annual purchases running at about half a trillion dollars.

Excluding routine payments such as for utilities, mortgages, car payments, and the like, nearly half of consumer purchases are paid by credit card, nearly four times as many as by check.

During the mid-1990s, Net cash payments (also called *e-cash, cybercash,* or *electronic payments*) were growing rapidly. However, they were still counted by the millions, were still reaching for their first billion dollars in yearly sales volume, were still less than 1 percent of purchases paid by credit card. As the last years of the century wind down, more and more pieces of the complex infrastructure required by Net cash payments are hammered into place. Now the various forms of Net cash payments are poised for enormous increases in volume.

Yet one barrier remains. To achieve the enormous volumes, this new form of value exchange needs a standard way of receiving, storing, and paying out cyber-money, e-cash, and electronic cash that we call Net cash. The standard way must include methods of keeping these payments secure, of transmitting them, and, when desired, of redeeming them with r-cash.

Competition may introduce several different standards, but the growth of electronic payments (Net cash) will be severely restrained until there's only one standard in use in the United States, and ideally in the entire world. The difficulties, practical, political, and otherwise, of putting the entire planet on one electronic payments standard boggle the mind. In this connection it's worth remembering the European Community's long struggle to create the Euro, a currency standard for all of Europe.

The standard for credit cards will almost definitely be set. But no standards for electronic cash have been proposed yet. Several product offerings for cash have been proposed by DigiCash, CyberCash, Citibank's Transaction Technology Systems, and NTT in Japan. Other cash solutions are based on smart cards such as VisaCash and Mondex will one day interoperate with the standard Internet payment system. So, the cash field is still wide open and changing very fast.

The growing success of the Internet will exert steady pressure in the direction of a single standard electronic currency, in spite of nationalistic misgivings rooted in twentieth century thinking. It may well prove to be far simpler to create the Earthbuck than the Euro. The *Earthbuck,* an international cyber-payments medium of exchange, could be electronically converted in a few nanoseconds from or to one regional or national currency at the latest exchange rates.

However, before the Earthbuck becomes a realistic proposition, the world's cyber-payments standards must be organized in simplified form.

Not only must the zloty, ruble, mark, schilling, franc, drachma, guilder, lira, escudo, peseta, krone, forint, krona, koruna, and the pound give way to the EuroEbuck; the yen, kip, yuan, won, nguitrum, ringgit, rupiah, bhat, kyat, taka, and the rupee need to fuse into an AsianEbuck.

The needs of international electronic trade would be better served by unity among the currencies of Africa: the rand, lilangeni, naira, birr, puls, dinar, dirham, kwanza, cedi, and others. In South America, a SudEbuck needs to replace the various currencies of that continent.

Where regional rivalries and enduring feuds are the norm, united currencies based on economic and cultural commonalities and alliances are more likely to emerge than are those based primarily on geographic location. Thus, we may see an ArabEbuck uniting the riyal, rial, dinar, dirham, and others.

But let's talk about the more immediate objective: one cyber-payments standard for the United States. Imagine how complex it would make daily life if there were three kinds of paper currency, with three sets of stores, each accepting only one of the three currencies. If you went to the post office, you'd need currency A. The drugstore down the street accepts only currency B. You drive into a gas station with an empty tank and discover the station only accepts currency C. Even though you have plenty of currencies A and B, you can't buy gas. The situation would be so intolerable it would force standardization on just one currency. The same thing will inevitably happen with cyber-payments.

Multiple standards for cash are possible, just like credit cards today (i.e., Visa, MasterCard, American Express, Discover). The different card brands have different rules and standards. When credit cards first showed up, most merchants would only accept one brand (Visa or MasterCard). Then their customers showed up demanding that they be able to use whatever card was in their wallet. The solution was *POS* (point-of-sale) *terminal technology,* allowing a single box to handle multiple standards. The terminal vendors took on the headache of doing the translation. The same thing may happen with electronic cash. Merchants may start out accepting just VisaCash or just Mondex, and then translation solutions will be developed by the terminal vendors to allow acceptance of all of them. In the meantime, just like it was with credit cards, it will be a major headache for merchants and an annoyance for customers.

The banks are already heavily involved in credit cards—a bank started credit cards. Since that's where both the money and the expertise for handling large volumes of money transactions are found, you must have banks behind Net cash payments.

Someone's got to be standing behind these electronic bits flashing around the world or sitting quietly on some plastic storage device. Banks, the natural structures to take on these responsibilities and opportunities, have to be there so you can readily convert r-cash (regular cash) into Net cash and back again. Hence the pressure to set up a single standard.

The ideal is to have one kind of Net cash that all banks sell, accept, or redeem at par. Net cash and r-cash would be identical in value—as they should be. Today, I can go into any bank in the United States with a twenty-dollar bill and get two fives and a ten. I can go into any grocery store and buy eggs with my r-cash money. Ideally, Net cash will gain the same universal acceptance and value. In fact, it's hard to see how such a development can long be avoided. The nation's expanding economy demands one kind of readily converted Net cash with the same value as r-cash. The improved monetary system should permit you to use Net cash payments—withdrawn from your bank account over the Internet, and loadable by you onto a chip card. The chip card would then allow you to pay for phone calls, copies at the copy shop, a beer at the local bar, gas, groceries, whatever.

Selling for Electronic Money Compared to Credit Card Sales

From the Merchant's Point of View

- Like r-cash (the long green in your wallet) cyber-money is immediately spendable. Credit card sales typically involve a delay of two to four days or more before the merchant's account is credited. During that time, the unavailable money is part of the banking industry's float and, as such, generally earns interest for the banks but not the merchants.

- There's more potential for fraud and problems with credit card sales than with verified Internet sales. Most merchants who innocently accept a stolen card for fraudulent purchases will have obtained approval from the verification authority, issuing bank, or credit card company. Verification lessens the risk to merchants. They get their money, and the authority takes the loss. Banks track fraudulent and uncollectable sales and cancel merchants whose record is poor.

From the Consumer's Point of View

■ One advantage of paying with Net cash is anonymity. You can't be logged unless, in a separate procedure, you choose to give your name and address. As the buyer, you can generally get away with telling the seller to pound sand if you don't want to reveal that information.

■ You're not handing over your credit card number. If I send a merchant $10 worth in Net cash, the worst thing that could possibly happen even on an insecure system, I lose $10. If someone steals my credit card number, there could be $9000 in charges rung up before I get home and realize my wallet's been stolen. Prompt action limits my loss, all right, but coping with the whole situation is still a big hassle that sometimes goes on for years.

■ With credit card purchases, when I hand you my credit card, you know who I am, who I claim to be—if you check the signature on the back of the card. However, most American merchants never do this.

■ You can add me to the mailing list you're selling to any scam artist who wants to buy it. This doesn't happen with Net cash. For most people it might not matter, but if you can preserve your anonymity and privacy from junk mail, and so on, it's very nice.

■ Finally, there are the credit card fees, transaction fees, interest, and annual membership fees. Whether the fees for Net cash transactions will be more or less, time will tell, but the early indications are that they will be less.

With either Net cash or r-cash, it's simpler. If I get smacked on the head and someone takes $40 from my wallet, say two twenties of r-cash, they're gone. With some forms of Net cash it may be possible in the future to block its use by a thief. So, in some ways Net cash payments are better than real cash or credit card cash.

Possible Low-Cost Web Site Development Methods

The credit card processing divisions of banks are generally most interested in getting your Web site up and running so they can make money processing your credit card sales. Charging you for software and technical assistance often is secondary.

However, the old axiom "Free advice is worth what you pay for it" may apply with great force here. Banks tend to be bureaucratic, conservative, and slow-footed. In the rapidly evolving and intensely competitive field of electronic commerce, dealing with them for your Web site development can be fraught with frustration, to say the least. Nevertheless, it can be a low-cost way to go.

Look into what Netscape's LivePayment can do for you. It's discussed later in Chap. 7.

In addition, several major banks are now offering, or will soon offer, Internet payment services, including Wells Fargo, Royal Bank of Canada, Bank of America, and First USA Paymantech, to name just a few.

Credit Card URLs

The information given below was valid at press time. It may change as each card's marketing people realize they're missing a low-cost way to speed their electronic growth by telling vendors how to do electronic business with them.

American Express

URL: http://americanexpress.com

This Web site offers plenty of individual card user information but nothing for vendors. However, you may be able to reach someone with vendor information by calling one of the several phone numbers given.

Diners Club

URL: http://www.dinersclub.com

You would think this credit card company, which appears to be struggling against its larger competitors, would leap at the opportunity to promote Diners Club to vendors at extremely low cost on the Web. Nah—its site ignores vendors and offers consumer information.

Discover Card

URL: http://www.discovercard.com

Negotiating Discover Card collections through local banks often is a bit dicey, and many merchant service companies can't process them.

MasterCard

URL: http://www.mastercard.com

An informative site with much information about late-breaking developments in chip cards and other aspects of e-selling.

Visa

URL: http://www.visa.com

Your local bank is probably well equipped to take over the burden of processing Visa card collections, as are the many merchant service companies.

Spotlighting Banks with Electronic Commerce Expertise

For additional information, check our latest update of App. B by visiting http://www.jamisongold.com/banks. Or, visit the Web sites of CyberCash and VeriFone. Or, call your local bank.

BankAmerica Corporation
Contact: Sharon Tucker, vice president
Phone: 415-622-2775
Fax: 415-622-6288
E-mail: sharon.tucker@bankamerica.com
URL: http://www.bankamerica.com

Also at Bank of America:
Contact: Jo Singleton, vice president, Electronic Delivery Services
Phone: 415-785-5933

Barnett Bank
URL: http://www.barnett.com

Citibank
URL: http://www.citibank.com
This Web site provides a great deal of information.

Comerica
URL: http://www.comerica.com

Nations Bank
URL: http://www.nationsbank.com

PNC Bank
URL: http://www.pncbank.com

Sanwa
URL: http://www.sanwa.com

Wells Fargo Bank
This venerable firm was merging with First Interstate Bank at press
time. Wells Fargo, well advanced in Internet transactions, was about to
add Microsoft Merchant Server to its payment processing solutions.
Apparently, First Interstate will capitalize on the Internet expertise
already developed by Well Fargo and will continue its Virtual Mall.

Spotlighting Companies Able to Provide the Electronic Transaction Expertise You Need

Suppliers of security software—such things as encryption/decryption
methods, firewalls, and intrusion destruction systems—appear in Chap. 7.
Here, we take a broad look at organizations concerned with facilitating
the development and operation of commerce-capable Web sites.

The following organizations, many of them pioneers in their specialties, can be of great help in coping with the complexities of cyber payments, as well as facilitating sales where credit cards are the method of
payment.

AMP eMerce Internet Solutions

P.O. Box 3608 (M.S. 84-26)
Harrisburg, PA 17105-3608
Phone: 717-592-6706
Fax: 717-780-7477
URLs: http://www.ampemerce.com
      http://www.connect.amp.com
Contact: Jim Kessler, AMP eMerce, 717-592-6706
E-mail: tchocker@amp.com

AMP, calling itself the world's leading supplier of electrical and electronic connectors and interconnection systems, "created the ground-breaking AMP Connect electronic catalog solution," according to Jim Kessler. It has since "leveraged the expertise gained" into a new division headed by him. The new division, AMP eMerce Internet Solutions, "specializes in customized electronic commerce solutions for clients in both business-to-business and retail operations. The division offers electronic commerce consulting, development of electronic catalog database and business transactions, Web site hosting and support, and systems integration for turnkey operations," he said.

The AMP electronic catalog was launched in January 1996 to serve its worldwide customers, offering product information in eight languages including Japanese, Mandarin Chinese, and Korean. The massive catalog contains 3-D models and charts of more than 70,000 AMP products. The catalog has more than 30,000 registered users.

"AMP is in a unique position to help clients harness the business potential of electronic commerce since we're doing it successfully ourselves," said Jim Kessler. "Many companies put up hundreds of static HTML pages on a Web site thinking they are conducting business-to-business electronic commerce. That is not enough. To serve the business-to-business market, companies need to create database-driven dynamic content that can be searched by requirements, not just browsed by keywords. Customers need immediate, accurate, product information."

We heartily concur, except to say that the need for dynamic content extends to Web sites devoted to business-to-consumer commerce as well. Nothing much can be accomplished by sites that do not exploit the interactive potential of the Web.

AMP uses OM-Transact Internet commerce software by Open Market.

Checkfree Corporation

4411 East Jones Bridge Road
Norcross, Georgia 30092
Phone: 770-734-3404
Fax: 770-734-3304
Contact: Matthew S. Lewis, vice president of corporate communications
E-mail: matt_lewis@atl.checkfree.com
URL: http://checkfree.com

As its name implies, Checkfree Corporation provides a secure system for paying electronically without writing and mailing a check. At present, the firm seems to be concentrating on the routine payments usually made by check rather than the random purchases usually paid for with a credit card.

Companies planning on heavy Internet sales should consider establishing an account with Checkfree so they can accept payments from new and old clients who use Checkfree. Make it as easy as possible for your buyers to give you their money.

The Checkfree home page.

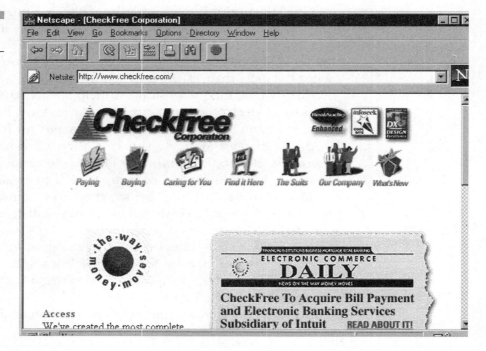

CyberCash

2100 Reston Parkway, Third Floor
Reston, VA 22091
Phone: 703-620-4200
E-mail: info@cybercash.com
URL: http://www.cybercash.com

CyberCash Sales and Marketing:
303 Twin Dolphin Drive, Suite 200
Redwood City, CA 94065
Phone: 415-594-0800
Fax: 415-594-0899
Contact: Cheryl Sullivan Lester, director of merchant marketing
Phone: 415-413-0155
E-mail: clester@cybercash.com

CyberCash bills itself as "the secure Internet payment system." Its system uses public key encryption technology for secure transmission of credit card data on the Net. Merchants never see an unscrambled credit

CyberCash uses public key encryption to transmit credit card data securely.

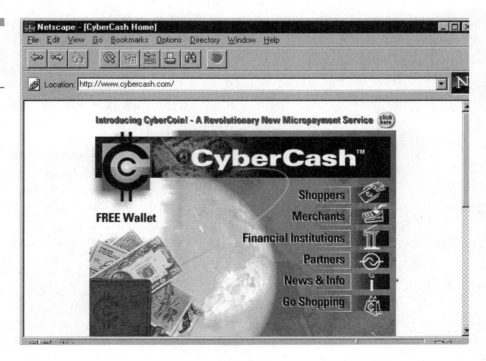

card number, thus relieving them of the responsibility for protecting a credit card number database from criminal access.

CyberCash has gone well beyond credit card transactions with its CyberCoin technology, which provides merchants a cost-effective way to sell electronic goods and services for small amounts of money, usually between $0.25 and $5.00, thus making it practical to provide games online and charge for their use on a pay-as-you-play basis.

When CyberCash, founded in August 1994, went public on February 15, 1996, it had lost $10 million and had no revenue. Nevertheless, Wall Street snapped up the IPO at $17 per share. On the first day of trading, the shares zoomed 60 percent to $28 per share.

The following month, CyberCash announced plans to team with SLI-GOS, one of Europe's leading providers of payment services, to take secure Internet payment systems to Europe. The two companies will integrate their technologies to increase European secure electronic commerce.

For more information, contact CyberCash's Deborah Claymon at 415-827-7065

In 1995, Magdalena Yesil wrote in *NetworkWorld,* "Internet commerce has grown more quickly in the past year than anyone had anticipated. Companies ranging from 1-800-FLOWERS to Wells Fargo to Silicon Graphics have begun to utilize this dynamic, versatile, and all-but-ubiquitous medium to reach potential customers."

The next year, 1996, saw the end of the beginning of Internet commerce. The number of Web sites had increased from the mid-four figures, 5 or 6 thousand, to mid-five figures, between 40 and 60 thousand. In fact there are no reliable figures on precisely how many Web sites are out there in cyberspace. A good case can be made that the total number is at least 100,000. In any event, it's generally agreed that Web sites are proliferating faster than Australian rabbits.

However, the theme of most of them seems to be, "Look at us; we're great." These sites, usually aimed at enthralling prospects with warmed-over brochure copy and masses of company-centric blurbs, rarely exploit the Web's enormous potential. Few of them are adequately promoted, and even fewer do much if anything to encourage repeat visitors. Indeed, a faintly grudging tone pervades many sites, as though whoever created them felt imposed upon to have that duty thrust at them.

Most sites don't provide interactive presale Q and A, a lead gathering system, customer service, or postsale tech support. Even fewer sites are capable of accepting orders and collecting payments. Of course, some products or services are unsuitable, if not impossible, for online commerce. However, that's not the reason why so few Web sites are commerce-capable; organizing a site for Internet commerce is considerably more difficult than merely putting up a ho-hum, brochure-warmed-over site.

Perhaps it's fortunate that so many companies have been slow to get involved in Web site sales. Already signs of overload are appearing on the Internet. Online commerce must compete for bandwidth with the enormous increase in e-mail. But too much is already at stake to allow the Internet to collapse—at least more than temporarily. New technology, we have grown accustomed to feel sure, will save the day.

Unlike 1995, enormous growth was widely anticipated in 1996. Many unrealistic expectations were not met. Reasonable expectations were amply fulfilled. Perfectly positioned companies selling on the Internet for payment via credit card or for cyber-money continue to grow at a giddy pace, with the result that every day late comers wait to enter the field, it makes it more difficult for them to successfully compete in the early adopters' niches.

EC Company

1705 El Camino Real
Palo Alto, CA 94306
Phone: 415-323-7500
Fax: 415-321-7816

Announcing its entry into the field in September 1996, EC plans to facilitate the easy integration of business-to-business electronic commerce solutions through its Global Alliance Program. The founding partners in EC are well-known software vendors including Ca\$hGraf Software.

Elcom Systems

400 Blue Hill Drive
Westwood, MA 02090
Phone: 617-407-5003
Fax: 617-407-5063
URL: http://elcom.com
Contact: Ms. Pat Breslin, director of marketing

Elcom Systems, a wholly owned technology subsidiary of Elcom International, developed and licenses the PECOS electronic commerce system. It customizes the PECOS technology to meet the specific needs of clients.

Elcom's PECOS technology automates the complete business-to-business transaction cycle, electronically linking licensees and their customers in real time throughout the product selection, ordering, fulfillment, and delivery process. In addition, the system facilitates customer interaction by enabling distributors and manufacturers to respond to inquiries immediately. As a result, the costs of customer support and manual order processing are minimized while administrative efficiency and productivity is increased.

IBM

The IBM Global Network
PO Box 30021
Tampa, FL 33630
Phone: 800-455-5056
E-mail: globalnetwork@info.ibm.com
          ibmdirect@vnet.ibm.com

As 1996 drew to a close, IBM was busily offering new technologies in various areas of electronic commerce. These new technologies will evolve during 1997; check with IBM for late developments. We will briefly discuss four of IBM's new projects.

■ *Cryptolope.* Cryptolopes provide a way to prevent the unauthorized distribution of publishers' works over the Internet. A *cryptolope* is basically a container or a package that holds a document as well as information about the document itself, such as terms of use, any licensing agreement, and the price of the document.

   When potential users gain access to a cryptolope container, they can view portions of its contents. A helper application (planned for release by Netscape) allows the viewing of everything within the cryptolope except the actual document. Once the users agree to pay for the document, they receive a key to unlock the cryptolope package.

   Cryptolopes don't require the user to purchase anything, either hardware or software. The helper application is available on the Web.

■ *Storefront.* Storefront is a new IBM system that provides industrial-strength electronic solutions to enable business-to-business transactions over the Internet. This development will facilitate EDI-like transactions between corporations.

■ *Integrion Financial Network.* For this project, IBM allied itself with several powerhouse financial institutions—notably Bank of America,

ABN AMRO, Bank One, Barnett, Comerica, First Chicago NBD, Fleet Financial Group, KeyCorp, Mellon Bank, Michigan Bank, Nations-Bank, PNC Bank, Washington Mutual Services Bank, and the Royal Bank of Canada. Over half the households in North America bank at one of these institutions.

The services IBM creates and provides through Integrion will be open to all banks, who can reach their customers through their own Web sites or through popular online services such as America Online, CompuServe, and Prodigy.

Integrion has the potential to become a far too powerful and popular combination to be ignored by Web sellers. Keep tuned to IBM's Integrion as it develops in 1997. If all goes well with it, make sure your Web site can quickly handle orders from businesses and consumers who want to use this method to pay for their purchases from you.

■ *CommercePOINT.* IBM claims this family of products is the first "designed to provide end-to-end electronic buying and selling on the World Wide Web."

"With the launch of CommercePOINT, we have accomplished more than electronic commerce on the Internet. CommercePOINT embodies all the processes of electronic business on a global scale," said Dr. Irving Wladawsky-Berger, general manager of IBM's Internet Division. "We've drawn upon our experience in networking entire industries such as health care, transportation, and utilities to bring a new way of doing business to the Internet."

World Avenue, a mall on the World Wide Web, offers retailers and other businesses a secure way to sell their offerings, whether products or services, to millions of consumers. IBM's Global Network, one of the world's largest, provides Internet access in over 700 cities and countries.

World Avenue had its grand opening in the fall of 1996 with about 20 retailers. Prices start at about $5,000.

iCat Corporation

1420 Fifth Avenue-Suite 1800
Seattle, WA 98101-2333
Contact: Jodi Sorensen, marketing programs manager
Phone: 206-623-0977
Fax: 206-623-0477
E-mail: jodis@icat.com
URL: http://www.icat.com

The iCat Electronic Commerce Suite is a package of iCat products that allow a business to build a commercial Web site. The Electronic Commerce Suite allows the company to set up a catalog online by creating the HTML needed to display its products.

Key Features

- Ability to import data from any database
- Supports extensive product information such as tables or complex specifications
- Predefined templates
- Supports all media formats including text, graphics, sound, movies, and Adobe Acrobat PDF files
- Optional dynamic page creation (on-the-fly)
- Secure online ordering; payment security via SSL, HTTPS, CheckFree Wallet, First Virtual, and leading systems. Optional real-time credit card authorization
- Customer preferences such as personal, editable shopping lists; in-product searches; and real-time order placement

The iCat Corporation home page.

- Customizable electronic billing forms
- Ability to receive, process, and track orders 24 hours a day

iCat Commerce Publisher System Requirements

- 486, Pentium, or higher PC running Windows 95 or Windows NT
- Any Macintosh, Power Macintosh, or Macintosh-compatible running System 7.0 or later
- 16 MB RAM and 15 MB free hard drive space

Microsoft Corporation

One Microsoft Way
Redmond, WA 98052-6399
Phone: 206-703-0403
Fax: 206-936-7329
URL: http://www.microsoft.com
E-mail: mkim@microsoft.com

Microsoft's huge Web site offers a wealth of information about its products, reachable via an effective search function.

Merchant Server is Microsoft's entry into Web site sales-enabling software. At press time it had just been announced.

For complete information, contact Microsoft's Michael Kim at 206-703-0403.

WebMate Technologies

960 Turnpike Avenue
Canton, Massachusetts 02021
Bob Trocchi, chief operating officer
Kimberly Polcari
Phone: 617-828-5600
Fax: 617-828-1911
URL: http://www.webmate.com.

WebMate's applications reduce the cost of entry into electronic commerce dramatically, thus opening this new medium to independent retail stores and other small businesses. Not only is the cost reduced, but the level of technical expertise required is sharply lower, making it eminently

WebMate strives to provide cost-effective Web applications for users.

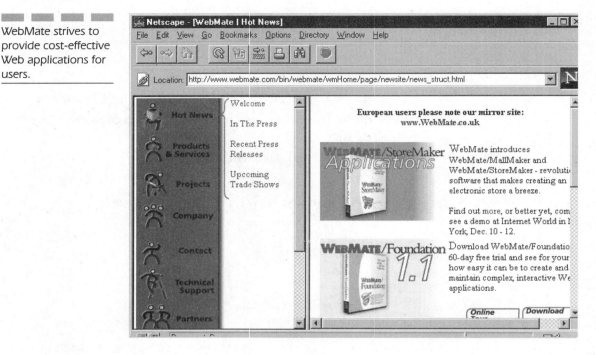

practical for small firms and stores to conduct retail business on the Internet.

All this is easily accomplished by utilizing WebMate's MallMaker and WebMate/StoreMaker. Revolutionary in concept, this electronic-commerce-enabling software became available in September 1996. As of that date, the following prices were in effect: WebMate/StoreMaker, US$995 for the first year and US$750 per year thereafter; WebMate/MallMaker is free to qualified operators with an annual fee of US$750 per store. Annual fees include all updates to the software and payment technologies as well as full support.

The company claims the applications will dramatically impact the trend of electronic commerce by offering a significant enhancement to what was previously available and by reducing the cost and complexity for both retailer and shopper.

WebMate/MallMaker enables a collection of stores to conduct retail business under one umbrella organization. WebMate/StoreMaker provides each merchant in the "mall," or stand-alone electronic store, a complete turnkey application for electronic commerce on the Web—a total solution customized for each store through a series of point-and-click templates:

- Multiple departments with product descriptions and pricing within each department. Picture graphics are available for each product.

- An electronic shopping cart that lets the shopper browse that store's products prior to selection. The customer has a continuous visual listing of all products in the cart with a running total. At any time, products can be removed or added prior to checkout.

- A built-in, fully integrated, and tested credit card RSA encryption product module with several encryption technologies. As encryption technology evolves or as new standards emerge, WebMate/StoreMaker will have these included as subsequent updates.

- Forms-driven modules that let the merchant add, delete, or modify product information and pricing with no technical knowledge.

ABOUT THE WEBMATE/FOUNDATION PRODUCT. WebMate/ Foundation is a comprehensive suite of tools and a server-based platform that includes built-in database functionality, a powerful yet easy-to-use scripting language, browser interface for rapid update of Web page content, plug-in modules for electronic commerce, interface to external SQL databases, and enhanced security features such as full data encryption. It runs with all popular HTTP servers, on most UNIX and NT platforms.

ABOUT WEBMATE TECHNOLOGIES. Founded in 1994, WebMate designs and markets software that lets users exploit the fastest growing part of the Internet—the World Wide Web. WebMate's experience building state-of-the-art Web sites for clients across all industry sectors, including WCVB-TV, EG&G, and the *New England Journal of Medicine*, has led to the development of the WebMate family of products.

WebMate's breakthrough software speeds the implementation of complex Web sites, makes it easy to implement electronic commerce solutions, maintains the highest level of security, and lets you easily maintain your own Web site.

WebMate/Foundation is the culmination of two years of work on various projects with major clients.

WebMate's expertise expands beyond WebMate products to assistance with electronic publishing on-demand, highly interactive database applications, private (intranet) applications with complex security or any other Web application. WebMate consulting services provide complete support to WebMate customers—from concept development and implementation to maintenance and hosting.

Saqqara Systems

1230 Oakmead Parkway—Suite 314
Sunnyvale, CA 94086-4026
Phone: 408-738-4858
Fax: 408-738-8345
Don Swenson, chief operating officer
E-mail: don@saqqara.com
Contact: Amer Ismail, manager, Operations
E-mail: amer@saqqara.com

Saqqara offers a wealth of information on building a successful business-to-business online catalog. Step Search Enterprise is its catalog offering authoring and dynamic database publishing software for the World Wide Web, which it says enables corporations to create a complete and structured product information database that provides users with simple navigation and search-of-product information online.

Spotlighting Credit Card Processing Companies

Credit card purchases will remain the dominant method in electronic transactions for at least the rest of the twentieth century. Thus, it's essential that any firm going online to do business be able to accept credit card sales from all the large credit cards. Sometimes this poses a problem.

In their efforts to avoid credit card losses, banks often throw the baby out with the bath water by denying credit card status to various classes of vendors, particularly new companies, small companies, and those that generate many small transactions. Some look with suspicion on firms that accept telephone orders; others are spooked by the idea of online transactions. It's the old fear of the unknown thing. This attitude will gradually wither away. The inexorable march of progress will force the profit potential of electronic commerce into the closed minds of stodgy bankers whose thinking is rooted in pen and quill practices.

Fortunately, there are solutions for most companies denied credit card account status. Merchant credit card service is a highly competitive field. AT&T's Business Buyer's Guide, which is a national directory of 800 numbers, lists dozens of card service companies under the heading "Credit Card and Other Credit Plans."

Rates and conditions change frequently. Selecting your card service firm is an important purchasing decision—shop around.

The following firms represent a small portion of those listed in the previous directory. The appearance here of any company is not a recommendation, nor is the omission of any firm a reflection on them.

National Data Payments

Phone: 800-367-2638

A California merchant reported great satisfaction with this Maryland company.

Americard Merchant Banc

P.O. Box 1197
Duluth, GA 30136
Phone: 800-552-1500
Contact: David Alcorn, president

This friendly organization specializes in serving the needs of smaller companies. It welcomes firms that sell on the Internet, says it has a high rate of acceptance, and usually approves and sets up a new account in seven working days. It works with American Express, MasterCard, and Visa.

Banc One Point of Sale Services Corporation

Contact: Steve Dieringer, group product manager
Phone: 614-248-3019
Fax: 614-248-4989
E-mail: steved@bancone.com
URL: http://www.bancone.com

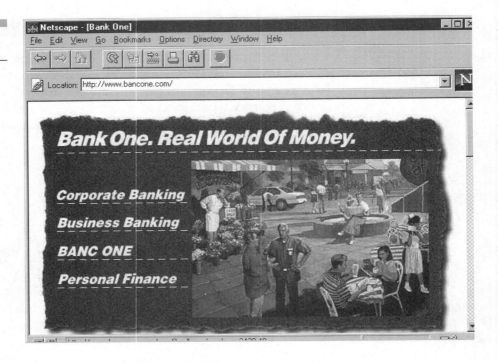

Bank America Merchant Processing Service

As the nation's fourth-largest processor of credit card transactions, this subsidiary of Bank of America generated $20.7 million in profit from $110 million in revenues in 1995. The Bank recently sold shares in this subsidiary in an IPO, although it says it will retain a controlling interest.

Card Service United

Phone: 800-370-4549

Its processing center is in Massachusetts; its bank in California. It advertises its acceptance of online transactions.

First Data Merchant Services

Phone: 800-237-2968

This service accepts Amex, Discover Card, MasterCard, and Visa.

First of Omaha—Merchant Processing

Phone: 800-228-2443

NPC Check Services

Phone: 800-334-9897

This New Jersey firm actually has a real live person answering the phone, so you don't have to go through the usual voice mail hell.

BBN Planet

Phone: 800-472-4565
　　　　617-873-2905
Fax: 508-694-4861
E-mail: net-info@bbnplanet.com
URL: http://www.bbn.com

To learn more about how BBN Planet can help you use the Internet for strategic advantage, contact it via the technology of your choice or contact Vaughn Harring, public relations manager at
Phone: 617-873-4659
Fax: 617-873-5620
E-mail: harring@bbnplanet.com
URL: http://www.bbn.com

Merchant Advantage is a secure business transaction service allowing merchants to sell goods or services from their Web site. Because it can accommodate business growth—without disruption to current operations or expensive reconfiguration—Merchant Advantage is the ideal electronic commerce solution for merchants of all sizes. Designed and operated for secure, reliable network management, Merchant Advantage delivers a cost-effective, easy-to-implement transaction channel for Web-based sales.

SECURE AND CONFIDENTIAL PROCESSING. The emergence of electronic commerce has introduced a dynamic new dimension to the World Wide Web. Because both merchants and buyers need security and confidentiality in their purchase transactions, Merchant Advantage

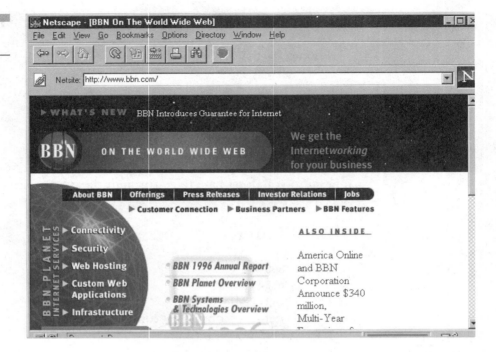

assures a critical prerequisite for online sales: a reliable, secure, and private method of exchanging payment for goods and services.

Merchant Advantage incorporates BBN Planet's high-end security technology to manage order verification and to authenticate commercial transactions to ensure that no tampering has taken place. An industrial-strength validation structure protects all data passing between the merchant's Web site and the Merchant Advantage server to protect the integrity of information. Sensitive data stored in the Merchant Advantage database is encrypted, as is all mail communication with the merchant. All communication with the buyer's workstation is protected by the SSL security structure—the most widely used security protocol on the Internet today.

An independent transaction service, BBN's Merchant Advantage service allows merchants the flexibility to operate their merchandising programs with minimal constraint. The service allows them to design and operate a commercial Web site to meet their electronic commerce goals and requirements. The merchant's server can operate on any UNIX-based server software with the merchant's Web site being physically distinct from the order processing server. This means the merchant can create and change content to describe the goods or services being offered for sale without disrupting order processing, technology, or operating schedules.

A COST-EFFECTIVE ELECTRONIC COMMERCE SOLUTION. Although electronic commerce is predicted to become a major distribution channel for goods and services in the near future, merchants don't have to make a large investment in order to incorporate it into their business. Merchant Advantage efficiently utilizes a comprehensive transaction processing facility that can serve many merchants simultaneously. As a result, merchants share the benefits of the processing facility for a very affordable cost of entry. Monthly fees are calculated and designed to reflect the merchant's increased success in using electronic commerce as a distribution channel.

A SERVICE THAT FITS. Integrating a new order stream into existing sales and fulfillment operations can pose significant technology challenges for merchants. Complex order management systems, comprehensive accounting systems, and multistage fulfillment programs can make the addition of a new channel of distribution very challenging. BBN's Merchant Advantage provides a series of system interfaces that enable merchants to build links to their existing internal operating structures.

SYSTEM REQUIREMENTS. Merchants must have an existing Web site, or plan to establish one, which describes the goods and services being offered. This Web site may be hosted anywhere. In addition, the following requirements must be met.

The Web server may operate any UNIX server software using HTTP-D and serving standard HTML. The Merchant's server must contain necessary information needed to describe the goods and services being offered, including prices and terms of sale. This information should contain required data needed to operate the service on the merchant's behalf. The Web site must be configured with the appropriate software to establish a secure transaction link between the merchant's server and the Merchant Advantage server.

SERVICE PROVISIONS. Merchant Advantage offers the Merchant a service capable of the following:

- Accepting orders using a secure link from a merchant's Web site.
- Verifying the validity of the order, adding the appropriate sales tax, shipping, and any other applicable order charges.
- Collecting buyer credit card payment information using a secure browser connection. Payment authorization is obtained from the credit card facility.

- Issuing the buyer a digital receipt which documents the transaction and manages a secure private key used in encrypting communications between the merchant and Merchant Advantage.

- Maintaining a record of the transaction in a database with 24 months of archived transactions. Notifies the merchant of each order and includes a description of the goods purchased, the customer's identity, and the necessary delivery information so the merchant can fulfill the order.

- Notifying merchants of orders via the technology of their choice: encrypted communications, file transfer, encrypted e-mail, or fax. Network operations are supported 7/24.

MERCHANTS USING MERCHANT ADVANTAGE SERVICE CAN OFFER THEIR BUYERS THESE OPTIONS:

- The option to register in a database. Registration offers buyers a means of storing purchase information for use in subsequent purchases.

- A shopping cart to hold goods until the buyer is ready to electronically check out.

- The ability to obtain a digital receipt to be used as purchase record. Buyers ordering electronic goods or software can use the digital receipt to enable immediate download from the merchant's server.

Beat the Security Bugaboo: Online Transaction Problems and Solutions*

---

* Portions of this chapter are courtesy of CyberCash, DigiCash, PGP, Netscape, VeriSign, and other companies listed in alphabetical order in this chapter. CyberCash is a registered trademark of Cyber-Cash Incorporated; DigiCash is a registered trademark of DigiCash, Incorporated. Pretty Good Privacy and PGP are registered trademarks of PGP, Incorporated. VeriSign and Digital ID are the registered trademarks of VeriSign, Incorporated. Other trademarks are the registered trademarks of their respective companies.

From the point of view of electronic commerce, why do you need security and why would you need cryptography?

Most of us think of *cryptography*—if we actually ever think of it at all—as something used by armies and navies to conceal their operations from the enemy during wartime and by governments everywhere to keep their secrets.

If you read the history of cryptography, you'll read a lot about the Enigma machine used by Nazi Germany in World War II. The Germans confidently believed messages sent via the Enigma machines were utterly unbreakable because Enigma applied a different code to each letter of a message. However, the human factor played a far larger part than the methodical German high command expected. In the final years of peace, an Enigma machine was smuggled out of Central Europe and handed to the British. They reacted in complete contradiction of their Colonel Blimp, muddle-through stereotype.

The British gathered an incredibly gifted and dedicated group of intellectuals from many fields at a manor called Bletchley Park and provided them with the world's most advanced computers of the time. Unknown to the Nazis, this motley crew of pipe-puffing university dons, gritty chess players, and assorted screwball geniuses cracked some of the Enigma codes early in the war and continued to decrypt Nazi messages of tactical importance right up to final victory.

Bletchley Park intercepted many vital orders and reports radioed to and from U-boats and other vessels at sea or to German army units from their headquarters. When they distributed the intelligence received, the British revised the decrypted messages to conceal their source.

As a result, during the war only a very few individuals knew the British were reading Hitler's mail. Those intercepts, code-named Ultras, were of immeasurable value in winning the war in Europe and Africa.

The Enigma machine could be said to have been anticipated by Julius Caesar 2000 years earlier. Caesar's system, laughably simple today, probably resisted cracking better than Enigma did. When sending messages, Caesar rotated each letter by a low number such as 3.

B thus became E. So, if Caesar ordered one of his legions to *march,* his message would encrypt to *pdufk.* Apparently this was enough to baffle the semiliterate spies of the era. For added security he could rotate letters by 5, 7, 15, or whatever number suited him. Unless you knew the code, the message would look like garbage whatever the rotation, especially if you were a Gaulish barbarian whose understanding of Latin and ability to read were shaky at best.

Something so simple apparently worked fine in ancient times, and probably during the Dark Ages as well. However, it's not a safe algorithm today because bright children can crack it before they finish their afternoon cookies. After all, there are only 26 possibilities with the alphabet.

On the other side of the world during the war, another democracy, the United States, was breaking the codes of its totalitarian enemy, Japan. It was a magnificent achievement, primarily made by the cryptanalysis team in Pearl Harbor. The task was so difficult the Japanese remained convinced throughout the war it hadn't been done because it couldn't be done. They held stubbornly to this belief in spite of repeated indications it had been broken.

Intelligence gained by the codebreakers set up the tactical situation leading to the astonishing American naval victory in the Battle of Midway against great odds. It was the turning point of the Pacific War. Before Midway, the Japanese never lost a battle; after Midway, their victories were small and rare, their defeats many and crushing.

The Japanese used a more advanced system than did Germany; no machines were necessary to code and decode messages. Their system, also thought to be utterly unbreakable, cracked in the face of determined assault. In the Japanese system, each word was represented by a randomly assigned set of five digits. For example, *78934* might stand for *Tokyo,* and *78935* for *refuel.* Every time they changed their codes, it might be months before the United States could read them again and, in fact, was never able to read more than about 20 to 30 percent of naval messages—but that was enough.

In spite of their ingenuity, the code systems used at both ends of the Axis were broken, at enormous cost to each nation whose security was breached. They were complacent about the security of their communications, and many of their leading figures paid for their obtuseness with their lives, forfeited in defeat.

Take the experiences of the Second World War's losers as a warning not to become complacent about your company's security arrangements. Review them frequently. Eternal vigilance! Install programs to detect attempts to penetrate your security. Change keys regularly. And, make sure the number of people who can gain access to your database is held to the absolutely lowest possible number.

At irregular intervals change the locks and reexamine whether everyone who had access yesterday actually needs access today. Your best protection against a disastrous inside job is an attitude of hard-boiled alertness.

The threats aren't confined to dusty history books; this is amply illustrated by the following discussions of current Internet security problems. Investigating measures to protect electronic commerce will provide valuable insights into defending against all kinds of internal or external hacker attacks on every type of the company's computerized operations and valuable databases.

Hacker Break-ins of Federal Computer Systems Get Wider Scrutiny

A Senate subcommittee, after finding Pentagon computers are hit with 250,000 break-ins a year, will focus next on the State Department. Investigators say State, often called "Foggy Bottom," has only a foggy notion of how many outsiders regularly invade its computers hooked to the Internet. The Justice Department has slowed computerization programs out of concern for hackers.

Only 1 in 500 break-ins is detected and reported to the Pentagon, which uses the government's most advanced hacker-awareness program. Two hackers used the Internet to gain access to an Air Force computer in Rome, New York. The hackers then used that connection to invade a computer system at NATO headquarters in Europe. Another of their victims is NASA, which apparently was tapped for coded passwords that the hackers sent to an unknown location in Latvia (Dow Jones News Services, *The Wall Street Journal,* 31 May 1996; copyright © 1996 The Wall Street Journal and used with permission).

Livermore Laboratories reports that attacks against corporations have also been carried on at a furious pace. AT&T Bell Laboratories used trap programs to search for attacks on certain servers it considered high security risks. During a two-month period, it recorded nearly 400 attempts to breach its security, including nearly 30 attempts to copy its password file. Had the team not developed its trap programs to monitor use, these attacks would have escaped notice. The implications are obvious for companies with valuable data that can be reached via the Internet, both data connected with electronic commerce and other company data.

Essential Know-How Nuggets About Cryptography

Business doesn't wage war with armies, bombs, and aircraft carriers. Nevertheless, all businesses, whether they are keenly aware of it or not, are engaged in an ongoing war against the criminal elements who would steal anything they can convert into cash. What better thing to steal than electronic cash?

However, this risk to businesses is usually greatly exaggerated. Ample means exist to render the theft of Net cash or credit card numbers extremely difficult.

It's much more straightforward to do electronic commerce without security, just as it's much more straightforward to leave your home unlocked and the keys in your car when you park on a downtown street at night. In most parts of the country, the age when doing such things would be safe is long past. While Internet commerce hasn't reached that point yet, we strongly advise against setting yourself up to be among the first to experience theft in your online selling operations.

Without using cryptography at all, you can simply send your credit card number over the Internet to a vendor who records it, charges your purchase to it, and ships your order out by mail or overnight express. Usually, that works just fine. However, the real world being what it is, some bad things can happen because everything is going in clear text.

Actual Internet Security Compared to Its Perception

Let's compare the security of the Internet as it's widely perceived today to reality. In reality, the Internet is much more secure than the perception—especially considering what people normally do with their credit card numbers. Many people freak out at the idea of sending their credit card number over the Internet.

However, only a small number of people in today's world have both the skills and the desire to steal credit card numbers. Very few people fit this profile. There are some, so there's danger, but the risk to the consumer is much smaller than is generally thought to be the case.

That risk should be measured against the standard usually applied. Consider the number of times you or the average credit card holder hands your credit card to someone who may be tempted to use it improperly. Think of the number of times over a given month that someone could make a copy of your credit card number. Every time you purchase something by handing your credit card to someone at a gas station, a hotel, a restaurant, or any other kind of store, do you make sure all carbons are destroyed and that the merchant's computer system is completely secure? Even if you do so, you have, by no means, eliminated all the security hazards. The plain fact of the matter is that you can't use a credit card in the normal fashion and maintain even minimum security.

Even not using credit cards is no guarantee against fraudulent charges against your credit card accounts. In fact, some credit card thieves concentrate on running up charges to unused cards on the theory that it won't be noticed, especially if they divert the billing to another address. Ah, yes, it's comparatively easy for someone to change the mailing address for your account—a phone call or letter will often do it. For this reason, if you don't get your regular statement on time, get on the phone and find out why. Prompt action could greatly reduce the hassle you'll go through if someone is pirating your account.

In any event, when used properly by its owner, there's always a hard copy of the charge lying around somewhere in the vendor's office. So, anytime you buy anything with your credit card, you're giving people the opportunity to steal the number, and over a month's time if you use your card two or three times a week or more, a lot of people are in a position to steal you blind. Maybe, after you walk away, they pick up the discarded copy from the trash and put it in their pocket.

The perception against the real threat is very skewed. Many people are paranoid about Internet transactions because they don't understand them, but they'll hand their card over without a qualm at stores and restaurants. This skewed perception is similar to driving a car versus flying a plane. Theoretically, on any trip, say one of a thousand miles, you're much safer in a commercial airliner and much more likely to die in an auto crash if you take to the highway. This holds true even if you're not riding with Cousin Oswald, who thinks beer lubricates the eyeballs and is far better at keeping a driver awake than coffee.

A car crash is much easier to understand, however, and passengers in a car feel they have more control than do passengers on commercial flights. In a car, you can poke a sleepy driver in the ribs or even take over the wheel. Automobile passengers understand how and why automobile accidents happen as opposed to air accidents, and so these familiar dangers are easier to accept. The perceived risk is much lower, even though when you look at the numbers, it's far safer to make a given trip by commercial air than by auto.

So, given that someone might steal your credit card number or otherwise interfere with your electronic commerce, if you want to do something about it, you need security. It's not much of a problem today, but as the volume of Net cash transactions becomes bigger, criminals will see ways to steal large numbers of credit card numbers quickly. Their methods will change as frauds are discovered and countermeasures put in place.

The knowledge base continues to expand. As it does, more people develop the capability to steal electronically, and electronic crime will become more of a problem.

What can you do to insure security when sending your credit card over the Internet? A lot of things can happen, so before you decide what to do about it all, evaluate the various threats.

A mistake often made occurs when a firm sets up a computer without security, it gets hacked, and then the firm decides, "We want security." It's far better to initially install at least a low level of security to discourage casual hacking before the site goes online.

Again, the analogy of protecting an auto provides insights. Many car thieves simply walk around looking in cars until they see one with the keys in the ignition. Then all they have to do is jump in, start the car, and drive away. None of that tiresome messing around with hotwiring, no sirens go off, no pesky devices prevent them from steering the car. So which are the first cars stolen? The ones with their keys in the ignition.

It's the same with Internet commerce. The first companies hit by hackers will be those with no security at all. It's easier, and hackers have limited time, energy, and patience, just like everyone else.

As an individual, what you do about the security of your personal credit cards is much like what you do to avoid having your automobile stolen. Whenever you drive into valet parking you hand the keys to your car to an attendant and take it on trust that you'll not only get your car back undamaged when you want it, but that it won't, in the meantime, have been used for a joyride or as a getaway car in a crime. Before you relinquish your keys, do you first run a background check on the parking attendant? Of course not. It's simply not practical.

Similarly, when you hand your credit card to a server or clerk, you trust that person—who has ample opportunity to record your credit card number for fraudulent purposes—not to misuse it. You don't have much choice, do you? Not if you want to use credit cards to make purchases.

Computer security is very similar. When you're discussing securing your car, you have to first identify the threats you're concerned about.

Types of Electronic Commerce Attacks

Different situations involve different threats. As a company executive considering how best to carry on money transactions on the Internet, first identify the threats you're really worried about and examine the different ways people could break into your system.

Denial-of-Service Attacks

One very simple threat that most firms can't do much to defend against is called *denial of service*. This form of attack occurs when someone does something to the network on the other end or garbles transmission so you can't communicate across the channel. Typically, that's not considered a threat that you worry about because there's not much you can do about it, especially over a public network such as the Internet.

If someone goes out and bombs all the routers in your city, or if someone's sitting outside your office inserting garbage on your Internet line or putting on junk with a magnetic field, they're denying you service and you can't do anything. No one's stealing credit card numbers, no one's getting charged for things they're not purchasing, no one's getting free products—but you're denied service. A case occurred in late 1996 when a vicious hacker attacked an ISP (Internet service provider) on the east coast. The attacker programmed a computer to swamp the service with torrents of undeliverable e-mail that prevented its legitimate customers from getting through. The volume of hacker garbage crashed the ISP's computer and threatened to put it out of business. While such things are rare, they remain a real threat—however, most executives choose not to address this risk.

As an individual, you may care a little about denial-of-service attacks because you can't get to your favorite Web site or use your ISP; as a business executive you should have a keen interest in denial-of-service attacks that could prevent customers and potential customers from reaching your Web site.

Passive Attacks

This seemingly oxymoronic phrase reflects the fact that attacks can occur without the victims being aware of them. *Passive attacks* involve the theft of information. A famous passive attack occurred in Ankara during World War II. The valet of the British ambassador to Turkey was a German spy, code-named Cicero, who gained access to the ambassador's safe. Instead of stealing documents, Cicero photographed them and sent the prints to Berlin. Since no documents were missing, Cicero was never detected. He disappeared when it became clear which side would lose the war.

Research in Germany after the war revealed that a potentially disastrous breakdown of security occurred when Cicero photographed a document showing Normandy as the site of the impending Allied invasion to liberate Europe. The real security breakdown lay in how this vital information got bandied about in diplomatic circles.

Hitler himself, it was learned after the war, said the warning from Ankara was an obvious disinformation trick, and so this priceless intelligence to Nazi Germany was ignored. Had it been acted on by committing the German Army units in the area to defending the Normandy coast, the American-British-Canadian invasion would have been driven into the sea with enormous losses.

In Internet business, a passive attack doesn't affect the transaction. Customers make their buys over the Internet with their credit cards; the sellers get their money; and the customers get their orders in due course. As far as either the merchants or the buyers know, everything went smoothly. However, if a passive attack occurred, some information was stolen (which could be a batch of credit card numbers or secret IDs or anything else secret). If the information itself is valuable (such as customers' credit card numbers) passive attacks must be addressed.

In many circumstances passive attacks don't matter much, such as where the information is not secret. In these cases, you may be more concerned with denial of service. If you want to log on to the Web site and you don't care who knows where you're going, and you don't care if someone else wants to steal bits, then you don't care about passive attacks.

Active Attacks Seeking Money

Active attack involves actively tampering with the communication such as when you could send your credit card with the order and someone goes in and changes the order or the name or somehow actively disrupts the communication. This is a more serious attack because you may think you're buying 1 CD and a malicious attacker could turn that into 100 CDs.

Malicious attackers can change the number of articles charged and divert the money thus freed up to themselves. Or they could divert the merchandise to themselves. Or, most serious for the merchant, attackers could merely divert the entire payment to themselves. When the charges show up on the customers' statements, they're likely to assume the *merchant* defrauded them by charging for merchandise not shipped. Furious complaints from customers may be the first indication to merchants of serious breakdowns in security.

Generally, in electronic commerce, you're not really concerned with denial of service. You're aware of the risk, so you're concerned to a small degree, but you don't put a lot of resources into combating the possibility. You worry more about the passive attacks so people don't steal credit card numbers, and you worry about the active attacks.

How do you deal with these risks? The simple answer is to *encrypt* things, which means coming up with some means to send a message over the communication link in secret code. You must have a way of creating the code; the person on the other end must have a way of undoing the code to get your message.

The terms usually used in cryptography are *plaintext* for the actual message sent, and *ciphertext* for the message after it's encryption. Encryption is accomplished by mathematically transforming the plain text by running it through an algorithm. This type of encryption is secure because it utilizes a *key,* a unique modifier to the algorithm that must be possessed in some form by the parties wishing to read the message. How this key is kept secure depends on the type of algorithm used, as discussed later in this section.

You can use various kinds of algorithms. The two basic cryptographic references are public key systems and private key systems. In private key systems, the parties on both ends must share the same key, if they're going to communicate securely over a link. This means they have agreed beforehand on some sort of shared key and use the same key to do the encryption and decryption.

Nonshared key (public key) algorithms also exist; they have separate keys for encryption and decryption. You can have your key to use for encryption and I can have a completely different key to decrypt the message. (This can be true in symmetric systems as well; the trick is that in shared key systems, the other key can be computed from whichever one you already possess.)

In certain public key algorithms, you encrypt in symmetrical algorithms and can interchange the functionality of the keys, but never the keys themselves. The private (normally decryption) key is *always* kept private, but may be used by its possessor to encrypt outgoing messages instead of decrypting incoming messages. Let's look at the basic idea: with a public key that anyone can access, anyone in the world (let's say in this case it is person A) can encrypt a message that only the holder of the private key (person B) can decode. In order to send a secure message back to A, B must have A's public key. B could encrypt the message with B's own private key, but everyone in the world has access to the public key that would be used to decode this message. This allows B to send a message that everyone knows must have come from B (a digital signature), but at the same time it is not at all a private message.

The completely secured and authenticated communication medium would be thus: person A sends message M to person B. M contains a small section encrypted with A's private key (for use as a digital signature). This entire message M (including the small encrypted section) is encrypted using B's public key. We now know that only B will be able to read this message. When B gets the message, B decrypts it with B's private key and can read the contents of M with one. exception—the small area encrypted by A's private key. Knowing that the message is supposedly from A (by looking at the message header), B can apply A's public key to the encrypted area to see if anything meaningful (for example, the digital signature) comes out. If it does, B knows that that segment must have been encrypted by A's private key, and the message is authentic. For B to reply to A, B would encrypt a small part of the message N with B's private key as a signature, then encrypt the whole thing with A's public key. And so on. We said it's simple, didn't we?

RSA is one of the pioneering public key systems. With RSA you can have the two keys and use one to encrypt or decrypt or vice versa, so it works both ways. You have to go through a special process to create the keys, where you create the key pair and then you can use one to encrypt or decrypt, and with the symmetric algorithms it can go either way. If A and B are your two keys, you can encrypt with A and decrypt with B or vice versa.

There are public key algorithms that are not symmetrical, which means you create A and B. One is the encryption key and the other the decryption key; in this case, you can't reverse them.

The nice part about the public key algorithms is that the two parties don't have to agree on a shared key. If we're on opposite sides of the country and need to exchange secure messages dozens of times a second, it becomes a problem. Banks with electronic commerce capabilities and large Internet marketers have to solve this problem of encrypting each plaintext message before sending and decrypting the ciphertext message after receiving it, and doing it at the speed of light. Fortunately, the problem has been solved.

Another nice thing about public key algorithms is you can use them for authentication by doing digital signatures. This allows any of your customers to send an order, a payment, or something else to you with their digital signature using any symmetrical public key algorithm such as RSA. Then you know who sent it with a probability of almost 1. The only risk—which, as a merchant, generally lies outside your range of control—is that someone other than the owner of the digital signature got onto his or her computer with fraud in mind. Some people will unwisely give someone else access to their private key. This is analogous to the situation where a movie actress decided she didn't have time to sign her own checks; so she trained her secretary to forge her name on checks. Before long, the secretary was writing checks to herself.

False Storefront Traps

This is a different sort of attack. Instead of trying to hack into electronic commerce, these crooks set up a trap and program it to rip off people who are trying to make legitimate purchases.

When you log onto a CD shop as a consumer to make a purchase, you want to know that you're actually connected to the CD shop. You want to be certain a hacker hasn't set up a look-alike Web site—a false storefront trap—to intercept incoming orders and credit card numbers.

As a merchant, you're concerned about this happening to your customers. Many of them will blame you for the resulting hassle. Even among those who realize it's not your fault, you'll lose a percentage. Once burned, they won't run the risk again.

Active Attacks Aimed at Embarrassing Your Firm Rather Than Stealing from It

It can happen to any organization. This was demonstrated late in 1996 when some Swedish hackers broke into the CIA's home page and changed its name to Central Stupidity Agency. (Yes, the CIA does have a home page; it gets more than half a million hits a month from all over the world.) The hackers replaced the agency's somewhat dry text with pictures of nude girls and their own nonsensical rantings. Even more humiliating, the CIA hasn't been able to find out who did this.

The incident had no practical effect except to briefly embarrass some Washington bureaucrats. These gentlefolk were sent scurrying to find out how their home page had been penetrated and distorted, rather than merely accessed. Security on the agency's mainframe computer that contains the nation's secrets is carried to far higher level, we're told, and was not compromised.

The same thing happened on the Justice Department's home page. It had to be shut down for a few days after hackers changed its front page to Department of Injustice and inserted pictures of Adolf Hitler and a swastika.

Strong Security Is Built In

Web sites are not easily changed from the outside; a strong level of built-in security will completely baffle anyone who is merely computer-literate. Your average Web surfer can't do it. However, as the previous examples indicate, skilled hackers can. Many are teenagers who become obsessed with this mental challenge and often with furthering some hair-brained cause.

You can be targeted by teenage pranksters, criminals out to steal money, or professional industrial spies. Because of these possibilities, assign someone to check your Web site every day to make sure no tampering has occurred. Give serious consideration to what usually is a less-expensive and more reliable alternative: installing Haystack's WebStalker. For more details, see the section entitled Intrusion Destroyers later in this chapter.

The Never-Ending War Between Codemakers and Codebreakers

It's never wise to assume a hacker or other attacker will use the expected approaches you're prepared to defeat. Recently the world of cryptography was startled to learn that Paul C. Kocher, a crytography consultant, had found a backdoor method of breaking encryptions previously thought unbreakable.

His method wasn't some elegant mathematical combination to enhance the effectiveness of a brute force attack. Instead, he suggested how a highly skilled hacker could enormously speed the process of gaining a secret key. The method: time the receiver's computer as it deciphers incoming messages or encrypts outgoing messages. A wiretap on the line carrying those messages makes it possible.

How does it work? Smart burglars don't crack safes, they guess the combination (or a small enough number of combinations to make it practical to open the safe by trial and error) by somehow observing how long it takes someone to twirl the dials. Instead of many thousands of combinations, they may wind up with only a few dozen, one of which must be right. For the same reason, a hacker acquires the exact amount of time—measured by computer in nanoseconds—that the target's computer takes to decipher a message. Once he's done that, he's very close to breaking the code by trial and error methods. Computerizing the attack makes it practical; methods exist to allow the hacker to build his solution step by step.

This concept compromises many of the digital certificates purporting to establish the user's identity beyond any reasonable possibility of error. However, Pretty Good Privacy (PGP), used to encrypt e-mail, has not been compromised in this particular battle in the ongoing war between codemakers and codebreakers.

Solutions to bar this backdoor attack were swiftly implemented—various easily accomplished defenses that would confound the attacking hacker. One is to build in brief delays, computer-generated at random—also measured in nanoseconds—so your computer doesn't respond with predictable timing. Another method, called *blinding*, causes the computer to multiply the message by a number it randomly selects, changing that number for each message. This raises the measure of difficulty the attacker must overcome to a far higher level. Now the attacker must find a way to discover what multiplier was used, and this information can't be extracted from a human operator because the computer selects the multiplier at random.

Theoretically, there are other methods of attacking highly secure codes. Possibly a criminal mind might devise a way to measure power consumption or the rate of heat dissipation of a chip. Far-fetched as this may sound, it does point up the fact that every fortress built by one person can be successfully stormed by another, sufficiently determined person. Like the struggle between offense and defense, between armor and missile, an improvement on one side tends to generate an improvement on the other. Eternal vigilance not only is the price of political freedom, it's also the price of security in Internet commerce.

To help put these problems in perspective, let's review a survey conceived by RHI Consulting and presented here with its permission:

Internet Security Causes Jitters, but Results Outweigh Negatives. CIO Survey Suggests That Security Issues Are Only a Minor Annoyance

If chief information officers (CIOs) are troubled at all by security issues on the Internet—and 57 percent of CIOs in a recent survey said they are—it hasn't stopped them from doing business online. Seventy-five percent of executives polled said that despite their concerns, they'll pursue business opportunities and everyday transactions via the Internet.

The survey was developed by RHI Consulting, a leading specialized-staffing service that provides information technology professionals on a short- and long-term basis. It was conducted by an independent research firm, which polled 1000 chief information officers from randomly selected U.S. companies having more than 20 employees.

Executives were asked: "How concerned are you with security issues associated with the exchange of confidential business and/or financial information via the Internet?" Their responses were as follows

Very concerned	32%
Somewhat concerned	25%
Somewhat unconcerned	8%
Not at all concerned	34%
Don't know/no answer	1%

CIOs were also asked, "Has this concern kept you from implementing or conducting business via the Internet?" According to Greg Scileppi, executive director of RHI Consulting, they said

Yes	23%
No	75%
Don't know	2%

Executives recognize the potential security risks associated with using the Internet, modems, Email and even internal networks, but the convenience and efficiency that these technologies afford is over-riding most of their concerns.

Because a breach of security can have serious repercussions, more companies are setting clear policies for protecting information and communicating these guidelines to employees.

While no system is entirely fail-safe, firms are increasingly block-ing access to unauthorized users by building firewalls, creating encryption and frequently changing users' passwords.

RHI Consulting is a leading provider of information technology pro-fessionals, helping companies meet the demand for supplemental and long-term technical expertise on projects ranging from multiplatform systems integration to implementation of local and wide area networks, client-server development, and help desk support. A division of staffing leader Robert Half International (NYSE: RHI), RHIC has 65 offices in the United States, Canada, and the United Kingdom. RHIC's Internet address is http://www.rhic.com. You can contact Reesa McCoy Staten of RHI Consulting at 415-854-9700 or at RHICToday@aol.com/.

Destroyers and Firewalls

All methods of protecting anything fall into just two classes: active and passive. To maintain the most formidable defense against electronic attack, use both. Let's talk about the active methods first.

Intrusion Destroyers

The only true attack-destroying software products available at the time of this writing are products from Haystack Labs of Austin, Texas. (See Chap. 6.) Running transparently behind your other programs, either its Web-Stalker or NetStalker will constantly prowl your computers and LANs looking for intruders or attempts at intrusion by hackers. Once an intrusion or attempt is detected, either on your Internet connection or your Intranet LAN, you hear about it immediately. The software can be instructed to page you, send you an e-mail, or just run the intruder off.

Where you're more interested in warding off attacks than apprehending the offender, have your WebStalker patrol behind the best firewalls you can erect. However, it should be recognized that firewalls only present an additional obstacle to attackers. If attackers are sufficiently motivated, they may continue to probe undetected until they discover a hole in your walls they can crawl through. That's why you need an intrusion attacker such as WebStalker. They offer you the prospect of knowing when attack attempts are taking place, thus giving you the option to take aggressive legal steps to put an end to them.

> Haystack Labs
> 10713 Hwy 620 North
> Austin, Texas 78726
> Phone: 512-918-3555
> Fax: 512-918-1265
> URL: http://www.haystack.com

WebStalker, which Haystack bills as the first automated management tool that patrols *inside* both your Internet and intranet Web sites, provides 7/24 protection for your Web server. Far more than a static, defensive firewall, WebStalker provides real-time detection and identification of external and internal attacks. You can program WebStalker to notify you of intruders through SNMP, pager, or e-mail, or it can simply kick intruders off. Haystack says you get total Web site security with no strings attached.

Firewall Vendors

Freemont Avenue Software
2825 Wilcrest, Suite 160
Houston, Texas 77042
Phone: 800-240-5754
        713-974-3274
Fax: 713-978-6246

One of the world's foremost suppliers of firewalls. Its subsidiary, Livermore Software Laboratories, International is discussed next.

Livermore Software Laboratories, International (LSLI)
2825 Wilcrest, Suite 160
Houston, Texas 77042
Phone: 800-240-5754
        713-974-3274
Fax: 713-978-6246
For product information, write portus info@lsli.com.
For product support, write portus@lsli.com.

LSLI and Freemont Avenue Software are the nation's leading suppliers of firewall technology to foil intruders. PORTUS Secure Firewall Version 2 is NCSA certified! Now, PORTUS Version 2.2 is available. Freemont Avenue Software, LSLI, and PORTUS are registered trademarks of Freemont Avenue Software, corporate parent of Livermore Software Labs.

Setting Cost-Effective Security Standards

When analyzing this decision, give some weight to the cost of a breakdown in your security measures. Sometimes it's useful to ask yourself, "What's the worst thing that could happen?"

Unfortunately, a realistic answer to this question could be scary for the managers of many companies. This conclusion might lead the company to impose stringent security measures too difficult for legitimate customers to penetrate, or to avoid going on the Web at all.

Any business making credit card sales over the phone has already assumed most of the risks involved. Having a Web site adds little new in the way of theft and fraud risk or customer complaints.

However, it does introduce the risk of hacker penetration of the Web site and, if the company's general computerized operations are on the same LAN, the more serious risk that the company's internal affairs and confidential information could be stolen or erased by hacker assault.

There's good news here. The risk of hacker penetration of a company's main programs through its Web site is easily foiled with absolute certainty by making sure there's no physical connection through a LAN between the Web server and the main company computer or network.

A simple and easily accomplished but extremely important office routine will make hacker penetration through your Web site into your main computer operations utterly impossible.

Dedicate a separate computer to be your Web server. If you use an outside service for your Web site, dedicate one computer to communicate with your Web site. Pull reports from your Web site daily with the computer dedicated for that purpose and have them scanned for material or messages that shouldn't be there before they are transferred by disk to your main computer network for further processing. *Always keep your Web site server separate from your other computerized operations. Never permit any cable connection between the two.*

This eliminates the possibility of hacker penetration through the Web site—an extremely difficult task in any case. However, it's imposing challenge seems to be the main attraction to the peculiar mentality of the hacker. Now let's look at the five basic ways to transact electronic commerce today.

In merchant sales to consumers, two methods stand out in importance: Net cash and credit card. Net cash, by its nature, is highly secure, so you have no realistic worries there.

However the dominant method right now is credit card sales. If I want to buy something online, I can follow a procedure very similar to calling an 800 number. I go to the Web site, give my credit card number, specify what I want, type in my address, and what I ordered comes in the mail. This can be done in plaintext, but increasingly, it's protected by one of the encryption methods discussed in step 8 of Chap. 2.

As a merchant, you use security there because you're worried about passive attacks—you don't want people stealing your credit card numbers. As a consumer, I'm concerned about active attacks—I don't want someone changing my order, diverting it from my house, or absconding with the cash.

Credit card sales on the Internet are already common; to a computer-literate person, it's easier than calling an 800 number to place an order. For merchants, it's relatively straightforward. They have software and hardware in place to charge to credit cards. All the merchant needs is the name, expiration date, and the card number of the customer. To consumers, the advent of the World Wide Web enormously expands their purchase-practical horizon; it literally puts the world's marketplace at their finger-tips. However, it's not entirely without a downside.

First, if you're sending your credit card number in plaintext to every merchant you buy from, you're creating a growing security risk—merely $50 if you act promptly to minimize your risk by notifying the credit card company if any problems occur. However, nobody compensates you for all the hassle involved in being a victim of credit card fraud.

Second, people know who you are and they could be watching what you buy. As far as I know, the Web site I buy CD's from could be logging everything I ever bought. It could put my name and address on mailing lists and sell those lists to firms and organizations I might not want to hear from. It might use the information to otherwise abuse my privacy.

Third, merchants dealing with credit cards have credit card overhead—usually at least 1.5 percent of the sale. Net cash is better because it *is* cash. Lots of companies are pushing their Net cash standards to address some of these issues.

Also, there's a growing consumer desire to be able to buy things over the Net without revealing to the merchant the buyer's identity or credit card number, especially. If the merchant can't track me, there won't be the opportunity for someone to steal my credit card number and charge $10,000 to my account. Sure, there's a limit to how much I'll have to pay if I report the matter promptly, but in any case it will be a frustrating hassle. The fallout may leave a huge blot on my credit history even though I would be completely innocent of any wrongdoing. Put it down to the blind operation of bureaucratic rules in credit reporting agencies.

Verification

If I'm buying something on my credit card from the online CD shop and I give my name, the CD shop should be very concerned that it's actually me. It can get the credit card number and my name, but that doesn't guar-antee that I am the true cardholder. The CD shop must ask me to send my digital signature to verify my identity.

Verification is done with two sets of keys, public and private. If I have a private key and you have my public key—anything that's encrypted with my public key, I can decrypt. So, if you take my public key and encrypt a message and send it, I'm the only one who can decrypt it.

Let's run through an example. You're the online CD store and I'm the customer. You've never heard of me but I electronically send you my American Express card number and an order for $1000 worth of purchases to be shipped immediately. What steps do you go through to make sure you're dealing with whom your Web site visitor claims to be? That is, how do you make sure you don't get stuck with a fradulent buy?

One way is verification. I want to know that you're really the CD store and you want to know that I'm who I say I am.

I'll take my private key and encrypt a message with it and you'll know my public key. (We'll come back to how you'll know that. For now, just assume there's a public directory of public keys that you can trust completely.) We know that anything encrypted with my private key can only be decrypted with my public key and vice versa.

We may have a standard protocol that if I'm going to buy something I will send you a message saying, "Hi, my name is B. Phillips," and I'll encrypt it with my private key. Your computer will in turn automatically decrypt it with my public key. If it appears to be the message you expect, you know I sent it.

Usually when I send a message, there'll be an unencrypted part that says, "This is an authentic message from B. Phillips." Attached to this would be an encrypted part saying, "Hi, I'm B. Phillips. This is encrypted with my private key." Then you look at the unencrypted part and know this was from B. Phillips. So, you get my public key and use that to decrypt the encrypted part. If it reads as it should, something like, "Hi, this is B. Phillips and here is my private key," you'll know I sent it.

The average consumer doesn't need to know any of this. It happens automatically within seconds. Right now Microsoft Internet Explorer and Netscape Navigator are both capable of automating Web site credit sales verification; more software solutions will certainly follow.

Going through a set-up process is necessary because I must have a private key on my computer. There has to be a public key as well. You, as the merchant who wants to sell to me securely, must be able to get that matching public key. You need some infrastructure so that it can all happen. Just because customers have credit cards doesn't mean they can start buying securely on the Internet.

Back to buying the CD. You, the merchant, are convinced that I am me. You send back a similar response with a digital signature that's something like, "Hi, we're the CD store, this is encrypted with our private key; decrypt with your public key." The customer's computer decrypts the message, everything matches up, and the transaction goes through without a hitch.

Today, probably 98 percent of the time the product is shipped, the merchant gets paid, and there are no problems relating to the method of ordering and payment. However, if the other 2 percent involves hacker crime, that 2 percent will likely account for 98 percent of the hassle someone in your store has to waste time straightening out. Two percent hacker fraud may be acceptable, but such things tend to grow with frightening speed.

The IRS's experience in this area deserves consideration. Some years ago the service realized people were filing false refund claims when no tax had been paid. The IRS decided it wasn't worth the effort to check more than 100 million W-2 and 1099 tax payment notices against the refund claims. As a result, this form of fraud exploded; losses soon ran into the multimillions and continued to increase exponentially.

What the IRS didn't seem to grasp was that crooks talk to each other. Once they find a scam that works one time, they can't wait to do it a hundred times. Meanwhile, these lowlifes bragged about it to their scumbag friends, of which they generally have many. Soon, even people already convicted of tax fraud were getting fraudulent refund claims paid to them in their prison cells.

Finally, the IRS saw the wisdom of making sure the tax had been paid before honoring a refund claim. It geared up to check those 100 million forms against the refund claims.

The moral of this story: If you invite theft by making yourself an easy mark, somebody will accept your invitation and steal your socks off.

Each company must decide for itself whether selling over the phone or on the Internet without security invites fraud, and at what point stronger security measures should be adopted. In case of doubt, choose the more secure alternative.

We've been making some assumptions as we went along. Let's go back and look at them in more detail. One assumption is that having these keys gives us security. Some supporting material for this assumption follows.

What Allows a Key to Make a Secure, Encrypted Message?

The problem of secure transactions on the Internet, financial or otherwise, is solved by one simple technology, one that most people should be familiar with—very large numbers. Electronic encryption technology currently focuses on using large numbers in an algorithm that modifies data so that, without having some knowledge of the large number, or a *key* to it, there's no feasible way to get back the original data. The basic premise is that if you select a large enough number to generate the key to encrypt data, no brute-force decryption will be able to break the encryption within a practical length of time. This time period of protection can be as arbitrarily long as the designer wishes. Of course, these very large numbers have some special properties that make them well-suited for this purpose. The foremost is that they are not easily factored into smaller numbers, since most modern code-breaking attacks use factoring as a shortcut. They are, however, factorable into two parts—these parts are used to generate the two keys used in the technique of public key encryption.

RSA public key cryptography has been established as a technique since 1978. Throughout that time, it has been beaten and abused by hackers, wily students, government security agencies, and anybody else generally interested in reading other people's private data. The result of all of this stress-testing is a simple truth—public key encryption is exactly as secure as its user wishes to make it, specifically in the assignment of the size of resulting keys.

The appropriate key length depends largely on the nature of the data being encrypted. Data that is sensitive only for a short period of time, such as debit or credit transactions to an online bank, could realistically use a weaker encryption standard because a transaction broken a year in the future would be of no value in most attacks—the bank would reject any additional attempts at performing a transaction that has already closed. It should be recognized that given a sufficiently large budget (around $10 million for special equipment), an organization could break today's weaker encryption standards fast enough to interfere with these types of time-sensitive transactions.

How weak is *weaker?* That depends on what type of cryptography is used—attacks on public key cryptography are of an inherently different form than those made on symmetric cryptography. Currently, in symmetric cryptography, anything using key lengths up to and including 56 bits should be considered weak encryption. In public key cryptography, a key length of 300 to 384 bits would provide a comparable level of protection.

Extremely sensitive data, such as trade secrets or items of similar importance, should rely on the strongest encryption available. Strong encryption, strong enough to survive prolonged attack by an organization with significant resources, typically uses 128-bit keys (for symmetric cryptography) or 2048 bits (for public key cryptography). It's a safe bet that the government is no longer relying on its 56-bit (symmetric) DES encryption keys for its most sensitive documents.

The U.S. government's sudden interest in encryption technology is another testament to the strength of public key encryption. It realized that merely by turning up the number of bits in an encryption key, any group can effectively prevent even the government from snooping through electronic data. In response to this, the government has begun to attempt to legislate its own backdoors into domestic security products (the primary idea behind the multiple Clipper and key-escrow proposals) and flat-out forbids the export of strong encryption. This is the reason behind the FBI's investigation of Phil Zimmerman for his release of PGP, the e-mail encryption tool. (See PGP under Service Providers in Chap. 7.) If the faceless federal bureaucrats lurking in the shadows of Washington fear something, you know it has to be pretty damn strong.

Getting the Keys

The next assumption is that we both have public and private keys. We have to get them somehow and there must be some method of distributing these keys. One way is to have a trusted central authority from which you can get both keys. VeriSign provides this service on the Internet right now. People can register there, pay the nominal fee, and get their keys.

I just installed a new version of Internet Explorer and one of the options is getting a personal certificate which means getting public and private keys and then storing them on your PC so you can do this kind of authentication.

We have to have the central authority that's trusted from which to get these keys. There's a bootstrapping problem in that I have this central authority, but how do I get its public key? Generally, it's assumed that VeriSign is reliable and you can trust the company. At some point with any security or cryptography if you get down to the basic axioms, there always is a leap of faith you have to take.

You have to address what your concerns are and decide what the real magnitude of the threat is. If you're doing $100 a week in business, you may not care about all this. If you're doing a large volume, weak security may be a real threat to your bottom line.

There's also the matter of looking up people's public keys. We have to assume we can trust the authority we're asking. If I'm a CD store and someone comes along who is looking to get some CDs without paying for them, that person may pretend to be someone else and use a stolen credit card. If the intruder sends back the correct public key, then I'm fooled. You have to put your trust in getting these keys.

There's an old saying in cryptography, "Everything is trivial except key distribution!" The hard part is distributing the keys without giving thieves a shot at them. As previously shown, once you have the keys in place it's pretty straightforward to do a secure transaction. However, for key distribution there really can be no perfect solution.

The best cryptographic algorithms are those where the algorithm is public and the secrecy rests with the secrecy of the private key. Criminals will be able to learn exactly which algorithm we use to communicate, but it doesn't matter. As long as they don't have the private key they can't crack the code.

Any cryptographic algorithm that relies on the secrecy of the algorithm is worthless. If anyone claims to have a proprietary algorithm and won't show it to you—assume it's worthless.

Examples are the encryption functions on Word Perfect and other PC applications that generally have really weak proprietary encryption formats. You can buy programs that allow you to crack those encryption formats if you forget your key because they provide such weak security. If you can do it easily, some sleazeball hacker can do it, too.

Once we get the keys in place, there is the assumption that I'm the only one who knows my key and you're the only one who knows your private key. If I lose my private key, someone steals it off my PC, or I loan it to my friend who posts it on Usenet, then the security is blown.

The code will be something like a thousand digit number so it won't be in your head. Chances are you won't write it down anywhere but will store it in your PC.

Systems to Authenticate E-Mail Are Not Perfectly Secure

You're only as secure as your private key. PGP offers an additional level of security on your private key—you can set it up so that you enter a password every time, or it won't work. This means you can put an arbitrary amount of extra security on top of its standard. However, this again is the same old convenience versus security trade-off.

Some people don't want to be bothered. They say, "Store it on my hard drive and don't ever ask me about it." That's very convenient, but it's not secure.

The most secure system imaginable would be a handheld device that produces one-time passwords for accessing the key on your machine. But it would be inconvenient. Few people want to go through all those antics every time they send e-mail. So, you're only as secure as your keys.

It's the same for Net cash—it's encrypted but you're not storing the keys, per se. All you're storing is the encrypted string which is your electronic cash. In a simple implementation, you get the Net cash from your bank and store it on your hard drive. Anyone who could copy those bits could spend your Net cash, like going into your wallet and taking out the money.

You can build up as many layers of security as you want on top of this. The key to your top layer of security, meaning a string of bits, has to be stored somewhere. You can put it on your hard drive and not worry about it or have a handheld device that goes into your wallet and an adapter on your PC. When you get more Net cash, you plug the adapter in and it stores the Net cash. But you could get mugged and it may be stolen the same way your ordinary wallet may be.

You could have a separate access card with a PIN number on it that must be entered on the device before you can spend the cash. You can go to any length to make it more secure. It's a trade-off with convenience. Every increase of security decreases convenience.

With most cryptographic algorithms, the more traffic (the more you use the keys), the less secure it becomes. So in the interests of maintaining a high level of security, use the keys as little as possible.

There are various types of cryptographic attacks. In general, the more data that's available, the easier it is to crack the code.

In *cryptanalysis*, the theory and art of breaking codes, the first step is to figure out the key—or steal it. Once that's accomplished, breaking into the encrypting algorithm is comparatively easy, which means the code-breaker extracts the plaintext message from the ciphertext. With most of the real algorithms in use today, it's very difficult to do—a brute-force computer attack would take 100 years on the fastest computers available today. So, in and of themselves, they're pretty secure.

But the devil's in the details. You may have an algorithm that's theoretically unbreakable and totally secure. However, there's the human link, because, while many links in the security chain can be computerized, humans have to do the programming. If your database is sufficiently attractive, criminals won't mess around trying to break the code the hard way; they'll try to suborn one or more of your employees or break in and copy your data. In other words, if you have a financially attractive target, it's unrealistic to rely simply on cryptography to protect yourself from theft through the Internet. You must also physically protect the computers and be ever watchful about the reliability of everyone who has or could gain access to them.

Most encryption algorithms are theoretically secure. However, people have to write the programs that actually perform the ciphering/deciphering operations, and they may screw the project up.

An implementation of DES, an encryption algorithm, fell victim to this. The algorithm underwent intense scrutiny, but the implementation did not. There was an error in programming the algorithm that caused messages not to be encrypted. As a result, people didn't immediately notice all this unencrypted traffic zooming around, messages they thought were secure but actually weren't.

The inherent weakness of the human factor pops up everywhere. Take, for example, the ordinary ATM card. From a practical standpoint, it's impossible to keep punching in numbers trying to hit the right one. A four-digit PIN has one less than 10,000 possibilities, a six-digit PIN has one less than a million possibilities. Even the dumbest crook won't stand in front of an ATM and try thousands of different PIN numbers. Like coyotes, criminals have a sixth sense for the easiest victim to pull down. So they will exploit the human factor by looking over people's shoulders and getting their PIN numbers. Then they knock the victims over the head, take their ATM cards, and use the cards to withdraw all their victims' money.

Another danger is from the thieves who steal company funds because they knows all the codes, perhaps as well as anyone in the company. A few years ago, the international department of a large American bank in Los Angeles detected the theft of several million dollars. The theft of that large a sum wasn't as easily discovered as one might think because the department routinely handled a large volume of multimillion-dollar transfers hourly. Furious checking revealed that the money was indeed gone, and the police were quickly brought into the picture.

The case was easily solved. Only a dozen people had the necessary knowledge. All but one of them showed up for work as usual the next day. Chit-chat with Zurich caused the Swiss police to bundle the man who missed work onto a nonstop flight back to Los Angeles. The LAPD met him at the airport with handcuffs. He doesn't miss work often anymore, although it's a fair bet he doesn't like his present occupation as well as working at the bank. Instead of buying personalized license plates, now he makes them in his prison's metal shop.

If you have your private keys stored on your hard drive, then criminals don't need cryptanalysis to break messages. When a computer is unguarded, they walk in, copy the private key on a floppy disk, and are gone in a minute, if they know what they're doing. If it's a network machine that someone else has access to in the Windows 3.1 or Windows 95 environment with no security at all, it's very easy to steal it. From then on they can break all your encryptions as easily as you can decipher them.

Most of us here at Jamison/Gold use Windows 95 on our personal computers. If we were all storing our private keys on our machines, it would be a trivial matter for me to steal any staff member's private key and send out mail pretending I'm that person. Windows NT offers additional security that helps prevent this.

Choosing cryptography is like choosing a doctor. You really have to trust who's doing it because if it's done wrong, you lose.

The vital security issue of authentication is well under control by VeriSign (discussion follows).

The U.S. Post Office—having seen e-mail cut huge chunks out of its most profitable operation, the delivery of first-class mail—has a plan afoot to get into the certification business. Apparently its plan is to charge about 32 cents to send each e-mail. Nice work if you can get it.

Message integrity verification, that is, methods to insure that software delivered over the Internet arrives in perfect condition, has been addressed by IBM (discussion follows).

A Quick Overview of Encryption Methods, Most of Which Are Available Now

Cryptolopes from IBM

IBM is creating a way to protect the unauthorized distribution of publishers' works over the Internet using a technology called *cryptolopes.* This technology is discussed in greater detail in Chap. 6.

CyberCash*

CyberCash, a leading developer of secure Internet payment solutions, uses public key encryption technology for secure transmission of credit card data on the Net. Merchants never see an unscrambled credit card number, thus relieving them of the responsibility for protecting a credit card number database from criminal access.

2100 Reston Parkway, Third Floor
Reston, VA 22091
Phone: 703-620-4200
Internet: info@cybercash.com
URL: http://www.cybercash.com

CyberCash Sales and Marketing
303 Twin Dolphin Drive, Suite 200
Redwood City, CA 94065
Phone: 415-594-0800
Fax: 415-594-0899

DigiCash

World Headquarters
Kruislaan 419
1098 VA Amsterdam
The Netherlands
Phone: 31.20.655.2611
Fax: 31.20.668.5486
E-mail: info@digicash.nl
URL: http://www.digicash.com

Branch Office in the United States of America
DigiCash Inc.
55 East 52nd Street—39th floor
New York, NY 10055-0186
Phone: 212-909-4092
        800-410-ECASH (800-410-3227)
Fax: 212-318-1222
E-mail: office.ny@digicash.com
URL: http://www.digicash.com/
        or http://193.78.226.2/
Anonymous FTP: ftp.digicash.com

Subsidiary in Australia
DigiCash Pty Ltd
Level 29, Chifley Towers
2 Chifley Square
Sydney NSW 2000, Australia
Phone: 61.2.375.2316
Fax: 61.2.375.2121

E-mail: andreas@digicash.com
URL: http://www.digicash.com/
    or http://193.78.226.2/
Anonymous FTP: ftp.digicash.com

Since beginning its operations in April 1990, DigiCash's mission and primary activities have been to develop and license payment technology products—chip card software only and hybrids—that are competitive in the market and show the true capability of technology to protect the interests of all participants.

DigiCash has pioneered development of electronic payment mechanisms for open, closed, and network systems that provide security and privacy. DigiCash's technology is based on patented advances in public key cryptography developed by the company's founder and chairman, Dr. David Chaum. Throughout its history, DigiCash has developed leading edge products and partnered with companies to provide advanced payment systems technology to the market.

MasterCard has licensed DigiCash technology for a demonstration system implementing the first smart card chip mask technology meeting the latest EMV (Europay, MasterCard, VISA) standard. According to DigiCash, these advances provide true dynamic public key authentication

DigiCash pioneered the development of electronic payments technology that provides privacy and security.

using the least expensive smart card chip available. DigiCash designed cards that included prepaid cash replacement functions and loyalty schemes, access control, and other applications for MasterCard's credit/ debit systems. DigiCash's advances in high security and reliability are integrated into the design. DigiCash developed a complete system including terminals, PIN pads, host computer, and all related software. Cooperation is ongoing.

Switzerland-based Crypto AG, the leading international manufacturer and distributor of cryptographic devices, nonexclusively licenses DigiCash encryption technology. For ultrafast processing of transactions, DigiCash developed a modular family of high-speed encryption boards that are manufactured and marketed by this licensee.

European Commission Project CAFÉ, founded and chaired by Dr. Chaum, is based on DigiCash technology implemented as a cross-border electronic wallet. This technology works with smart cards and infrared point-of-pay electronic wallets. The project consists of a consortium of firms including Gemplus, France Telecom, and PTT Netherlands. Project CAFÉ was selected by the European Commission to install a trial card and electronic wallet system in its headquarters buildings in Brussels, which was begun in third quarter 1995.

Other leading organizations that DigiCash has worked with in technology development include VISA International, IBM, and Siemens, as well as various European telecoms.

DIGICASH; NUMBERS THAT ARE MONEY.   Net cash by DigiCash is a new concept in payment systems. It combines computerized convenience with security and privacy that improve on paper cash. It adds value to any service involving payment. And its versatility opens up a host of new markets and applications.

Electronic cash is not just a step on the way to tomorrow's payment system technology. It *is* that technology, and it's here now.

DigiCash works with payment system and service providers in all phases of electronic cash innovation. One of its people says, "We help you develop and refine the concept, and we see it through every step to final implementation."

The DigiCash team brings together top cryptographers and payment system specialists with some of Europe's best software and hardware specialists.

VERSATILITY.   Wherever value is exchanged, between business, government, customer, client, or citizen, electronic cash is the medium of choice. For computerized payments over the phone, the user needs only the special software from DigiCash. Users can pay directly at a counter, kiosk, or phone booth with current smart cards as the platform; with the pocket-size card readers DigiCash has developed, they can even make payments to each other.

SECURITY. The security provided by electronic cash is unmatched in scope and cost-effectiveness. There's no need for an acquirer of value to contact a central system more than weekly, because the technology is secure against cheating and misuse even without online connections. Since electronic cash is digitally signed by the issuer, there's no room for dispute over payments, and no mutually trusted center is necessary. All parties need only select and protect their own hardware; the DigiCash software does the rest.

PRIVACY. Electronic cash, unlike even paper cash, is unconditionally untraceable. The blinding carried out by the user's own device makes it impossible for anyone to link payment to payer. But users can prove unequivocally that they did or did not make a particular payment, without revealing anything more. Besides appealing to consumers, this level of privacy limits exposure to future data-privacy legislation and reduces record-keeping costs.

ELECTRONIC CASH (NET CASH) APPLICATIONS. Here are some of the opportunities for Net cash applications DigiCash has been working on:

At the point of sale. Prepaid cards, credit cards, vending

For telepayment. Phone cards, teleshopping and telebanking, conditional access to services, network payments

SECURITY—FOR ALL CONCERNED. Neither the user nor the payee can counterfeit the bank's signature. But either can verify that the payment is valid, since each has the bank's public key; and the user can prove that the payment was made, since the user can make available the blinding factor. But because the user's original note number was blinded when it was signed, the bank can't connect the signing with the payment. The bank is protected against forgery, the payee against the bank's refusal to honor a legitimate note, and the user against false accusations and invasion of privacy.

What prevents users from spending the same note twice? One obvious method is checking the bank's signatures online against a database of spent notes. For most systems, which handle high volumes of low-value payments, this is too expensive. DigiCash has found better solutions. Before accepting an offline payment, the payee's equipment issues an unpredictable challenge to which the user's equipment must respond with some information about the note number. By itself, this information discloses nothing about the user. But if the user spends the note a second time, the information yielded by the next challenge gives away the user's identity when the note is ultimately deposited. For enhanced practical protection, smart cards can also be programmed to prevent double spending at the moment it is tried.

MORE POSSIBILITIES.   DigiCash has devised a number of variations on these basic systems. For the bank to issue users with enough separate electronic coins of various denominations would be cumbersome in communication and storage. So would a system that required payees to return change. To sidestep such costs, they use an electronic *check*—a single number that contains multiple denomination terms sufficient for any transaction up to a prescribed limit and to which the appropriate value is assigned at payment time. What's more, the values of the denomination terms can be made variable. In this way, users can receive interest on their unspent checks, the bank can receive interest on credit payments, and the same check can be spent in different currencies.

Just as the form of Net cash (electronic cash) itself can be varied, so can the hardware configurations needed to apply it. Rather than having their accounts debited at a bank, users can insert hard currency into terminal equipment. The user's equipment can be an ordinary smart card, a public-key-capable smart card, or a personal computer. DigiCash has also developed a pocketable smart card reader with its own keypad, display, and infrared link.

Documentation and technical details for these and other options are available on request from DigiCash. Patents have been issued and are pending in most major markets.

DigiCash has demonstrated performance in each phase of payment system development—from conception, through feasibility studies, breadboards and prototypes, to production management.

Digital Signatures

Let's take a brief stroll down technical alley. We'll go just far enough to convince everyone but genuine, dues-paid techies it's not the most useful place to wander.

In the RSA public key cryptosystem used for electronic cash, both encryption and decryption are done by raising the message—here, the note number—to a power that is the appropriate key. These exponentiations are done in a modular arithmetic system: one that saves only the result of division by a fixed number called a *modulus*, which needs to be quite large, usually at least 150 digits.

Any questions so far? Good. On we go.

First Virtual Holdings

11975 El Camino Real, Suite 300
San Diego, CA 92130-5545
Phone: 619-793-2700
E-mail: info@fv.com
URL: http://www.fv.com

First Virtual (FV) is an unusual company in many respects. After its startup in 1994, it operated for 15 months without a physical office. It's system of Internet payments does not use public key encryption but does require that both buyer and seller be registered with it.

FV facilitates electronic commerce with what appears to be a reasonable degree of security by a unique system. It separates the nonsensitive information which is sent over the Internet from the sensitive items (such as credit card numbers) which are never sent over the Internet.

"A higher level protocol based on Email callbacks" is the heart of FV's system. Buyers and sellers may establish contact in any way, online or offline. When a transaction is decided upon, they submit the transaction to First Virtual via standard e-mail or via FV's SMXP protocol. FV verifies the buyer's identity and requires an e-mail reply before processing the transaction. FV uses offline methods—snail mail, express, or e-mail—to obtain sensitive information.

Although FV freely admits to glitches, bugs, and unanticipated limitations, it claims to have worked effectively to control them. It also reports some operational problems stemming from its Internet-centric method of operation and discusses its advantages. For example, customer service operators, often physically disadvantaged, work with effective devotion from remote locations, usually their homes. As a result, FV gives no office space to, and pays no rent for, that function, which in many companies requires considerable resources.

First Virtual's URL provides several lengthy documents that any executive considering electronic commerce should read.

GTE

GTE has thrown its hat into this ring with a new technology called Cybertrust. For information, contact:

77 "A" Street
Needham, MA 02194
Phone: 800-487-8788
E-mail: WaltonC@mail.ndhm.gtesc.com
URL: http://www.Gte.com

Microsoft

Its solution to Web site problems will be ready by the time you read this. For the latest information, call Michael Kim at 206-703-0403

Netscape Communications Corporation

501 East Middlefield Road
Mountain View, CA 94043
Corporate Sales Phone: 415-937-2555
Fax: 415-528-4124.
E-mail: info@netscape.com
URL: www.home.netscape.com

Netscape got off to a fast start in April 1994 by quickly introducing and widely distributing Netscape Navigator, a World Wide Web browser. It followed this with its Suitespot software to provide secure Internet business solutions. These include LivePayment, which allows the Internet to provide a point-of-sale terminal.

Netscape says its Commercial Applications "can be used individually or in combination to create almost any kind of online business." Among its users are the online sites for the Discovery Channel and the *New York Times*.

PGP

555 Twin Dolphins Drive, Suite 3570
Redwood Shores, CA 94065
Phone: 415-631-1747
Fax: 415-631-0599

E-mail: support@pgp.com
URL: http://www.pgp.com

The corporate aim of Pretty Good Privacy is to stem the erosion of privacy in the information age. It envisions a global electronic community with private communication enabled by encryption that is

- Transparent
- Ubiquitous
- Trusted

Toward this end, PGP plans to continue and expand its role as the industry standard for trusted, open digital encryption products that enable secure digital communication and storage.

The firm provides encryption solutions for secure communications and storage of data to users, corporations, and original equipment manufacturers (OEMs). Developed by founder Phil Zimmermann, the company's initial product, PGP for e-mail, released in 1991 as freeware on the Internet, is now the de facto standard for Internet mail encryption.

Zimmermann, a privacy rights advocate, made it possible for individuals to send, for the first time, uninterceptable information via e-mail.

PGP's family of encryption products includes all forms of digital information: e-mail, data, telephony, fax, image, and video.

Millions of users around the world rely on PGP's e-mail product for secure electronic messaging. The freeware version of PGP for e-mail is a command-line version of the product, not intended for commercial use. The Massachusetts Institute of Technology (MIT) distributes PGP's e-mail product within the United States only. It is available from a controlled FTP site that has restrictions and limitations to comply with export control requirements. Since 1994, the MIT distribution site alone had distributed free copies of PGP at a rate of 500 to 1000 downloads daily.

PGP incorporated in March 1996 to market commercial versions of what had already become a popular product among computer enthusiasts around the world. Personal and corporate editions of PGP for e-mail will soon be available with easy-to-use graphical user interfaces, technical support, additional documentation, and upgrades. These will replace the commercial versions of PGP's e-mail product currently being sold by ViaCrypt. ViaCrypt and its parent corporation, Lemcom Systems, were acquired in July 1996 by PGP.

Today, Phil Zimmermann is building a company that is synonymous with electronic privacy, with the help of well-known Internet and networking executives including Jonathan Seybold, founder of Seybold Seminars, and Dan Lynch, founder of Interop and currently chairman of CyberCash.

Surety Technologies

One Main Street
Chatham, NJ 07928
Phone: 201-701-0600
Fax: 201-701-0601

In 1992, Bellcore researchers Scott Stornetta and Stuart Haber won Discover Magazine's Award for Technological Innovation in computer software for a prototype of the Digital Notary Service.

Scott and Stuart founded Surety in 1994 to commercialize these award-winning, patented Bellcore technologies, which focused on electronic records management. Today, Surety's mission is to provide corporations and professionals with a simple, unimpeachable way to prove the integrity and authenticity of all their electronic records.

WHAT PEOPLE ARE SAYING

"...a software system that may do more than any other to advance the cause of the paperless office..."

—*Computer Technology Review,* April, 1995

"This company offers an exciting new technology. We look forward to great synergy between RSA and Surety Technologies."

—Jim Bidzos, president, RSA Data Security

"...while digital notarization doesn't make it possible to transmit credit-card numbers over the Net, it addresses a more important problem: the intrinsic mutability of electronic documents."

—*Computer Letter,* November, 1995

Digital Notary, Digital Audit Trail, and the Surety logo are trademarks of Surety Technologies. All other trademarks used are the properties of their respective companies.

VeriSign

VeriSign approaches security from the standpoint of verification, which it accomplishes by encryption. Verisign, then, is a *certificate authority.* It issues and processes digital signatures such as the ones SET will use.

VeriSign provides trusted digital authentication services and products to enable the adoption of secure electronic commerce solutions.

Contact Stratton Sclavos, CEO, or Rebecca L. Repka, marketing communications associate for more information.

2593 Coast Avenue
Mountain View, CA 94043
Phone: 415-961-7500
Fax: 415-961-7300
E-mail: rebecca.repka@VeriSign.com
URL: http://www.verisign.com

CORPORATE MISSION. The corporate mission of VeriSign is to provide trusted digital authentication services and products to enable the deployment and adoption of secure electronic commerce solutions.

COMPANY DETAILS. VeriSign has 80 employees. It was founded May 1995 as a spinoff from RSA Data Security. It is privately held. Among the principal investors are RSA Data Security, Security Dynamics, and VISA International.

PRODUCTS ON THE MARKET NOW. Digital ID (also called certificates) in four escalating levels of identity assurance is now available.

CLIENT PARTNERSHIPS. VeriSign provides Digital ID's for client applications from the following partners: Banyan Systems, ConnectSoft, CyberCash, Deming, Frontier Technologies, FTP, IBM, Microsoft, Netscape, OpenSoft, PrEmail, and Worldtalk.

SERVER PARTNERSHIPS. VeriSign provides Digital ID's for server applications from a long list of partners including AOL/Navisoft, Apple, CompuServe/Spry, IBM, Lotus, Netscape, Open Market, O'Reilly & Associates, and Oracle.

Success Stories
on the Net

The first entrepreneurs and companies to grasp—and act on—the enormous potential of Internet commerce have already established formidable electronic networks in a few product or service areas. In some cases, late-starting me-too competitors will find it difficult to duplicate the success of the first firms to offer electronic purchase in their particular niche. What is most likely to work in these cases is a new approach offering customers something of value the original seller in the field does not—and ideally cannot—provide.

Successful Product E-Sellers

Although a few fields have already been seized by the most nimble entrepreneurs, vast numbers of product lines await their first effective electronic sellers. One of the most impressive cases of Web exploitation by an alert entrepreneur occurred in the field of book selling, traditionally a low margin field. This achievement is all the more laudable because it occurred when dozens of well-established independent bookstores were being driven out of business all across the country by the rapid proliferation of superstores.

CDnow

Jason Olim, president
Matthew Olim, vice president
Penllyn, PA 19422
URL: http://www.cdnow.com

The American Dream is alive and shining brilliantly in two 27-year-old twin brothers. One, a pony-tailed extrovert. The other, a soft-spoken introvert. Together, starting from their parents' basement, they have accomplished what any business owner will respect—they've built a highly successful business entirely on the Internet.

CDnow is growing at a rate of 15 to 20 percent a month. Some 450,000 Web shoppers visit the site each month, selecting from more than 200,000 CDs, albums, cassettes, music videos, CD-ROMs, laser discs, T-shirts, and other music-related accessories. The company expects its 1996 volume to exceed $6 million.

The CDnow Web site is rich with information and allows users to make purchases easily.

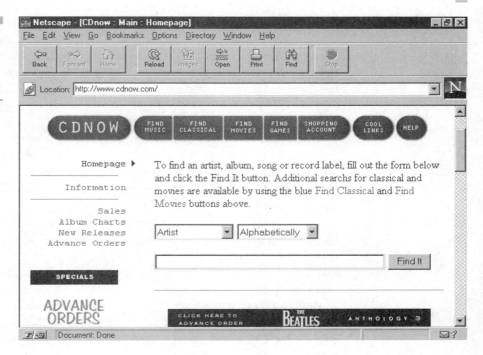

Movienow, a 35,000-video database of movies and special-interest videos, also featuring reviews and entertainment news, has been added. A separate home page offering videos is planned.

Jason, the outspoken one, says, "Our goal has always been to build an information environment so rich, so compelling, and so easy to use consumers can literally program it to their precise musical interests and tastes—to create a new paradigm in retailing."

It's something he calls *inter-cast* marketing. "When individuals explore CDnow, the site adapts to them, creating a customized environment where they can easily access only the information they desire and need to make a purchasing decision."

The idea for CDnow dates to when Jason, a long-time classic and alternative rock fan, acquired a taste for jazz. Problem was no one at the local music store could suggest anything more than a few artists and titles.

"Traditional retailers just weren't helpful in expanding my knowledge of music, in helping me learn more so I would buy more," remembers Jason. He spent his college years at Brown University, playing in local bands and banging around ideas with friends on how to better market music to consumers.

After graduating with a degree in computer science in 1992, Jason was employed as a computer consultant. He kept his goal in mind to improve the way music is marketed. In 1994, as opportunity on the Net blossomed, his idea crystallized. Why not provide the in-depth musical information he craved as a music consumer over the Internet and then sell CDs and accessories to those who would browse the information?

The next day, Jason recruited three college buddies for his venture. Within weeks, he was negotiating deals with music distributors to supply product to his company. After a month, however, his partners lost interest. Jason was left with the awesome task of programming hundreds of thousands of lines of computer code necessary to create a leading-edge Internet site.

Twin brother Matthew offered to help. The only trouble was Matthew—an astrophysics student at Columbia University—had no formal training in computer programming, let alone in the complex programming Jason needed to manage the depth and breadth of information he planned for CDnow.

But Matthew was up to the challenge. He grabbed a copy of the bible of C-based programming, the 1978 edition of Kernighan and Ritchie's *The C-Programming Language*. In a couple of weeks, he was writing code and had become proficient enough to argue with Jason (the resident computer expert) about how to implement complex data structures.

Matthew became singularly focused, spending endless days (and nights) designing and building the intricate interfaces. "For months it was all I could think about." Not wanting to miss a beat, he would even brush his teeth in front of the computer. Says Matthew, "It was so much fun to build the site. I could experiment and play. It was a wonderful intellectual process."

"Matthew evolved into a 'super-programmer.' He is a true mathematician," Jason says. "In ten lines of code he does what would take other programmers as five to ten times as many. What he accomplished in his first year would reasonably have taken three or four programmers working full-time and cost more than $1 million."

The Olims rewarded their dedicated sons with a timely five-figure loan, plus the use of their basement to enable their dream venture to take off. CDnow opened its virtual doors on August 1, 1994, just six months after Jason conceived the idea. With some fine-tuning to their system, one of the most sophisticated sites on the Internet resulted.

CDnow operates off 40 databases, all linked to one another through an intricate network of billions of pathways. This allows cyber-surfers to glide smoothly through the ocean of information about music and music-related topics, making connections between artists, musical genres, and influences. CDnow contains biographies of more than 12,000 artists, complete with listings of every album and CD they ever recorded. Browsers can read some 175,000 reviews from some of the most respected musical critics in the world.

Promotions for CDnow are posted on inline chat rooms and other music-related sites. Using inter-casting, customers are categorized based on buying patterns and preferences. E-mail promotions are targeted to specific interest groups so as not to be a turn-off. Jazz hounds don't get Beethoven bulletins; Prokofiev lovers don't hear about Duke Ellington.

After a blur of plus-15-hour days, the brothers moved into new offices and now employ 28 full-time employees. Fifteen percent of sales come from outside the United States, with Canada and Australia generating the heaviest volume. Japan follows close behind. CDnow ships regularly to over 60 countries.

"Going online was easy," says Matthew. "Now the pressure is on to make sure the orders are flowing and the system is running smoothly." But the basic tenets still hold true. "The key to cyber-marketing is providing a rich resource of information in an easy-to-use format." This, perhaps, represents the ultimate wisdom for Internet marketers.

As Jason puts it, "CDnow is as much about information as it is about selling. When you provide a location where people can learn about a keen interest of theirs, and when they can customize information to suit their needs, then electronic commerce is the natural outcome. And for businesses, this is the real promise of the Internet."

Eventually, CDnow plans to market in a one-on-one manner where personalized messages are sent to customers in real time while they shop. Artificial intelligence programs will track a customer's path, offering specials and other targeted purchasing opportunities.

Future plans envisioned include broadcasting live concerts from their Web site. Jason foresees significant revenue from advertising sales on their site and in licensing CDnow's technology to others.

The Internet's jumping with the first Jukebox at http://www.interjuke. com created for the customers of CDnow. The site allows the cyber-listener to hear the latest musical release from a wide range of musical genres without waiting the usual 10 to 20 minutes to download the file. Anything from Juliana Hatfield's latest album to Loop Guru's "Duniya" to Mozart's "Piano Concerto No. 9" to "Mongo Santamaria."

CDnow's Internet Jukebox is made possible by the technology of Progressive Networks and the encoding capabilities of the Muzak Corporation.

CDnow's use of RealAudio's advanced 2.0 Live Streams technology (the software can be downloaded from http://www.realaudio.com.) makes it possible to instantly receive a steady stream of musical vibes. Depending on the receiver's modem, the system can reproduce FM quality sound at 28.8 baud or AM at 14.4 baud. The Internet Jukebox and the 2.0 version of Live Streams were simultaneously launched

Special technology from Corel was developed to enhance retail fulfillment. Purchasers' credit card numbers are protected by CDnow's Netscape Commerce Server and PGP (Pretty Good Privacy) encryption software. Retail transactions are tracked by Soundscan Reporting, the authoritative source for the music industry.

Virtual Vineyards

Robert Olson, CEO
Palo Alto, CA 94303
URL: http://www.virtualvin.com

Founded in 1994 by Peter Granoff and and Robert Olson, the business was born when the two halves of an idea found each other over dinner. Granoff had long been put off by the pretense of "wine speak" and had been distressed by the trend in the industry to reduce wine marketing to a numerical scoring system. He felt this trend was particularly harmful to his favorite producers, the small artisan wine makers.

Olson's background is in the computer industry. He had been studying the potential of interactive electronic marketing for several years. With the advent of the Web, he felt the time was ripe to put his ideas into practice, but he lacked an appropriate product. As he and Peter explored potential product ideas over a bottle of wine, they realized they had the answer in hand.

By using the Web to sell wine, they could give potential customers in-depth information about the wines being offered and the people who made them. The information could be provided in ways site visitors would find pleasant and unintimidating. They would feature only the best wines from the best vintners, so customers could count on getting a great bottle every time.

And they would develop sophisticated software tools to make shopping as easy, convenient, and enjoyable as possible. One of the first of their innovations was Peter's "Ask the Cork Dork" page, where visitors can type in what they're looking for—price range, variety, and so on—and receive expert wine recommendations.

In response to customer demand, they introduced specialty foods and the freshest of produce in addition to their fine wines. They now employ 12 employees who bring together expertise in the food and wine business, software and information technology, and customer service. The company's commitment is to high-tech, high-touch marketing and service.

The Web site opened for business in January 1995, and reactions from both customers and the media has been very positive. According to CEO, Robert Olson, they are receiving 20,000 visits each week and are growing at around 20 percent a month. International business accounts for 8 percent of total revenue. They installed Netscape Secure Commerce Server for safe encrypted transactions and are very pleased with its security features. They continue to enhance their software systems.

Olson says he's amazed at how companies hurriedly slap together a site and then wonder why it isn't performing up to expectations.

"Provide your customer with new and inventive reasons to return to your site. Just throwing money at it will not guarantee the customers will necessarily come. Build it smart and bring them there. Give them a reason to come."

Amazon Books

Jeffrey Bezos, CEO
Seattle, WA
URL: http://www.amazon.com

This newcomer to book selling is a pioneer in electronic commerce. The firm began in a 500-square-foot building with seven employees. Within a year, its fourth physical expansion moved Amazon Books into a 45,000-square-foot facility in Seattle staffed by 89 employees. By the time you read this, it may well have expanded again—a distinct possibility if it continues its 34 percent a *month* growth rate.

It chose the name because it lists over eight times as many books as any superstore. The Amazon River carries more than eight times as much water as any other river.

According to CEO and president Jeff Bezos, Amazon's catalog lists 1.1 million book titles. This is essentially every book currently available from recognized publishers. Amazon stocks a limited number of best-selling titles and it ships within 24 hours after receiving an order on its Web page. Another 350,000 titles can be quickly supplied from wholesalers, with an additional 750,000 titles coming direct from publishers.

Amazon's Web site allows users to search through over a million titles.

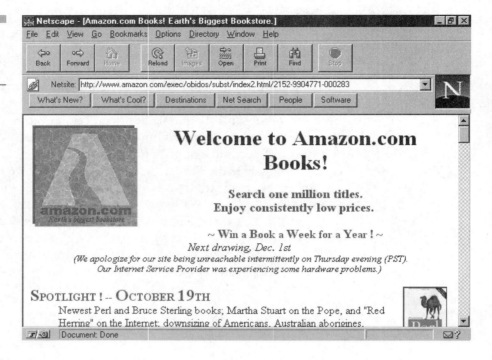

The Sharper Image

Richard Thalheimer, CEO
Joshua Tretakoff, manager of alternative media
San Francisco, CA 94111
URL: http://www.sharperimage.com

This techno-savvy retailer, long known for its upscale gifts, completed a major transformation of its Web site in May of 1996. It teamed with Next Software (Steve Jobs, CEO), using WebObjects tool kit, a $25,000 set of object-oriented tools. This allowed it to link orders from the site directly into a IBM AS/400 computer system to process orders.

The company had revenue of $280 million for 1995, half a million of it from its Web site. Its original goal was to triple Web sales in 1996. As the fourth quarter began, it was ahead of the goal and confidently anticipating Web sales of over $2 million for 1996.

The logistics of getting its entire catalog of almost 1000 items plus its 500-item quality Home Furniture Collection and Spa Merchandise online presented a challenge. Its in-house databases store thousands of images. Joshua Tretakoff, Sharper Image's manager of alternative media, said, "Rather than

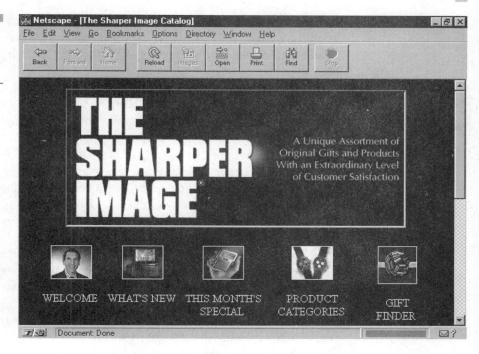

having to create static pages one by one, spending time and effort on design and dumb stuff, we used a number of templates to dynamically generate the pages on the fly. It's a database-driven system which allows for an amazing degree of customization." It also permits easy updating.

It plans to preview exciting new functionality online to tempt the customer. "They won't be able to keep their fingers off the keyboards," says Tretakoff. The Sharper Image introduced the "Gift Finder" which allows gifts to be selected by interest. Plans are underway to actively survey its customers seeking critiques on items it's considering carrying on the Web. "It gives immediate feedback and demonstrates how much we value our customers' opinions," said Joshua.

When a Web customer asks for a specific product, the information requested—copy, photos, graphics, pricing, and promotional offers—is taken from several databases automatically formatted with HTML tags and popped onto the customer's Web browser. It happens very quickly.

"We wanted to ship orders from the www on the same day they are placed," says Tretakaoff. "We're doing it now. Under the old system, orders took 48 hours to process. The new Web system, automatically checks on availability and inventory stock." Even though the server is in Arizona, Joshua is able to run the site effectively from his office in San Francisco.

The Next program allowed it to dramatically increase its presence without a major allocation of resources. With millions of catalogs mailed yearly and paper prices soaring, the idea of a paperless Web catalog was very appealing.

WebObjects' architecture sits between the Web site and Sharper Image's back-office computers. "WebObjects gives us this added protection—not just on the functional side, but on the heightened security as well," says Tretakoff.

Sharper Image offers a variety of ways to pay over the Internet. One of the two most secure is Secure Sockets, available if the customer's browser supports Secure Sockets Layer (SSL). Customers enter payment and shipping information on their Netscape Secure Server.

The second is Secure Keypad, Sharper Image's own secure feature for entering payment information. This system was developed by Evergreen Internet as part of its CyberCat ordering system. Instead of simply transmitting your credit card number, it does things differently. When you trigger the secure keypad, it generates a random dynamic keypad—basically a graphic image. Each image is only good for one session. As you type your credit card number, the system transforms each digit into image map coordinates for transmittal, along with a unique key only Sharper Image's computer can decipher.

The only data transmitted are image map coordinates, sent one by one. Given the complexity of the Internet, the message's several packets might travel different routes from buyer to seller. This presents a hacker with a daunting task of interception. Assuming these interceptions could be accomplished successfully enough to reconstruct the entire message, the hacker would then have to break the individual codes for each digit, which requires a unique, dynamically designed image map.

Not surprisingly, Sharper Image has experienced no problems with either secure system. It also accept orders via fax and those phoned to its 800 number.

Regarding Web sites, Joshua says, "For some strange reason because this is a new medium, business people throw their common sense out the window while throwing money at their Web sites. 'Get me one of those—now,' seems to be the knee-jerk reaction. Two months later management takes another look and are astounded at how expensive the project was. You certainly wouldn't pay at this level for any other form of business. I hear about companies spending $250,000 on their sites and I cringe."

He advises to treat this like any other aspect of business. Don't, under any circumstances, feel that just because it's the Web, you'll pay exorbitant fees. "Four or five months from now you'll have the stalest site on the Web and you're married to it."

Sharper Image was conceived when CEO Richard Thalheimer advertised a sport watch in a runners' magazine in 1981. He was so encouraged by the number of responses he started a small catalog operation. It flourished. Today there are 4 Spa Collections and 80 stores (75 percent in upscale malls), with locations in Switzerland, Australia, and Korea, with the newest opening recently in Saudi Arabia.

Ben and Jerry's Homemade

Ben Cohen, founder
Joe Wilkins, self-described Webhead
South Burlington, VT 05403
URL: http://www.benjerry.com

Ben and Jerry's was founded in 1978 in a renovated gas station in Burlington, Vermont. Childhood friends Ben Cohen and Jerry Greenfield used a $12,000 investment ($4000 of which was borrowed) to fund their venture. They soon became renowned for their innovative ice cream flavors.

The company's mission statement calls for it to operate a profitable business and to enable the community to profit by the way it does business. It donates 7.5 percent of pretax earnings to Ben and Jerry's Foundation—managed by a nine-member Employee Board—which funds community action teams at five Vermont sites. Corporate grants help children, families, disadvantaged groups, and the environment.

The company is actively pursuing enhancements for online commerce. One coming innovation will be a "virtual Ben and Jerry" who will take the visitor on a voice-interactive tour where the "tourist" may ask either founder a specific question. If your virtual tour guides are unable to answer directly, they will take you to the person within the organization who can. This program will utilize Shockwave Narrative and RealAudio.

Cyber-ice cream fans can fire an "ICBM" (Ice Cream By Mail) to their friends or their own homes. An ICBM from Ben and Jerry's is six packs of ice cream packed in liquid nitrogen and over-nighted by Federal Express. A relative recently sent an ICBM to a family member serving in the armed forces on a ship off the coast of Bosnia!

Light-hearted fun is the core of this Vermont company. The sounds of Missy the cow's mooing and the trademark cowhide make this site "a fun happening place." Animated graphics are built by Netscape including a "cemetery" for discontinued ice cream flavors where a delivery truck chugs alongside dancing skeletons. Contests are a big hit. "The Real Scoop," a book for kids with recipes, company history, and trivia is a recent award winner.

Offerings of special orders at local shops via the Net are under consideration. Gifts such as "Nerd Packs," (pocket protectors), hats, and T-shirt sales are also planned.

Netscape Commerce Server is the server of choice. Home.com will be managing its expanded Internet Shop.

Ben and Jerry's are in all 50 states. Offering "euphoric ice cream" abroad are outlets in Benelux, Canada, France, Israel, the United Kingdom, and Russia. Plans are to locate in many European and Asian markets in the future, but management is not plunging swiftly into the Asian market. "It's easy to do a *lousy* job but it takes time to do a *good* job," Ben Cohen says.

ONSALE

Jerry Kaplan, CEO
Mountain View, CA 94043
URL: http://www.onsale.com

This online computer store recreates the fun and excitement of bidding at an electronic auction, where prices and availability change in response to customers' actions. By searching for close-out and refurbished computer bargains and bringing them to the online community, ONSALE strives to bring the perfect products to the perfect audience at the perfect time.

The company began in May 1995. It is growing at 20 to 30 percent a month and projects revenue of more than $30 million for 1996. Its Web site is attracting 1 million visits a week.

CEO Jerry Kaplan knew there was an overabundance of computer stores and to succeed he must use the new medium of the Internet and capitalize on its interactive opportunities.

He envisioned a live auction, where computer customers bid on everything from CPUs to zip drives. He wanted bidders to experience the excitement of a live auction. Orders are transmitted to the participating merchants, who process the orders and collect payment. Two cycles of bidding are conducted weekly.

Computer buyers often revisit the site knowing a continuous flow of new computers, software, and components are being showcased. Over 50,000 cyber-bidders have vied in this virtual auction house for coveted computers, software, and components.

AMP eMerce Internet Solutions

Jim Kessler, director
URL: http://www.ampemerce.com

AMP eMerce Internet Solutions was launched on September 9, 1996, as a subsidiary of AMP, Incorporated. With revenues of $5 billion annually, AMP is the world's largest supplier of electrical and electronic connectors and interconnection systems. It currently features 72,000 parts in its online catalog and will have close to 100,000 parts cataloged early in 1997.

Jim Kessler, director of AMP eMerce Internet Solutions, says the new subsidiary was formed to offer AMP's experience and hard-won know-how to other companies seeking to develop large catalogs on the Net. He likened developing a Web site to dancing with an 800-pound gorilla, "You only stop when the gorilla wants to!"

"You can go from a hero to an absolute loser in this game if you're not attentive to what's out there," Kessler cautions. "Carefully evaluate what you want your site to do for you. What business problem are you addressing? Answering those questions often means thinking about your Web site in a way similar to how an editor views a magazine ad.

"Use all the communication skills available. Think carefully about content. Are you reaching the right audience? How do I get the audience to return? How do I measure my success?"

Kessler puts a high priority on front-end planning and avoiding false or inaccurate expectations of what can be accomplished.

AMP uses Open Market Software for authorizing and verification to accept payment over the Internet. "Small and medium users can benefit from a service provider capable of acting as a clearinghouse," said Kessler.

eMerce suggests doing a test version of your Web site and then using the information gained to hone your site into exactly what's needed. "The moment you ask for customer input, be prepared to operate a 24 hour facility and to respond within hours. This can be a black hole into which you throw unlimited resources. Make sure you can handle it before it's offered. It's important to be cautious. Look hard at what practical returns you can anticipate via your Web site."

Kessler has noticed many sites whose makeup strongly indicates they are the emotional reactions of executives who felt their companies needed a presence on the Net. As a result of taking the emotional approach, these Internet appearances were developed without considering what the sites could accomplish. As a result, they accomplish nothing.

"We made sure some identifiable savings could be realized. The paper catalogs published by AMP are an expense item of between $7 million and $10 million a year. Offloading some requirements for those paper catalogs onto the Internet has the potential of effecting considerable savings.

"Many companies put up hundreds of static HTML pages, thinking they are conducting business-to-business electronic commerce. This is not enough. To serve the business-to-business market, companies need to create database-driven dynamic content searchable by requirements, not just browsed by keywords. Customers need immediate and accurate product information."

At a cost of $0.70 to $2.00 each, AMP was faxing 40,000 responses to product information requests each month before its Web site went online. Through the Internet the same information is supplied to AMP's 30,000 registered Web site users in superior fashion at considerable savings. Formerly it was only practical for AMP to respond to its international clients in English. The cost and time delay involved in translating its huge print catalogs into the variety of languages needed could not be justified. Now AMP has the capability of responding individually to product information requests in French, Italian, Spanish, German, Japanese, Mandarin Chinese, and Korean. Before its Web site went active, this didn't make economic sense.

Electronic catalogs are the foundation of business-to-business electronic commerce. When manufacturers and distributors have thousands of products or configurations presented in hundreds of pages of paper catalogs or static HTML pages, finding the correct product can take days. AMP eMerce Solutions have cut product-location time from days to hours.

In dealing with 45 countries worldwide, it found translation can be cost-prohibitive without a dynamic database. It uses the Oracle 7 database. It cut translation costs from in the millions of dollars to in the thousands.

No single company can provide a complete solution to the problems of electronic commerce, Kessler believes. It requires multiple strategic partners to bring your electronic commerce site together in its most effective and profitable configuration. A variety of disciplines need to be tapped; database expertise; search engine and other Web site promotion; high level graphics and image skills; simple, fast, and accurate processing of authenticated orders, to name a few. Then, the talents of good HTML development comes in as the glue to hold the whole thing together. The AMP catalog uses proprietary navigator technology from Step Search, jointly developed with SAQQARA Systems. This allows the user to control the direction of the search within the catalog guided by high-resolution graphics, 3-D models, and charts. SAQQARA also provides the search engine. Products and technologies from Lucent Technologies, Open Market, Oracle, DataBase Publishing Software, and netImage are also utilized.

If your site will take orders on the Internet, you must put infrastructure in place to support all the complexities involved. "Think through what business problem you are addressing," Kessler says.

Internet Shopping Network (ISN)

URL: http://www.isn.com/
E-mail: service@internet.net.

A pioneer when first launched in 1994, ISN is now a leading computer products retailer on the Internet. The firm offers a huge selection of computer products at some of the industry's lowest prices. Through innovation and by taking advantage of new capabilities and technologies, ISN leads the pack in making online commerce easy and convenient.

The Internet Shopping Network has taken advantage of new electronic commerce technology to make buying computers and related items easy online.

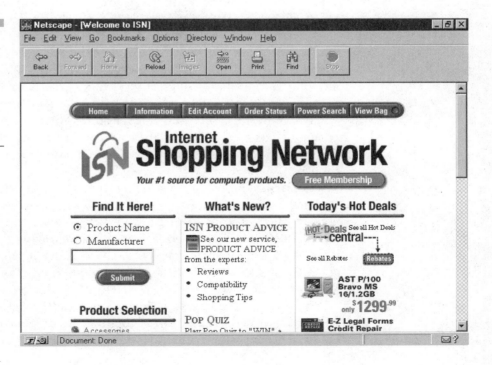

ISN carries a complete selection of 35,000 computer hardware and software products from over 600 manufacturers. It also offers immediate access to some of the most popular software carried in its Downloadable Store.

Comprehensive product descriptions, specifications, and performance benefits are provided to help buyers make the right purchase decision. Real-time capabilities allow ISN to bring its customers up-to-date pricing, product changes, and inventory updates so they can always have the latest product information.

Wall Street Camera

Eli Kurland, partner
Andy Czegledi, partner
New York City, NY 10005
URL: http://www.wall-street-camera.com

Wall Street Camera began 45 years ago amidst imposing Manhattan skyscrapers. In 1987, Andy Czegledi and Eli Kurland, after working together for five years, decided to buy the business. They now employ 20—make it 21 if you count Kurland's trusty white German shepherd who watches over everyone. Their clientele includes photographers, corporate, medical, and legal professionals. Says Andy, "Wall Street customers are seeking top value with great service. We give them those things with a friendly smile and maybe a little joke to brighten their day."

Their Web site is very new but the added Internet business has already paid for their computer and all costs associated with the site design and launch on the Net. In fact, the investment was made back in the first month.

The firm's monthly advertising budget is in the five figures for national and international periodicals. When the New York newspapers got too pricey, it stopped advertising there. The partners are pleased their ads on the World Wide Web are appealing to tourists worldwide—including many from Japan. When visiting New York City, many Japanese camera enthusiasts make a beeline for the photography store they saw on the Web. Mail order accounts for 65 percent of total sales.

Wall Street is the largest dealer of Leica and Rolleiflex in the country. Its inventory includes 2000 top-of-the-line new cameras and photographic equipment items. Rare cameras priced at over $30,000 are available.

Serious collectors think they've died and gone to heaven at Camera Heaven, where 50,000 to 75,000 pre-owned cameras, movie cameras, and projectors together with lenses and filters are stocked. New clients seem to be going for the used cameras in a big way—particularly international Web shoppers. Some of these collectors spend hundreds of thousands of dollars a year.

Sam's Wines and Spirits

Fred, Darryl, and Brian Rosen, owners
Chicago, IL 60614
URL: http://www.sams-wine.com

When Brian Rosen recognized the business potential of a Web site, he studied the possibilities with great care, analyzing demographics of the Internet shopper. He tried to visualize what those special customers' needs might be.

The Sam's Wines site tries to cater to its users' needs.

He then researched how to put together his own site. In November of 1994, Sam's Wines Web site went online. He is pleased with the site's performance which accounts for about 10 percent of overall company revenue.

Posting the company's URL on all business cards, stationery, mailings, advertisements, catalogs, and phone book listings is given high priority. Rosen feels certain this policy has contributed mightily to boost the site's average to 3200 hits a week.

Sam's Wine and Spirits began in 1945 and now has 100 employees. Brian, Fred, and Darryl Rosen have celebrated the opening of the firm's second half-century by opening a new and larger location.

Brian updates the site monthly, offers special promotions, and sends out e-mail bulletins to attract repeat business. He recognized the importance of keeping the Web site simple and swift for the time-pressed Web shopper.

He cautions people charging in to designing a Web site without considering the ramifications of the project. Clearly defining who he was trying to reach and making it as easy as possible for customers were important factors he considered.

Franklin Electronic Publishers

Morton E. David, chairman and CEO
Burlington, N.J.
1-800-BOOKMAN
URL: http://www.franklin.com

Franklin's Web site contains many of the features needed for successful electronic selling over the Internet. We recommend a visit to this site to examine how it's doing it.

Customers who access Franklin's Web site can choose among the following links to Franklin-related subject matter:

- *Franklin News.* For background information and breaking news on the company

- *Product Information.* Product-line catalog with detailed descriptions

- *Try a Franklin.* Interactive product demonstrations which replicate functions and graphics of Franklin's handheld electronic books such as the *Merriam-Webster Collegiate Dictionary*

- *Franklin Challenge-online.* Trivia game with fun facts taken from Franklin products
- *Cool Links.* Hot links are planned to Web sites of Franklin's publishing partners such as Starfish Software, Bertelsmann, McGraw-Hill, Oxford University Press, Macmillan Publishing USA, Zondervan, and Harper Collins

CEO Morton E. David says, "The Internet is a natural medium on which Franklin successfully markets its products."

Successful Service E-Sellers

Since the pricing for many Internet services escapes competitive pressure and is benefit-based rather than cost-based, it can be highly profitable.

Auto-By-Tel

Pete Ellis, president
Irvine, CA 92612-1400
URL: http://www.autobytel.com
Prodigy: Jump: Auto-By-Tel
CompuServe: Go: Auto-By-Tel
America Online: Internet Connection: World Wide Web

The automobile industry was in the dark ages in the opinion of auto tycoon Peter Ellis and health industry innovator John Bedrosian. So they cofounded Auto-By-Tel in 1995. It is the nation's largest dollar volume Internet sales program according to president Ellis.

Projected sales are 250,000 vehicles for 1996. They are receiving 30,000 purchase requests a month. Ellis predicts up to 50 percent of all auto sales will have Internet involvement within five years. "Auto-By-Tel's amazing growth has even astounded me," says Ellis, "and it proves the Internet is the most viable marketing tool in the information age."

This program links informed auto buyers with attentive car dealers via the Internet with commercial online services. Within the first 10 months, 65,000 requests for new vehicles were processed. Around half of those requests resulted in sales totaling more than $300 million.

Marketing over the
Internet allows Auto-
By-Tel to quote buy-
ers substantially
lower prices and save
them many hassles.

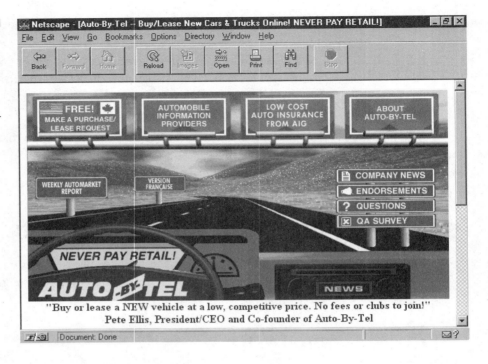

The network has over 1400 dealers in the United States and Canada. Dealers pay as low as $250 monthly to belong. The firm is able to quote lower prices due to sharply lower or eliminated advertising and sales commission costs. Consumers stand to save thousands of dollars and avoid the major hassles associated with car buying. Only those who enjoy kicking tires and fighting off sales pitches pine for the old way of doing business.

Auto-By-Tel has an agreement with Microsoft CarSource where auto information searches and purchase requests can be done on the same Web site. There is no charge for this service.

Most requests for quotes are fulfilled within 48 hours. Auto-By-Tel dealers know they're dealing with savvy cyber-customers and realize their price must be deeply discounted or the sale is lost.

Auto-By-Tel reflects the demographics of the Internet—average age is 35; most own their homes worth about $225,000, and their average household income is over $80,000.

IBM is making available an Internet service to help banks and dealers approve car loans faster.

Low-cost auto insurance is available through American International Group (AIG) via the Auto-By-Tel Web site. Because quote requests are facilitated by in-house customer service representatives, the company passes along the savings.

CitySearch

Charles Conn, CEO
Thomas H. Layton, chief operating officer
La Crescenta, CA 91214
URL: http://www.citysearch.com

CitySearch was featured in *Fortune* magazine as one of the "25 Very Cool Companies" and was ranked fourth in NetGuide's listing of the top 100 Internet sites. This California company, with ties to Steven Spielberg, has unveiled a one-stop interactive resource guide to local communities in Pasadena and San Francisco in California; Raleigh, Durham, and Chapel Hill in North Carolina; Austin, Texas; Salt Lake City, Utah; and New York City, where CitySearch works with Metrobeat, a local online information service. The company expects to cover 30 cities, including Paris, Madrid, and Sydney by the end of 1997.

The idea for this company came to Bill Gross when he needed a haircut in New York City. He choose a barber from the Yellow Pages and as his cab delivered him to the address, found it was not the kind of business he had imagined. He knew if he'd had the benefit of photos of the various barber shops he could have made a decision based on facts—not guesswork.

Instead of doing a slow burn or dismissing this as a "bad haircut day," the entrepreneur put his inventive genius to work and founded City-Search. Gross had headed up Lotus Development and then formed Knowledge Adventure the "edutainment" software profiled in *Forbes, The Economist,* and other periodicals.

He formed a start-up team of young, aggressive developers with deep collective experience in the software, Internet, and retail industries. CEO Charles Conn was a leading management consultant and partner at McKinsey and Company, where he led many new product development and retailing projects. He was a Rhodes Scholar and first in his class at Harvard Business School. Jeffrey Brewer was the former online applications developer at Knowledge Adventure. COO Thomas Layton was president of a high-growth start-up, Score Learning Corporation, and has extensive experience in other entrepreneurial firms and venture capital.

Through extensive testing, CitySearch has created an intuitive interface to allow consumers, including newcomers to the Internet, to browse community information or conduct sophisticated searches by keyword, time, and location. Information such as weather, sports reviews, profiles of community leaders, movies, shopping areas, and museum exhibits are easily accessible.

Customers can find a new restaurant, view its menu and interior seating, locate it on a map, and even place a take-out order. There are also listings for charitable organizations, community calendars, churches, government services, club activities, miscellaneous visitor information, plus historical and cultural listings.

Investors include AT&T Ventures; Goldman-Sachs; Bill Melton, president and CEO of CyberCash; venture capitalist Ben Rosen; and cinema magnate Steven Spielberg. The company's board chairman is Robert Kavner, formerly head of AT&T's multimedia division and director of new media efforts at Creative Artists Agency.

CitySearch is not an electronic yellow pages or newspaper. This new service provides the current community and business information adapted to the visual, searching, filtering, and interacting power of this new medium. It is built bottom-up from within the community. It employs 250.

CitySearch becomes a part of the community it puts online by building a team in each city. Local writers report on community happenings, meetings, and entertainment.

Eventually the company plans to offer online classified ads with large newspapers in targeted cities. In San Francisco, the company will offer a 3-D virtual view of communities, shopping districts, and buildings. Future services include a chat function enabling users to make comments to various sites.

Small- to medium-size businesses that can't quite afford their own Web site can contract with CitySearch, which has developed a variety of preformatted Web pages. For $29 to $89 a month, a company can have its own stylish electronic storefront under the CitySearch umbrella.

CitySearch is a full-scale Java application, the first of its type, with a proprietary search engine and server, and a custom Illustra database. The company has formed strategic partnerships with Silicon Graphics, Borland, Illustra/Informix, Etak, and Database America.

1-800-Flowers

Donna Iucolano, director of interactive services
Westbury, NY 11590
URL: http://www.800flower.com
CompuServe: Go:Fresh
America Online: flowers

Jim McCann acquired 1-800-Flowers when it was losing a whopping $400,000 a month. He swiftly focused efforts toward exceptional service, with developing repeat business as the number-one priority. The company now has 1000 employees and is the world's largest florist.

Donna Iucolano, director of interactive services, said, "The 80s was the decade of telephone ordering and the 90s is the decade of electronic orders." Its Web site debuted in April 1995 with e-sales accounting for 10 percent of total revenue, or $25 million in 1996. Netscape Commerce Server is in use insuring secure credit card transactions. It attracts 30,000 page views a month. To keep visitors returning, the site is completely redesigned twice a year.

Interactive advertising on the Net is its fastest-growing area. It is constantly updating the site to keep it fresh, offering new services and contests. Currently the cartoon character Dilbert promotion has attracted heavy response. Its United Airlines frequent flyer miles offering has also been a big hit.

The company ushered in a tidal wave of advertising in the electronic media to attract the Internet surfer. It was on eight online services and promotions on four interactive TV channels plus listings in a number of Internet directories and search engines.

"This medium is moving by leaps and bounds daily," says Iucolano. "Four to six months is an eternity on the Internet, so don't put your Web

To keep visitors returning, the site for 1-800-Flowers is redesigned twice a year.

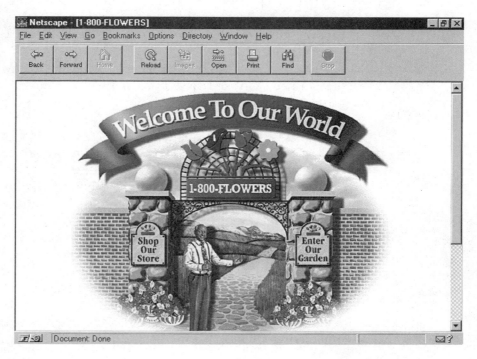

site up and forget it. These sites require constant attention." She advises businesses to check out the Web site developers, carefully taking time to check references. "Make sure they can do what they promise. These things always take longer and cost more than originally thought," she says.

The company's first experience with electronic retailing was with CompuServe's Electronic Mall in 1992. It is currently considering electronic retailing at AT&T's Marketlive, Time-Warner's DreamShop, and IBM Corporation's World Avenue.

With America Online's Marketplace, users can view 250 gifts and floral arrangements. The electronic Gift Concierge prompts you via e-mail when a birthday, anniversary, or special occasion is approaching. The gift registry holds up to 50 dates.

America's Brightest LLC

Chip Meyers, founder and president
Santa Monica, CA 90403
URL: http://www.americasbrightest.com

This Web site offers a package of business and career resources including one-on-one interaction with experts in a variety of fields. The interactive site is divided into two areas: small business and the working professional.

The company was started in early 1995 after Chip Meyers, now 29, realized a need. Unlike large corporations, which can afford to hire the consultants they need, most small businesses must do without. Nevertheless, they need to consult with experts who specialize in career and small business issues. "For a small business or an individual, a lot of services are out there, but most are expensive and therefore not accessible," said Meyers. When he started his first two businesses he realized he needed a team of lawyers, recruiters, accountants, and business consultants but couldn't afford all the expertise. So, he set about to put them all in one place in his third business venture.

His services include Lucy Lawyer (career-related legal issues consulting), Job Swami (job-hunting and career expert), and Uncle Sammy (tax and personal accounting advice), Vito Scallini (private investigator), and Frankie Hollywood (public relations). Also included are several major business magazine subscriptions, Quarterdeck Web Talk software, discussion groups, and discounts and services from its nationally recognized marketing alliances with AT&T, the *Wall Street Journal*, Kinko's Copies,

Block Financial Services, NetCom, and *Entrepreneur* magazine. The fee to business subscribers is $49.95 monthly or $499.95 a year. This permits posting questions by e-mail to the various experts. Members are guaranteed a response. The individual working professional subscription is $9.95 monthly or $99.95 per year.

A data base of "perfect employees for your current job openings" is available online, and the service offers background checks of employees. Also offered is assistance with newsletters, travel tips, and discounts.

The Web site was activated in August 1996. Meyers's goal is to attract 3000 individual and 300 business subscribers. The site is updated consistently by offering new services and promotions. One hundred percent of his business is generated over the Internet.

GolfWeb

Gary Allen, product manager
Cupertino, CA 95014
URL: http://www.golfweb.com/

An oasis of lush green color provides a calming backdrop to the GolfWeb site where the latest tournament results, golf gear catalogs and brochures, golf magazines, and a pro shop can be explored. Also featured are celebrity interviews and columns by or about top golf personalities, industry news, and special events. The viewer could encounter the likes of Clint Eastwood beaming a welcome from Pebble Beach via your computer screen. Some of GolfWeb's pages feature miniprograms of RealAudio for sound bites and Java.

A popular addition is FORE!ground, located at the top of the home page. Classified ads, a golf chat room, and tips and instruction are also showcased.

GolfWeb was founded in 1994 by a team of experts in marketing, publishing, and Internet engineering; golf aficionados; and one former golf pro. It currently has 25 employees. Its Web site launched in January 1995 and has been processing electronic orders since May 25, 1996.

GolfWeb's ProShop, using iCat Commerce Publisher for the online cataloging, opened with 250 items, spanning 900 pages.

It began by posting 35,000 Web pages. Currently it offers visitors access to its database with details about 20,000 golf courses. The main site averages 550,000 hits a day by users in 80 countries.

GolfWeb has attracted advertisers such as Lexus, MCI, and Wilson, where ad packages range from $5000 to $6000 per week. It was awarded the

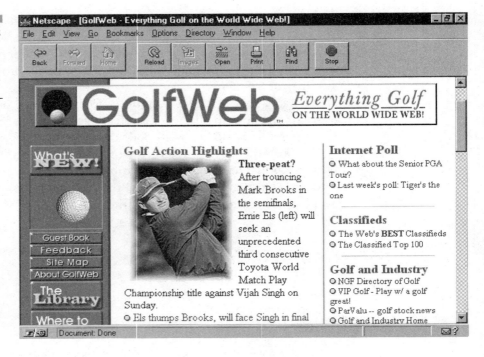

The GolfWeb site was voted the "Best Professional Sports Site" by Global Network Navigator.

"Best Professional Sports Site" by Global Network Navigator; POV ranked GolfWeb as one of the Web's 100 best sites.

Secure online transactions are through an agreement with Checkfree Corporation and a joint marketing effort with NetCom. Backoffice transaction capabilities are handled through OM-SecureLink through a partnership with Open Market.

E*TRADE SECURITIES

Bill Porter, chairman
Christos Cotsakos, CEO
Palo Alto, Calif.
URL: http://www.etrade.com

E*TRADE's founders were the first to develop and introduce electronic brokerage services for the individual investor. You can place stock or option orders, get quotes, and track your portfolio 24 hours a day with their leading edge technology. They are a subsidiary of E*TRADE Group.

The E*TRADE site provides financial information, news, charts, and deep discounts on commission rates for investors.

This site offers access to financial information, news, charts, and other data. It offers deep discount commission rates. "This will be the seventh time we have cut prices since beginning service in 1992," Bill Porter said. "Our strategy has always been to offer investors the latest in online trading capabilities. The efficiency of the technology allows us to control costs and pass the savings on to customers."

The Web site offers free stock market quotes to the public together with a stock market game and a trading demo in its visitor center. Accounts can be opened on the Web site as well.

The company has been expanding at more than 10 percent monthly and, at this writing, has a customer base of 82,000.

All customer account transactions on the World Wide Web are secured by a Netscape Secure Commerce Server. When customers log in, a key symbol in the lower left-hand corner of the screen confirms private and encrypted communications.

Access to the customer-only trading and account area requires a private E*TRADE User ID and password, available exclusively to E*TRADE account holders.

HomeScout

Geof Barker, CEO
Seattle, WA 98101
URL: http://www.homescout.com

HomeScout is the brainchild of The Cobalt Group. It allows home buyers to search a central database to locate the perfect property.

HomeScout works much like the other Internet search engines. With more than 500,000 summary listings in one database, it allows home buyers to search one Web site for comprehensive housing inventory in a given location. When buyers find property listings matching their search criteria, they can review the complete, detailed listing which is located at the source Web site. HomeScout's inventory is updated continuously.

In addition to maintaining the largest inventory of real estate listings on the Net, HomeScout maintains directories of real estate agencies, insurance agents, mortgage brokers, attorneys, contractors, landscaping services, and so on. Tips, tools, and articles in the HomeScout Guide are also available online.

This site is receiving 125,000 page views weekly and forecasts one million total in 1997.

The company developed its Web site in-house. Geof Barker cautions businesses on rushing their Web pages onto the Web. "It always takes longer than you think," he said. This company is actively attracting advertisers on the site and collections are handled electronically.

The Cobalt Group is a team of executives, developers, designers, and marketers formed to develop various classified and marketing publications on the Internet.

YachtWorld

Seattle, WA 98101
URL: http://www.yachtworld.com

YachtWorld, another venture of The Cobalt Group, offers a searchable database of 2000 yachts on the Internet with multiple photos, specs, and text. Links to the central listing agent are included.

A photo library of bare boat and crewed charter yachts from around the world links to charter brokers, yacht management companies, and charter companies.

There are 15,000 marine businesses listed in the Boating Yellow Pages, which can be searched by industry category, company name, and state or country. By clicking on the business name, the visitor can view the marketing brochure of a growing number of companies which display their products and services on the Internet.

It offers an exclusive business directory of boat builders, designers, services, products, associations, and events in the large yacht industry. YachtWorld is the exclusive Internet marketing partner of the Super Yacht Society and Superyacht Northwest.

Capt'n. Jack's Tide Guides and Nautical Software features monthly tide information for 50 locations in the United States. Visitors can browse a catalog of 80 nautical software products.

The Armchair Sailor bookstore has over 1800 nautical book and video reviews.

YachtWorld receives 200,000 to 300,000 page views a month.

Quotesmith Corporation

Robert Bland, president
Darien, IL 60561
URL: http://www.quotesmith.com

Historically, the only source of insurance pricing information has been from insurance salespeople, most of whom represented only one, two, or three companies. Quotesmith changed all this by making the full resources of continually updated insurance databases instantly available on the Internet. Because insurance is a state-regulated industry, there was no centralized source of insurance pricing information. Twelve years ago, Quotesmith developed its databases, and the information is now available directly to consumers on an interactive basis.

Anyone can find out the best term life prices being offered by 140 top-rated term life insurers without having to spend time with any insurance salespeople.

Bland said,

Our databases tell us price variances of up to 600 percent exist in the marketplace among different companies for identical term coverage. This underscores the importance of shopping around before buying term insurance. The Quotesmith price comparison service makes it easy for people to instantly understand what the marketplace has to offer in terms of price, coverage, and safety before a buying decision is made.

Our simple Web site won't win any awards for bells, whistles or glitz but it does provide comprehensive up-to-the-day insurance pricing information which is not available from any other single source. This will be very useful information to the 57 million Americans who own a term life policy and the 4 million Americans who buy term life policies each year. The allure of the huge market outweighed the insurers' traditional dislike for having their policies compared on a price basis. We were able to convince the insurers the business opportunity for them is enormous.

The Quotesmith Web site went online May 1, 1996, and is working beautifully for the company. The site accounts for the most rapidly rising area of profitability—accounting for 30 percent of its revenue, which is 6 million a year. It employs 44 people.

The president advises against using self-serving hyperbole on your Web site—say as little as possible, but make it count. Be clear and specific and don't waste the customer's time.

There are plans to offer insurance plans for health and long-time care in the future.

Quotesmith's new Web site provides a simple one-stop application-ordering menu which allows a customer to instantly request applications and apply for insurance from any of the 140 companies 24 hours a day.

MovieLink

Alissa Robinson, associate MovieLink product manager
Phone: 777-film
URL: http://www.moviefone.com

This site provides information and ticket purchase at movie theaters in 26 metropolitan areas. Moviefone is expanding to include many more cities in the coming months. Its listings include each film's running time.

The company was formed in 1992 and currently has 50 employees. Its Web site went online in July 1995. It was redesigned and relaunched in July 1996. It receives 3000 unique visitors through the index every day. Electronic cash transactions are processed by its secure server.

One of the newest services introduced is Movie Previews, which provide brief descriptions along with information on who's starring in the picture.

Visitors to the MovieLink site can obtain movie information and purchase tickets online.

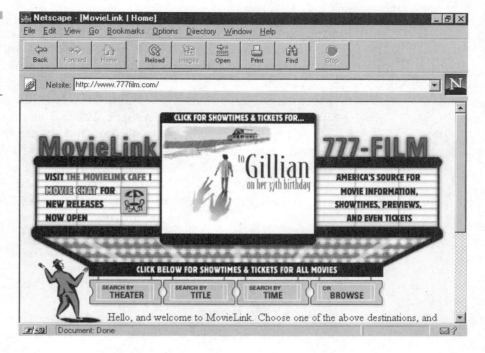

SportsLine USA

Michael Levy, president and CEO
Fort Lauderdale, FL 33309
URL: http://www.sportsline.com

SportsLine USA was founded in February of 1994 by Michael Levy, a pioneer in both the high-speed data communications industry and in high-tech applications for sports. The Web site was launched August 1995. The company has chosen to build its own brand rather than license content from existing sports information providers. Mike Kahn, a former NBA writer, oversees a staff of 14 writers and 50 freelance sportswriters. Total employment is 120.

Seventy percent of the company's site is free to users. Subscribers pay $4.95 monthly for exclusive, member-only content, daily features, and newscaster-style game coverage. The box seat subscription charge is $39.95 per year.

SportLine's fully interactive content is retooled and updated each day. Proprietary editorial content from award-winning sports writers, including RealTime audio and video cybercast, is proudly featured.

Its extensive Merchandise Mall features secure electronic transactions. A sports industry job bank and sport-related travel packages are included. Many promotional contests will be offered throughout the year. This dynamic company is shifting its focus toward star athletes, entertainment, and memorabilia sales.

SportsLine is the exclusive home to Shaquille O'Neal, who left Microsoft Network for a joint venture Web site (Shaqworld.com).

Sports enthusiasts can read columns and exchange e-mail with Pete Sampras and Monica Seles, Joe Montana and Arnold Palmer among other mega sports stars. There are fan clubs and chat sessions.

The site has secured 16 million dollars in financial backing from venture capitalists Kleiner Perkins, Caufield, and Byers, Reuters New Media, and New York Life Insurance Company.

In 1996, the site was generating more than two million hits and more than 500,000 page views a day, compared to an average of 60,000 hits a day in 1995. It expects 10 million hits a day by early 1997. The majority of SportsLine's revenues will come from advertising. Pepsi, AT&T, and American Greetings are some of its sponsors.

The site has been endorsed by Bob Costas, Arnold Palmer, and Joe Namath. It is the official online service of the NFL players, FedEx Orange Bowl, Bolletieri Tennis, Sports Academies, and Sports Byline USA (the largest syndicated sports radio talk show in America).

Levy sees similarities in the Internet and the early days of cable television. He suggests companies try to make it big, fast in their Web site ventures and to be prepared to budget the funds required to do it right.

Travelocity

Neal Checkoway, president and CEO,
Worldview Systems Corporation
Terrell B. Jones, president, SABRE Interactive and SABRE Computer
    Services
URL: http://www.travelocity.com

On March 12, 1996, Travelocity launched its one-stop travel site. In the first three months of operation, more than 1.2 million visits were recorded, making it one of the most frequented travel sites on the Internet.

The new megasite features 200,000 pages of travel destination information from Worldview, combined with dynamically generated travel reservation information allowing instant SABRE bookings, the world's most powerful travel computer reservation system.

Travelocity is one of the most frequented travel sites on the Net, offering visitors useful services and continuously updated travel information.

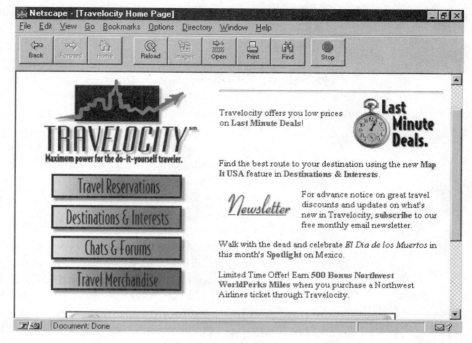

By linking databases, the two companies have created the largest collection of integrated and searchable travel information on the Internet.

The site features the latest in Web technology including a home page which gives users the ultimate online travel planning and booking experience.

Some of the services include the following:

- *Travel Reservations.* Available online at Travelocity are 700 airlines, 31,800 hotel properties, and 50 car rental agencies.

- *Destinations and Interests.* A continuously updated multimedia travel guide with searchable information on dining, lodging, business services, and entertainment activities in thousands of destinations worldwide.

- *Merchandise.* Luggage, books, videos, and hundreds of travel products, accessories, and unique items from around the globe are offered.

- *Chats and Forums.* Live chats with travel experts, bulletin boards to swap ideas with fellow travelers, contests and games to test visitors' travel savvy.

- *Map-It Geolocating.* Detailed street maps for points of interest at featured destinations in the United States.

A trip can be completely booked in 5 or 10 minutes including even restaurant reservations. Merchandise and travel can be securely purchased online.

IVN Communications of San Ramon offers more than 1500 custom video clips, multimedia displays, and still images illustrating featured destinations of the world showcased in Travelocity's Destinations and Interests department. It offers 400 travel video titles including programs produced for Reader's Digest, Fodor's, and Rand McNally.

Magellan's of Santa Barbara, California, features travel accessories, appliances such as dual-voltage hot beverage makers and travel irons, pocket currency exchangers, and security items.

Lanier Publishing International of Petaluma, California, has guidebooks to hotels, condominium vacations, guest houses, and bed and breakfast inns worldwide.

Travelocity's Business Information sections includes where to rent a laptop if yours malfunctions. You can also check out the Foreign Protocol Etiquette listings to learn local customs, such as where you should dress conservatively or when to keep your feet on the ground (in some countries it's considered insulting to show the soles of your shoes to anyone!).

Travelocity has 144,901 members since launch and is registering members at 65,799 per month. Site visits are at a current rate of 559,320 per month.

The number of pages viewed since launch is 13,663,032, at a current rate of 6,115,123 per month. The number of hits since launch is 47,715,958, with the current rate of 20,745,525 per month.

Travelocity's distribution partners include the following:

GE Business Pro—GE Information Services (http://www.gebusinesspro. com).   Travelocity is featured in the GE BusinessPro Internet-based productivity tool targeted for small- and medium-sized businesses.

Infoseeker and Infoseek Guide—Infoseek Corporation (http://www.infoseek. com).   Travelocity is the official sponsor of Infoseek's travel information section, one of 12 U.S. Select Topics. Travelocity's travel experts provide site reviews and develop content highlighting special themes and destinations.

StarText—an online service of the Fort Worth Star—Telegram (http://www.startext.net).   Travelocity is linked to StarText, the local information and Internet access service of the Fort Worth Star—Telegram, which provides complete news coverage, weather, classified ads, stock and financial information, entertainment news, humor, forums, discussion areas, and more.

USA TODAY Online—USA TODAY (http://www.usatoday.com). Travelocity cohosts the travel section "Your Travel Guide," which features
extensive travel and entertainment destination information and
travel reservations from Travelocity.

FreeLoader—Individual, Incorporated (http://www.freeloader.com). Free-
Loader provides Travelocity with a customized version of its unique
offline downloading service to "surf the Net while you sleep."

WOW! from Compuserve. WOW! from CompuServe is a powerful new
online service created specifically for home use. It offers each
household member easy access to information, entertainment, and
communication—including the Internet. Travelocity is the exclusive travel reservation and destination information provider.

PCR Personal Computer Rentals Corporation

Jim Clark, director of marketing
Cranbury, NJ 08512
URL: http://www.pcrrent.com

PCR Personal Computer Rentals, the only national franchiser of computer rentals, announced its site on the World Wide Web October 1, 1996.
The company started in 1983 and now has 75 locations and 400 employees.

Users may click on Request a Quote, and have a rental price for almost
any large city in the United States. The user specifies what equipment is
needed, where and when, and PCR will return a cost estimate.

Potential customers may also search through Hot Links in the classified section of PCR's home page to find special offers and pricing for
used equipment. "Each PCR location will have their own sub-pages linked
to our main page so there are updated price specials monthly," says Jim
Clark, PCR's marketing director. "The Web site makes it easy for customers
to make arrangements right on the Internet from anywhere in the world
and get immediate response with less paperwork. Businesses sometimes
need additional computers for meetings or seminars, training classes, con-
ventions, special projects and seasonal work loads," he added.

The Web site is providing approximately 15 to 20 leads per week. An outside programmer designed the site and the process took approximately
three weeks. Clark suggested keeping it simple at first—avoid cramming
too many ideas onto the page which will dilute the main message. Pay
close attention to speed and dynamics and stay away from slow-loading
graphics. PCR is constantly working out ways of speeding up and improving the site. Approximately 1 percent of its volume comes over the Internet.

The company also rents laser and other printers, larger-screen monitors, CAD/CAM systems, projectors attached to computers, laptops, desktops by IBM, Compaq, Apple, Epson, and Hewlett-Packard. Multimedia hardware is also available. PCR delivers, installs, maintains, and picks up rented computers and peripherals. PCR can provide equipment usually within a single day and can provide a toll-free number for customers who need 24-hour hotline technical support.

The Rainforest Alliance

Ann Ziff, chairperson
Daniel Katz, executive director
New York, NY 10012
URL: http://www.rainforest-alliance.org

With a membership of 14,000 and 40 employees, The Rainforest Alliance is dedicated to the conservation of tropical forests. This through education, research in the social and natural sciences, partnerships with businesses, governments, and local people.

The econavigators are ushered into the misty and mystical world of a virtual jungle journey. They are given examples of how humans depend on the rainforest during this adventure. There's also the fun and educational Rainforest Kid's Zone.

Internet members receive an electronic bimonthly newsletter on rainforest conservation and Rainforest Alliance activities update. This international nonprofit organization refuses to do wasteful mass direct mail campaigns and depends on its site via the World Wide Web to raise awareness. Memberships start at $15.

Contest giveaways, such as an all-expenses-paid ecotour to Costa Rica and tickets to major concerts featuring top performers, are offered during the year.

Site guide includes conservation programs with the ecology and economy of the Amazon River basin. Conservation Media Center, which won the 1995 Drucker Award for Nonprofit Innovation, is revolutionizing tropical agriculture including the production of bananas, coffee, cocoa, oranges, Brazil nuts, and natural rubber.

Resources feature Schoolhouse and the Press Room. Detours offers a link to Know Your Place and Jungle Journey. Partners in Marketing allows forward-thinking businesses to highlight their commitment and dedication to conservation through a variety of creative marketing

At the Rainforest Alliance site, visitors experience a virtual jungle journey and can enter to win contest giveaways such as an all-expenses-paid trip to a rainforest.

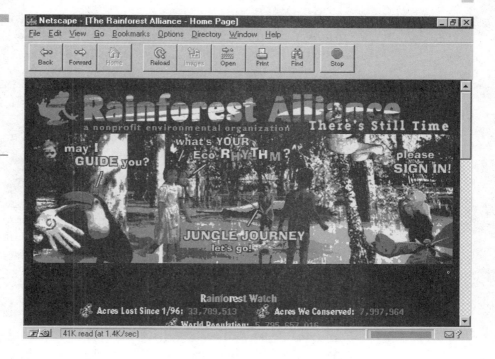

options. It allows consumers to exercise their social conscience in purchasing decisions and support environmentally friendly companies.

This inventive site was voted "Best of the Net" by the *Village Voice* in October 1996.

Successful Microniche E-Sellers

Hawaii's Best Espresso Company

Maui Coffee Roasters
Nicky "Beans" Matichyn, owner
Kahului, HI 96732
URL: http://www.planet-hawaii.com/bec/

Nicky "Beans" Matichyn has been in the coffee business since 1972. He and his college friends opened Cafe Primo right after graduating in upstate New York.

He has always enjoyed good coffee. When he discovered the "extreme beans" from the bountiful islands of Hawaii he decided to move near the source.

Nicky started Hawaii's Best Espresso Company on Maui in 1992. He was using Italian espresso beans until he journeyed to the other side of the island and found Maui Coffee Roasters' and its flavorful Kona and Espresso blends.

Says Nicky, "Our motto, 'Extreme beans: Multi-dimensional Coffee with Full Visual Effects,' reflects our philosophy to push coffee to the extremes of good taste."

When his "money-mad" landlord raised the rent, Nicky Beans could have done a slow burn. Instead he burned rubber to the information superhighway, and launched the business from Front Street to the Internet.

Now the company ships the finest coffees from Kona on the Big Island, Maui, Kauai, and Molokai to the four corners of the earth. Over 30 coffee selections are offered, including Chocolate Macadamia Nut flavored brew. Also available are espresso machines, Maui Coffee Roasters mugs, and fresh macadamia nuts from the islands.

Its Web site went up at the end of 1993 and business has been increasing steadily ever since. It receives 3000 page visits a month and will do a volume of one and a half million in 1996. It attributes 20 percent of its business to Internet sales. Nicky is looking into shopping-cart software for 1997. Monthly promotions, offered with a light and humorous touch, mirror another of Nicky Beans's philosophies: "If you can't have fun and enjoy your business, you're in the wrong business."

He advises companies not to rush the project through because it will show. "Don't expect too much out of the Web page at first," Nicky said. "A successful site must evolve with much thought and care to showcase your products and services in their best light." This company updates its site once a month.

Jenny's Floral Studio

Tanya Wolff-Molson, owner
Sarnia, Ontario, Canada
ON N7V 2N6
URL: http://www.virtualflowers.com

Shane Molson had an innovative idea for his wife, Tanya. He suggested her Web site allow anyone with a computer and an e-mail address to send a colorful graphic "virtual flower" bouquet to a person of choice anywhere in cyberspace for free. The idea has been a smashing success. Virtual bouquets are sent to 5000 to 6000 people every day. This site receives 3.5 million hits a month. The site debuted February 1, 1996.

The recipient receives an e-mail with a claim ticket number signed "The Virtual Bouquet Delivery Robot." The receiver then clicks on the pick-up window at the virtualflower.com Web site to view the "flowers" and a personal note from the sender. With so many complimentary "virtual bouquets" zipping through cyberspace, when a need to send real flowers arises, many remember the free service and give Jenny's Floral the business. Users select from eight creative floral arrangements shown in colorful graphics on the Web page.

The company was formed in 1985 and now has 12 employees. Approximately 30 percent of its business flows from its Web site. It is currently testing secure servers and will offer encrypted service by the end of 1996. A special cash card which will allow repeat customers VIP express service is also in the works. There are plans to offer plant and floral care tips as well.

CanWeb Services is its server of choice.

"Every day is a learning experience," says Tanya. This company is constantly fine-tuning its site. One of the biggest challenges has been coping with the volume of requests so customers will not have to wait.

Hot.Hot.Hot

Perry and Monica Lopez, owners
Pasadena, CA 91105
URL: http://www.hothothot.com

The Lopez's launch on the Internet was as lively as their spicy hot sauces. Monica was locked out of her store one day. As she waited for her husband to bring the keys, the president of a Web-design company happened by. The two had a conversation and before long Hot Hot Hot was online.

Available on the site are 450 sauces and related products from all over the world. Offerings such as Scorned Woman, Ring of Fire, Dave's Temporary Insanity, or Satan's Revenge account for 25 percent of sales via the Web site. It averages 1500 visits a day.

Monica, 34, has a film degree, and Perry, 37, a graphic designer, thought long and hard about their Internet involvement and both were hands on in its development. They labored to present the origins of their hot sauces and how they are made in a fun and intriguing way, using colorful icons to describe fiery, extra hot, hot, and medium. They wanted to make the ordering process and the navigation easy.

The Lopezes sent e-mail to various organizations including Marketing News and The Chili Heads group announcing the online service. In less than an hour after their Web page debut, the first order was received. Monica estimates reaching as many customers as they do via the Web site would cost $50,000 a month in catalog mailers compared to the $100 a month of Internet charges she pays. They are actively looking into encrypted credit card servers. They do not store credit card numbers on any tapes or disks attached to any of their computers or machines.

They enjoy meeting Web shoppers from the United Kingdom and Germany who "drop by while vacationing. Internet customers are given very attentive service to preserve good will," Mrs. Lopez said.

The only time she got "flamed" with an angry e-mail critique was when someone stumbled onto the site seeking racier fare. Tapping into a Web site named hot.hot.hot, probably anticipating a peek at a hot-looking model, the user was dismayed to find the computer screen filled with red hot chili peppers instead.

"In 1994, when hot.hot.hot went online there were 5,000 Web sites compared to 300,000 in 1996," says Monica. Electronic sales have doubled each year compared to a 15 percent increase in walk-in sales. This company adds four to five new employees during the holidays.

Dean and DeLuca

Pat Roney, president
URL: http://www.dean-deluca.com

In 1982, long-time friends Dean and DeLuca decided to open a grocery store in the community where they lived—SoHo, the art center of New York. They did, and it, like the art community, grew beyond all expectations. Dean and DeLuca were tired of the second-rate foods being promoted as "gourmet" or "exotic." To them, good food is good food, whether it comes from grandma's farm kitchen in Michigan or a four star restaurant in Paris or Florence.

They currently have 500 employees.

Their Web site boasts 600 gourmet food items from fresh fruits and vegetables, game, and smoked salmon to exotic teas and coffees. Plans to introduce a brand new and extensive line of kitchen accessories and additional gourmet ingredient items in 1997 to their customers are in progress.

When setting up this company's Web shopping site, Pat Roney had many of the same concerns and problems facing any business going online: who should we work with, what are the costs, and when can we expect to be online? Initial price estimates for getting its more than

600 products onto a Web site through an outside source ranged up to $40,000.

After researching the possibilities, it settled on an iCat Electronic Commerce Suite. The company contracted with iCat Corporation's Technical Services Group (TSG) in Seattle to handle production.

Scott, the graphic designer responsible for Dean and DeLuca's paper catalog design, mapped out the Web shopping site. Scott trained for two days at iCat's headquarters, and problems were later worked out by phone. Scott supplied TSG with the appropriate graphics with the art department directing the production work.

TSG extracted product names, descriptions, prices, and other text elements from the QuarkXpress files of the print catalog and transferred the information into a database in iCat Commerce Publisher, the first product in the suite. Transferring the product text into the database involved a tagged import process using text-only, or ASCII, files.

To add product images to the site, TSG batch-converted PICT files provided by Dean and DeLuca to the Web-friendly GIF format. The conversion process took roughly half a day. From there, TSG linked the graphics to the database through an automated import process and added ordering templates to the layout for secure online transaction.

The catalog was created in about 20 days with the assistance of one member of TSG. The full catalog was created with five HTML page templates: three templates incorporated the iCat Command Language and served to produce all of the product pages for the 600 product catalog. One additional HTML template acts as the home page and the other provides company information.

Notes CEO Roney, "We liked the idea of having the world's finest food emporium available at all times to anyone interested in cooking. And when we learned we could be up and running with our entire product line within a month, we jumped at the chance."

The Web site went online in April of 1996 and had 1000 requests in the first few weeks.

Royal Publishing

Walters Speaker Services
Dottie Walters, owner
Glendora, CA 91740
URL: http://www.walters-intl.com

Dottie Walters began a tiny advertising business on foot, pushing two babies in a broken-down baby stroller in a rural community with no sidewalks. She built the business into four offices with 285 employees and 4000 continuous contract advertising accounts. Then, she sold this large business so she could concentrate on her own speaking career.

Conducting seminars, writing with her "Speak and Grow Rich" program, recording audio cassette programs on selling and speaking success, and publishing her own newsmagazine, *Sharing Ideas* are some of this talented entrepreneur's activities and accomplishments. She is a consultant for businesses and speakers' bureaus and author of numerous articles in publications around the world.

The publishing business was formed in 1977, followed in 1981 by the speaking bureau. The Web site went online in May of 1996. The site is providing approximately three strong leads per week.

Lilly Walters suggested offering free tips on your Web site—something the customer will value. "Getting linked to every search engine possible is critically important," she said.

"Take care to make it faster and simpler to navigate with a minimum delay to the client," advises Walters.

APPENDIX A

Who to Call: Companies That Are Eager to Help You Jump into E-Selling*

You can download the latest update of this appendix from:

http://www.jamisongold.com/eager

To have your company considered as an addition to the online appendix (and to the next edition of this book) or to make corrections, send an e-mail to wjamison@jamisongold.com and be prepared, when requested, to express your press kit and other information about your company's contribution to e-cash commerce technology.

AMP eMerce Internet Solutions
P.O. Box 3608 (M.S. 84-26)
Harrisburg, PA 17105-3608
Phone: 717-592-6706
Fax: 717-780-7477
URLs: http://www.ampemerce.com
       http://www.connect.amp.com
Contact: Jim Kessler, AMP eMerce, 717-592-6706
E-mail: tchocker@amp.com

AMP eMerce Internet Solutions "specializes in customized electronic commerce solutions for clients in both business-to-business and retail operations".

Atomic Software, Inc.
2837 Peterson Place
Norcross, GA 30071
Phone: 770-417-1228
URL: http://www.atomic-software.com
Contact: Thomas McCole, president

Atomic, whose target market is small- to medium-size businesses, provides credit card authorization software for Windows 95 and NT servers.

---

* To the best of our knowledge, every company listed here is reliable and its products and/or services are effective. However, we have not necessarily seen, used, or evaluated every technology mentioned. Therefore, a listing here is not to be taken as our recommendation, nor is the absence of any firm or product a reflection on its integrity or value.

Additional details on companies and products are given in the preceding chapters.

CashGraf Software, Inc.
2901 58th Avenue N.
St. Petersburg, FL 33714
Phones: 813-570-5555
Fax: 813-578-0238
Toll Free Sales: 800-872-3902
Solution Center: 813-528-2579
Solution Center Fax: 813-526-5053
URL: http://www.cashgraf.com
Contact: Larry Deaton, president and CEO

This company offers functionally rich solutions in easy-to-use software for small businesses including home offices.

Checkfree Corporation
4411 East Jones Bridge Road
Norcross, GA 30092
Phone: 770-734-3404
Fax: 770-734-3304
Contact: Matthew S. Lewis, VP corporate communications
E-mail: matt_lewis@atl.checkfree.com
URL: http://checkfree.com

This corporation provides a method for consumers and businesses to make payments electronically.

Corel Corporation
Ottawa, Ontario, Canada
Phones: 800-772-6735
          613-728-3733
URL: http://www.corel.com

Corel offers several reasonably priced products to help you design your own Web pages.

Cybercash, Inc.
2100 Reston Parkway, Third Floor
Reston, VA 22091
Phone: 703-620-4200
E-mail: info@cybercash.com
URL: http://www.cybercash.com

CyberCash Sales and Marketing:
303 Twin Dolphin Drive, Suite 200
Redwood City, CA 94065

Phone: 415-594-0800
Fax: 415-594-0899
Contact: Cheryl Sullivan Lester, director of merchant marketing
Phone: 415-413-0155
E-mail: clester@cybercash.com

This company supplies public key encryption technology for secure transmission of credit card data on the Net. Merchants never see an unscrambled credit card number, thus relieving them of responsibility. Also available is CyberCoin technology, a cost-effective way to sell electronic goods and services for between $0.25 and $5.00.

DigiCash, Inc.
World Headquarters
Kruislaan 419
1098 VA Amsterdam
The Netherlands
Phone: 31.20.655.2611
Fax: 31.20.668.5486
E-mail: info@digicash.nl
URL: http://www.digicash.com

U.S. Branch Office
DigiCash, Inc.
55 East 52nd Street—39th floor
New York, NY 10055-0186
Phone: 212-909-4092
        800-410-ECASH (800-410-3227)
Fax: 212-318-1222
E-mail: office.ny@digicash.com

Subsidiary in Australia
DigiCash Pty Ltd
Level 29, Chifley Towers
2 Chifley Square
Sydney NSW 2000, Australia
Phone: 61.2.375.2316
Fax: 61.2.375.2121
E-mail: andreas@digicash.com

This company provides chip card software and electronic payment mechanisms providing security and privacy, based on patented advances in public key cryptography developed by the company's founder.

EC Company
1705 El Camino Real
Palo Alto, CA 94306
Phone: 415-323-7500
Fax: 415-321-7816

This company provides business-to-business electronic commerce solutions.

Elcom Systems, Inc.
400 Blue Hill Drive
Westwood, MA 02090
Phone: 617-407-5003
Fax: 617-407-5063
URL: http://elcom.com
David Wolf, president
Contact: Ms. Pat Breslin, director of marketing

This company licenses the PECOS electronic commerce system that automates the complete business-to-business transaction cycle.

First Virtual Holdings Incorporated
Phone: 619-793-2700
E-mail: info@fv.com
URL: http://www.fv.com

First Virtual's system of Internet payments does not use public key encryption; instead it requires both buyer and seller to register with this company.

Freemont Avenue Software, Inc.
2825 Wilcrest, Suite 160
Houston, Texas 77042
Phone: 800-240-5754
        713-974-3274
Fax: 713-978-6246

Freemont is one of the world's foremost suppliers of firewalls to protect electronic commerce from hackers. (See its subsidiary, Livermore Labs.)

Haystack Labs, Inc.
Phone: 512-918-3555
Fax: 512-918-1265
URL: http://www.haystack.com

Intruder-foiling Stalker products by Haystack patrol inside both your Internet and intranet Web sites, providing 7/24 protection.

IBM
Phone: 800-455-5056

Big Blue has several developments in the works for electronic commerce. Call your local IBM office.

iCat Corporation
1420 Fifth Avenue—Suite 1800
Seattle, WA 98101-2333
Contact: Jodi Sorensen, marketing programs manager
Phone: 206-623-0977
Fax: 206-623-0477
E-mail: jodis@icat.com
URL: http://www.icat.com

iCat Electronic Commerce Suite facilitates building an online catalog by creating the HTML needed to display products.

Livermore Software Laboratories, Intl. (LSLI)
2825 Wilcrest, Suite 160
Houston, Texas 77042
Phone: 800-240-5754
        713-974-3274
Fax: 713-978-6246
E-mail, product information: portus info@lsli.com
E-mail, product support: portus@lsli.com

PORTUS Secure Firewall Version 2.2 is NCSA-certified. Livermore is a subsidiary of Freemont Avenue Software. LSLI and PORTUS are registered trademarks of Freemont Avenue Software. LSLI and Freemont Avenue Software claim to be the nation's leading suppliers of firewall technology to foil intruders.

Microsoft Corporation
One Microsoft Way
Redmond, WA 98052-6399
Phone: 206-703-0403
Fax: 206-936-7329
URL: http://www.microsoft.com
E-mail: mkim@microsoft.com

Netscape Communications Corporation
501 East Middlefield Road
Mountain View, CA 94043

Phone: 800-638-7483
Fax: 415-528-4125
URL: http://www.netscape.com

Netscape provides an inexpensive but excellent Web site creation tool, along with the acclaimed Navigator browser.

NeXT Software, Inc.
Phone: 415-366-0900
Fax: 415-780-3929
URL: http://www.next.com

This company claims to be the leading provider of custom development software for the World Wide Web and other applications.

Terisa Systems, Inc.
Menlo Park, CA
Contact: Ken Mohr
Phone: 415-919-1776
E-mail: ken@terisa.com
URL: http://www.terisa.com

This company provides the SecureWeb toolkit combining S-HTTP and SSL into a single development package, ensuring interoperability with both protocols. SecureWeb is a trademark of Enterprise Integration Technologies Corporation.

THISoftware Company, Inc.
Houston, Texas
Phone: 800-804-6545
         713-785-4357
URL: http://thisoftware.com
THISoftware offers another low-cost Web site design package.

VeriSign, Inc.
2593 Coast Avenue
Mountain View, CA 94043
Phone: 415-961-7500
Fax: 415-961-7300
E-mail: verisign.com
URL: http://www.verisign.com

VeriSign provides trusted digital authentication services and products to enable the adoption of secure electronic commerce solutions.

WebMate Technologies Inc.
960 Turnpike Avenue
Canton, Massachusetts 02021
Contact: Bob Trocchi, chief operating officer
Kimberly Polcari
Phone: 617-828-5600
Fax: 617-828-1911
URL: http://www.WebMate.com.

Webmate's applications reduce the cost of entry into electronic commerce dramatically, thus opening this new medium to independent retail stores and other small businesses. Not only is the cost reduced, but the level of technical expertise required is sharply lower, making it eminently practical for small firms and stores to conduct retail business on the Internet.

APPENDIX B

Banks Advertising E-Cash Capability and Merchant Credit Card Service Companies

You can download the latest update of this appendix from:

http://www.jamisongold.com/banks

To have your bank or merchant credit card service company considered for addition to this online appendix (and the next edition of this book) or to make corrections, send an e-mail to wjamison@jamisongold.com and be prepared, when requested, to express your press kit and other information about your company's contribution to e-cash commerce technology.

Banks

Atlanta Internet Bank

Don Shapleigh, president
Phone: 770-392-4990

Forward thinking bankers have launched the world's first cyberbank in Atlanta. When its cyberdoors opened for business late in 1996, its services were available to AT&T WorldNet Service subscribers.

Atlanta Internet Bank's initial products included interest-bearing checking accounts, direct deposit, electronic bill payment, account transfer capability, and ATM cards.

The bank has announced the launch of its "anytime-anywhere" service with special interest rates on money market accounts. The initial announcement stated that for a limited time, Atlanta Internet Bank would be offering 7 percent interest (annual percentage yield of 6.18 percent) on NetVantage money market accounts to WorldNet subscribers.

"This is the beginning of a new era in financial services," said Atlanta Internet Bank president Don Shapleigh. "We're using bits and bytes instead of bricks and mortar and passing the savings on to our customers. This will allow us to maintain very competitive rates after the introductory rate offer expires."

Future services planned by the new bank include loan products, brokerage services, IRA accounts, and credit and debit cards.

"Atlanta Internet Bank has taken a giant step into the electronic commerce marketplace," said Jeffrey Feldman, AT&T's Advanced Network Solutions vice president. "AT&T's Advanced Network Solutions team firmly believes that banks and other financial service providers will win customer loyalty by offering their own branded, electronic environments that deliver real value to end users—just as Atlanta Internet Bank has demonstrated."

Atlanta Internet Bank's services are provided through Carolina First Bank, Greenville, South Carolina, a wholly owned subsidiary of Carolina First Corporation.

BankAmerica Corporation

Contact: Sharon Tucker, vice president
Phone: 415-622-2775
Fax: 415-622-6288
E-mail: sharon.tucker@bankamerica.com
URL: http://www.bankamerica.com

Also at Bank of America:
Contact: Jo Singleton, vice president Electronic Delivery Services
Phone: 415-785-5933

Barnett Bank

URL: http://www.barnett.com

Citibank

URL: http://www.citibank.com

This Web site provides a great deal of information.

Comerica

URL: http://www.comerica.com

Nations Bank

URL: http://www.nationsbank.com

PNC Bank

URL: http://www.pncbank.com

Sanwa

URL: http://www.sanwa.com

Credit Card Processing Companies

Merchant credit card services is a vigorously growing and highly competitive field. AT&T's Business Buyer's Guide, a national directory of 800 numbers, lists dozens of card service companies under the heading "Credit Card and Other Credit Plans." For more information, see Chap. 6. For our latest update, visit:

jamisongold.com/banks

To have your merchant credit card services company considered for addition to the online appendix (and to the next edition of this book) or to make corrections, send an e-mail to wjamison@jamisongold.com and be prepared, when requested, to express your press kit and other information about your company's ability to facilitate electronic commerce and credit card sales over the Internet.

Banc One Point of Sale Services Corporation

Contact: Steve Dieringer, group product manager
Phone: 614-248-3019
Fax: 614-248-4989
E-mail: steved@bancone.com
URL: http://www.bancone.com

National Data Payments

Phone: 800-367-2638

A California merchant reported great satisfaction with the rates, responsiveness, and general service of this Maryland company.

Americard Merchant Banc

P.O. Box 1197
Duluth, GA 30136
Phone: 800-552-1500
Contact: David Alcorn, president

This friendly organization specializes in serving the needs of smaller companies. It welcomes firms that sell on the Internet, says it has a high rate of acceptance, and usually approves and sets up a new account in seven working days. It works with American Express, MasterCard, and Visa.

Bank America Merchant Processing Service, Inc.

As the nation's fourth-largest processor of credit card transactions, this subsidiary of Bank of America generated $20.7 million in profit from $110 million in revenues in 1995. The bank recently sold shares in this subsidiary in an IPO, although it says it will retain a controlling interest.

APPENDIX C

Today's Best Search Engines

They can change rapidly as new technologies strike down yesterday's best. In the Internet software jungle, no prisoners are taken, no mercy shown. Unless you're the best in your niche, you're soon gone.

To get our latest take on Today's Best in Search Engines, visit:

http://www.jamisongold.com/search

A *search engine* is a tool for sifting through the huge mass of information on the Internet. It's a database. Strictly speaking, it's a piece of software. As such, it could be called *search software* or *search program,* but *search engine,* being a far more vivid term, caught on.

Search engines are indispensable for speeding the search through the enormous fund of Internet information in order to find what you need.

What each search engine offers is a different approach to the mammoth and possibly insurmountable problem of indexing, categorizing, and sorting through this ever-changing pile of information. Because not only is the Internet growing at a phenomenal rate, but some parts of it are dying as well.

Alta Vista

URL: http://www.altavista.com

Alta Vista attempts to database the Internet—a staggering task that it has done a fairly good job at accomplishing.

Excite

URL: http://www.excite.com

Excite uses complicated language-based rules to refine and enhance standard search requests. Among Excite's partners are Apple, AOL, and the *Los Angeles Times.*

The Alta Vista home page.

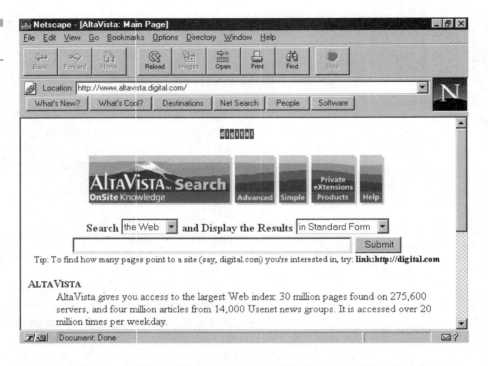

The Excite home page.

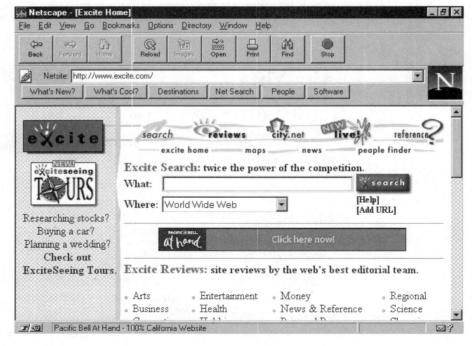

HotBot

URL: http://www.hotbot.com

Operated by Hotwired, this extensive collection of Web pages—now more than 54 million documents—is an excellent research tool.

InfoSeek

URL: http://www.infoseek.com

Now in the works for the immediate future: a super spider searcher. InfoSeek has strategic relationships with NetCom, Netscape, Sun, Verity, and Xsoft, among others. Leads all others in advertising revenue.

Lycos

URL: http://www.lycos.com

Lycos lists over 51 million URLs to back its claim that "If it's out there, it's on Lycos." It was recently reported to be second in advertising revenue, and closing.

Magellan

URL: http://www.mckinley.com

Magellan offers reviews and ratings for over 40,000 Web sites and provides an index to another 2 million sites. Partnerships include AT&T, Europe Online, IBM, Microsoft, Nynex, Time Warner, and others.

WebCrawler

URL: http://www.webcrawler.com

WebCrawler began as a research project at the University of Washington. Now the university credits the WebCrawler's transformation into a successful commercial product to the explosive growth of the Internet. With laudable restraint and modesty, the university remarks, "Since its

HotBot can search through more than 54 million documents.

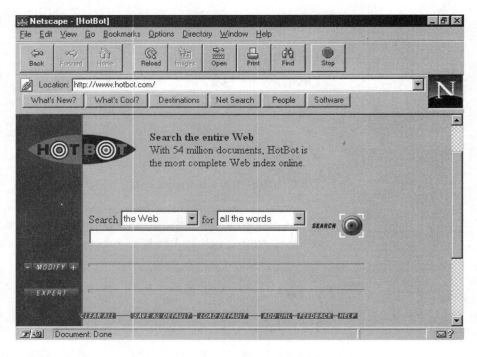

The InfoSeek home page gives users several search options.

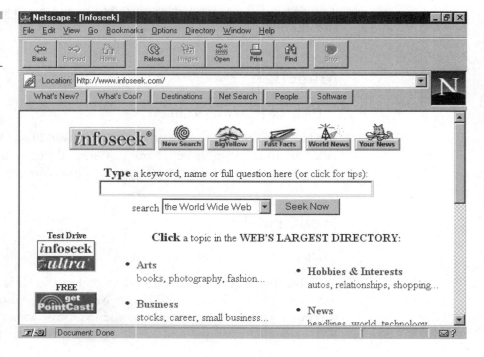

The Lycos home
page.

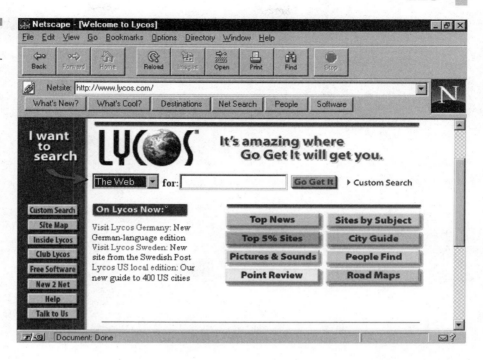

inception as a research tool, the Internet has seen many similar stories
whose collective message is clear: research and development activities can
have a profound effect on the direction our society takes." Certainly,
immaculate timing was essential to WebCrawler's incredibly rapid ascent;
yet this would have been for nothing without the project's brilliant concept and its determined and skillful implementation.

In early 1994—eons ago in terms of the Internet—a forward-thinking
member of the Department of Computer Science and Engineering's faculty had the insight to gather the faculty and students in an informal
seminar to discuss the early popularity of the Internet and the World
Wide Web.

Students often float their ideas in small projects at these seminars, and
several were started. The WebCrawler was Brian Pinkerton's project. It
began as a small single-user application to locate information on the Web.

Other students talked Pinkerton into building a Web interface for the
WebCrawler that could became widely usable. When first released on
April 20, 1994, the WebCrawler's database contained documents from just
over 6000 different servers on the Web. The WebCrawler quickly became
an Internet favorite. By October 1994, this pioneer search engine was
receiving an average of 15,000 queries a day.

WebCrawler began as a University of Washington student's research project and has turned into one of the most heavily used full-text search engines on the Web.

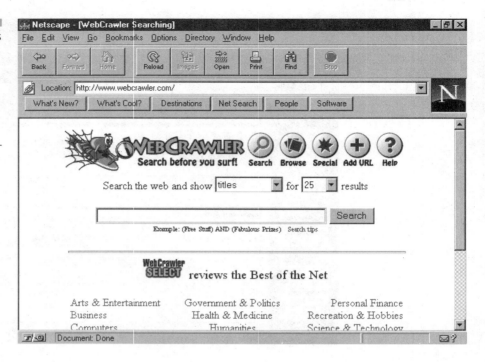

The Web continued its amazing growth. Before long it became clear that in order to keep up with that growth, the WebCrawler would need far more resources than the university was ready and able to provide. Dealernet, a local Seattle company, became WebCrawler's charter sponsor by donating a new server to the effort. In return, its logo was displayed on the WebCrawler's sponsor page as a supporter of the WebCrawler research effort.

At about the same time, Starwave, a departmental affiliate, became the second sponsor by donating a second machine and funding Pinkerton to focus his time on the WebCrawler effort. In doing so, Starwave was strengthening its ties to the department and funded work that was daily becoming more relevant to its business.

During the WebCrawler's early development, Pinkerton worked as a research assistant and on WebCrawler at night and on weekends. The Starwave funding was provided on the basis that Pinkerton would focus on WebCrawler as the basis for his thesis.

In general, growth is a good thing. However, too much of a good thing can become unmanageable. In January 1995, about nine months after it went online, WebCrawler became the heaviest consistent user of CSE's network. In February, major changes to the service were necessary to accommodate the new load. In March, the daytime load became so high the service was usable only at night. The pressing need to finance this effort with serious money became overwhelmingly obvious. It was clearly seen that unless important money came galloping to rescue WebCrawler, its popularity would choke it to death.

Until then, the WebCrawler project had been run by a grad student with just enough faculty supervision to ensure that the work could support a thesis. The primary problem became locating an organization willing to fund a service with the goal—proven in popularity but unproven in profitability—of providing a search engine to a million Internet users throughout the world.

Outside sponsors would fund the effort in exchange for advertising on WebCrawler. However, this made it more than awkward for the service to continue operating at the university. The solution was clear. WebCrawler, sold to America Online and moved to San Francisco on March 29, 1995, became a commercially operated and supported engine.

WebCrawler was the first full-text search engine on the Internet. Several competitors emerged within a year of WebCrawler's debut: Lycos, InfoSeek,

Yahoo indexes subjects on the Web.

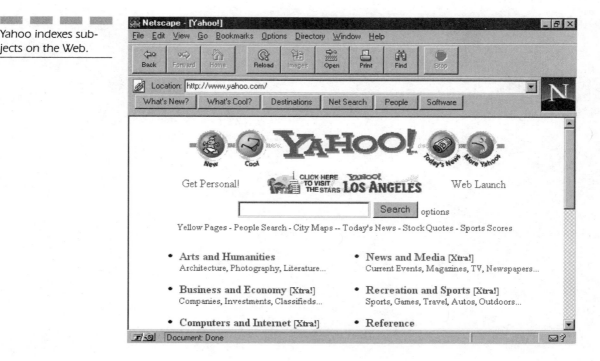

and OpenText. They all improved on WebCrawler's basic functionality, though they did nothing revolutionary. WebCrawler's early success made their entry into the market easier and legitimized businesses that today constitute the small but vital industry of Web resource discovery.

WebCrawler remains popular today. Over 2 million people use it each week, on average making more than 3 million queries a day. As part of America Online's GNN service, WebCrawler continues to evolve and improve.

(Adapted from material by Global Network Navigator, Incorporated.)

Yahoo

URL: http://www.yahoo.com

In the strictest sense, Yahoo is an index rather than a search engine. It recently added Alta Vista's Super Spider to its online capabilities. Yahoo has prestigious partners including Reuters, Ziff-Davis Publishing, and Agents Incorporated.

APPENDIX D

The Capabilities and Track Record of Jamison/Gold, LLC

Capabilities

Jamison/Gold, LLC is a complete multimedia production company headquartered in Marina del Rey, California. Formed in 1994, the firm provides cutting-edge custom design and development services for Web sites and other new media platforms. The firm is also engaged in software research and development, specializing in creating custom software application technologies that expand the potential of multimedia applications.

The Jamison/Gold team was built to the purpose of providing a highly effective integration of excellence and innovation in technical development, design, and marketing communications. J/G's software engineers are classically trained, having been taught at top computer engineering schools such as MIT.

Jamison/Gold is well known for developing the first commercial-quality interactive game on the Internet (Adventure With An Attitude), which was featured on the Sony PlayStation Web site and has received over 20 million hits to date and numerous awards including Interactive PR's "Web Site of the Year" for 1995.

Track Record

Jamison/Gold's clients include the following:

Sony Computer Entertainment

DreamWorks Interactive

Nissan Motors

Infiniti Motors

Columbia Tristar

Pretty Good Privacy (PGP)

Bell Research Laboratories

TBWA Chiat/Day Advertising

Hill and Knowlton Public Relations
Fleishman-Hillard Public Relations
Psygnosis

Jamison/Gold LLC

4551 Glencoe Avenue—Suite 160
Marina del Rey, California 90292
Phone: 310-823-6345
Fax: 310-448-7109
E-mail: jamisongold.com
URL: http://www.jamisongold.com

GLOSSARY

Buzzwords, Acronyms, Computereze, and Anti-technobabble Missiles That Put You in Control When the Discussion Turns Nerdy

For our latest update, visit:

http://www.jamisongold.com/buzz

Throw some of these terms into discussions about electronic commerce and Web sites from time to time. Vendors and subordinates will be mystified as to how much you know about the subject under review. This will help keep them straight as to their ability to handle the responsibilities they want to assume. All that's necessary to gain this power is to know several buzzwords well enough to use them correctly and confidently.

Computer people find it difficult to talk about their specialty without using jargon for the same reasons attorneys and doctors can't talk about the law or medicine in everyday language. Jargon is necessary speed talk in every field from agriculture to zoning, without which move-ahead communication would be greatly hampered, if not stopped altogether.

Essential as jargon is to honest communication, it becomes dishonest technobabble when used primarily to impress, baffle, and overwhelm the uninitiated.

On the theory that a good offense is the best defense, this glossary explains some buzzwords you may enjoy using when you feel you're about to be buried in technobabble. Buzzwords change rapidly in electronic commerce.

The ***italicized boldface*** terms are those you really should know before you involve your company in electronic commerce. Terms in *italics* you'll probably never encounter and can ignore. However, their obscurity makes them especially effective when you need to fire an anti-technobabble missile to shoot a discussion down before it escapes into jargon orbit. The following are some terms in common use when this went to press.

Bit An electrical impulse a computer recognizes as being either a zero or a one. Eight bits make a byte.

Browser A software program capable of translating the Web language computers understand and the Internet transmits into information, attractive graphic presentations, and programs on the visitor's screen.

Byte   A group of eight bits (zeros or ones) that represent a letter, a digit, or many other symbols.

CAFÉ   Conditional Access For Europe.

CCP   Compression Control Protocol. A method for negotiating data compression over PPP links so that multiple data compression methods such as those with compression ratios of up to 4:1 can be supported.

CDMA   Code Division Multiple Access.

CGI   Common Gateway Interface. A powerful attribute of the Web. Without CGI, the Web would be limited to just text and pictures. CGI allows you to create programs on the Web ranging from simple ones capable of processing survey or order information to extremely complex programs or games with animation and sound.

CPU   Central processing unit. On desktops, this is the metal box that holds the brains of the computer.

DME   Distributed Management Environment. OSF's multi-vendor distributed database support. Includes management of hubs, bridges, and routers.

DNS   Domain name server(s) take easily remembered names such as www.sony.com and translate them into the hard-to-remember Internet addresses (generally a series of digits and dots) that computers recognize. In addition to the obvious benefit of not having to use Internet Protocol (IP) addresses such as 106.2.107.11, DNS makes it easy to change the physical location of your Web server without changing the name of your Web site. For example, if Sony should move its Web site from a computer in California to one in Texas (or Timbuktu), users do not need to change the address they have for Sony. It's all done automatically through DNS.

DOS   Disk operating system. (See **OS**.)

EFTS   Electronic Funds Transfer Systems.

FTP   File Transfer Protocol. The most common method used over the Internet to copy files from computer to computer, including programs and graphic images. FTP is not used to view Web pictures—a different protocol (HTTP) accomplishes this.

GIF   Graphics Interchange Format. A file format for storing 256 raster (not vector) graphic images. Most images used on the Web are in GIF format.

HTML   HyperText Markup Language. The language used to organize Web pages in ways that permit font size and color, backgrounds, graphics, and positioning to be specified and maintained.

HTTP   HyperText Transmission Protocol is used to transmit Web messages between browsers used by Web surfers to the Web page being accessed.

INTERNIC   Internet Network Information Center. Partly funded by the National Science Foundation, INTERNIC performs the following functions:

■ Provides Internet information services

■ Supervises the registration of Internet addresses and names

■ Helps users obtain access to the Internet.

IP   Internet Protocol.

IRC   Internet Relay Chat. A multiuser chat system where everybody types and everybody reads in real time. Messages are not stored on IRC, but are broadcast to all listeners.

ISDN   Integrated Services Digital Network. A technology that relies on existing telephone lines (the twisted pair of copper wires in use since phone service began) to connect with the Internet. However, instead of converting the digital signal to analog to go over the telephone line and then reconverting it at either end, ISDN uses digital adapters to send the information in an entirely digital format and thus provide up to five times faster transmission than conventional modems can deliver.

ISP   Internet Service Provider. Any company that specializes in providing access to the Internet. Some outfits specialize in providing commercial access or individual access.

JAVA   A computer language that allows applications to be programmed so they will work on a variety of platforms such as Windows, UNIX, and so on. The disadvantage is that some loss of speed in involved.

JPEG   (jay peg) Joint Photographic Experts Group. The name of the standard lossy data compression system for digitalized still images. JPEG is the second-most common format images are stored in on the Web after GIF. JPEG images may contain far more than the limited 256 colors found in the GIF format.

LAN   Local Area Network. Two or more computers connected (usually located close to each other, as in the same office) by cables to permit data residing on one to be accessed by the other computer(s). If one of a LAN's computers is connected to a modem and telephone line, the entire LAN can be accessed by outsiders unless adequate security measures are in force. Compare to WAN.

NCSA   National Center for Supercomputing Applications.

OS Operating System. A software program containing the basic instructions computers must have before they can do anything. These instructions permit computers to execute application programs such as word processing, spreadsheets, and many others. Windows 95, DOS, UNIX, NT, OS/2, and Apple Macintosh systems are among the operating systems in widest use today.

OS/2 Operating System—2. An operating system from IBM.

OSF Open Software Foundation. A nonprofit development and research group set up in 1988 by potent computer and software companies such as DEC, HP, IBM, and others to provide multivendor distributed database support. Includes management of hubs, bridges, and routers. OSF creates software with standardized and publicized interface specifications. OSF/1 is up and running on DEC's Alpha processor. Other implementations are in the works.

PCS Personal Communications System(s).

PPP Point to Point Protocol. The most common protocol used by individual users to access the Internet. A protocol used by TCP/IP routers and PCs to communicate over dial-up and leased-line WAN connections. PPP sets up a standard way for routers and computers connected over a WAN link to establish, monitor, and exchange data.

Router A server that directs messages along the information highway to their intended destination.

Search engine A search engine is a tool for sifting through the huge mass of information on the Internet so you can find what you're looking for more quickly. It's a database. Strictly speaking, a search engine is a working piece of software; that is, it's a search program—but *engine* sounds cool so we use that. Each search engine offers a different approach to the mammoth and—for the individual, insurmountable—problem of indexing, categorizing, and sorting through this ever-changing mountain of information that is the Internet.

Secure transaction An encrypted message transferring money in some form from a buyer to a seller in return for goods or services.

Server A computer that supplies information to other computers.

S-HTTP Secure HTTP. (See **HTTP**). Used to encrypt specific Web documents rather than the entire session.

SSL Secure Sockets Layer. An open standard proposed by Netscape Communications for providing secure (encrypted and authenticated) messages to and from Web sites, along with other applications such as e-mail, FTP, and Telnet. Uses RSA public key encryption for messages concerned with electronic commerce payments.

SQL Structured Query Language. If you talk like a programmer, SQL resembles English. It provides language that defines and manipulates data in a database server in ASCII text.

T-1 Digital Transmission Rate 1. Connected to the Internet, a T-1 provides data transmission at rates up to 1.54 mbps.

TCP Transmission Control Protocol.

Telnet Runs terminal sessions on remote computers.

UNIX A complex, high-speed operating system used primarily by mainframe computers.

URL Universal Resource Locator. Jargon for *Web address,* usually something like http://www.(company name).com. For example, our URL is http://www.jamisongold.com.

VAN Value Added Network.

VRML Virtual Reality Modeling Language. A specification for describing 3-D worlds and objects that can be transmitted across the Internet.

WAN Wide Area Network. Usually provided by a public carrier, a WAN is a data communications network spanning any distance. You get access to the two ends of a circuit and the carrier does everything in between. Typically the carrier's part appears on network diagrams as a gray blob because nobody ordinarily cares how the carrier does its work. In contrast, a LAN typically has a diameter (the maximum distance between any two stations) measured in a few meters, or kilometers at the most, and is entirely owned by the company using it.

INDEX

ABOUT THE AUTHOR

Brian Jamison and Josh Gold are co-founders of Jamison/Gold, LLC, an interactive agency that specializes in World Wide Web site production, using such cutting-edge technologies as VRML, Java, Shockwave, and CGI. They have developed Web sites for Nissan Motors, Infiniti Motors, Sony, Greenworks, and other major companies.

Warren Jamison, a former manufacturer and sales executive, has written, co-authored, or edited ten books, including *The New Toughness Training for Sports, How to Master the Art of Selling, Ed McMahon's Superselling,* and *How to List and Sell Real Estate in the 90s.*